THE POVERTY OF POWER

Energy and the Economic Crisis

Barry Commoner

BANTAM BOOKS · TORONTO · NEW YORK · LONDON

RL 11, IL 9-up

THE POVERTY OF POWER

*A Bantam Book / published by arrangement with
Alfred A. Knopf, Inc.*

PRINTING HISTORY
Knopf edition published May 1976
Bantam edition / September 1977
6 printings through July 1980

*A substantial portion of the material in this book
appeared in* THE NEW YORKER.

ISBN 0–553–14315–8

Published simultaneously in the United States and Canada

*Bantam Books are published by Bantam Books, Inc. Its trade-
mark, consisting of the words "Bantam Books" and the por-
trayal of a bantam, is Registered in U.S. Patent and Trademark
Office and in other countries. Marca Registrada. Bantam
Books, Inc., 666 Fifth Avenue, New York, New York 10103.*

PRINTED IN THE UNITED STATES OF AMERICA

15 14 13 12 11 10 9 8 7 6

CONTENTS

1. THE PROBLEM 1

2. THERMODYNAMICS,
   THE SCIENCE OF ENERGY 6

3. THE FOSSIL FUELS: OIL 30

4. THE FOSSIL FUELS: COAL 61

5. NUCLEAR POWER 76

6. THE SUN 113

7. THE USES OF POWER 145

8. THE PRICE OF POWER 198

9. THE POVERTY OF POWER 221

NOTES 250

ACKNOWLEDGMENTS 284

INDEX 287

1

THE PROBLEM

IN THE LAST TEN YEARS, the United States—the most powerful and technically advanced society in human history—has been confronted by a series of ominous, seemingly intractable crises. First there was the threat to environmental survival; then there was the apparent shortage of energy; and now there is the unexpected decline of the economy. These are usually regarded as separate afflictions, each to be solved in its own terms: environmental degradation by pollution controls; the energy crisis by finding new sources of energy and new ways of conserving it; the economic crisis by manipulating prices, taxes, and interest rates.

But each effort to solve one crisis seems to clash with the solution of the others—pollution control reduces energy supplies; energy conservation costs jobs. Inevitably, proponents of one solution become opponents of the others. Policy stagnates and remedial action is paralyzed, adding to the confusion and gloom that beset the country.

The uncertainty and inaction are not surprising, for this tangled knot of problems is poorly understood, not only by citizens generally, but also by legislators, administrators, and even by the separate specialists. It involves complex interactions among the three basic systems—the ecosystem, the production system, and the economic system—that, together with the social or political order, govern all human activity.

The *ecosystem*—the great natural, interwoven, ecological cycles that comprise the planet's skin, and the minerals that lie beneath it—provides all the resources that support human life and activity.

The *production system*—the man-made network of

agricultural and industrial processes—converts these resources into goods and services, the real wealth that
sustains society: food, manufactured goods, transportation, and communication.

The _economic system_—the recipient of the real
wealth created by the production system—transforms
that wealth into earnings, profit, credit, savings, investment, taxes; and governs how that wealth is distributed,
and what is done with it.

Given these dependencies—the economic system on
the wealth yielded by the production system and the
production system on the resources provided by the
ecosystem—logically the economic system ought to con-
form to the requirements of the production system, and
the production system to the requirements of the ecosystem. The governing influence should flow from the
ecosystem through the production system to the economic system.

This is the rational ideal. In actual fact the relations
among the three systems are the other way around. The
environmental crisis tells us that the ecosystem has
been disastrously affected by the design of the modern
production system, which has been developed with almost no regard for compatibility with the environment
or for the efficient use of energy: Gas-gulping cars pol-
lute the environment with smog; petrochemical factories
convert an unrenewable store of petroleum into unde-
gradable or toxic agents. In turn, the faulty design of
the production system has been imposed upon it by the
economic system, which invests in factories that promise increased profits rather than environmental compatibility or efficient use of resources. The relationships
among the great systems on which society depends are
upside down.

Thus, what confronts us is not a series of separate
crises, but a single basic defect—a fault that lies deep in
the design of modern society. This book is an effort to
unearth that fault, to trace its relation to the separate
crises, and to consider what can be done to correct it at
its root.

Energy plays a decisive role in the interactions among
the three systems. Energy, radiated from the sun, drives

the great ecological cycles. Energy, derived from fuels, powers nearly every production process. Most of the recent increases in the output of the production system and in the rate of economic growth are due to the intensive use of energy to power new, more productive machinery. The intensified use of energy is responsible for the rapid drain on fuel supplies and for much of present environmental pollution. And, as we shall see, the intense application of energy to production processes is closely associated with two of our main economic difficulties: unemployment, and the less visible but equally dangerous shortage of capital.

Thus, the energy crisis is so tightly linked to the crucial defects of the system as a whole as to offer the hope of leading us out of the labyrinth of interwoven crises—if we can but understand it. And we do not. This is made painfully evident by the sudden, unperceived onset of the energy crisis. For years the United States and most of the world used energy as though it were a freely given resource, its availability and uses understood as well as those of water or air. Suddenly the availability of energy can no longer be taken for granted; it has become a huge problem, strongly affecting almost every aspect of society.

In the last few years, energy supply problems have disrupted daily life; they have triggered an economic depression; they have led to a bitter confrontation between Congress and the President; they have altered the political relations between the industrialized countries and the developing ones; they have generated lightly disguised threats by the President and the Secretary of State to invade oil-producing countries.*

The energy crisis illuminates the world's most dangerous political issues, as it wrenches back into open view the brutality of national competition for resources, the festering issues of economic and social injustice and the tragic absurdity of modern war. The crisis forces us to make long-avoided choices. If we must give up present energy sources and find renewable ones, cur-

---

*Factual information and quotations are referenced, and sometimes amplified, in the Notes section beginning on page 250.

tail the wasteful uses of energy and the blind replacement of meaningful human labor by energy, where and how will the necessary decisions be made? Can these decisions be made, or even debated, without re-examining the precepts of the economic system which now govern how energy is produced and used?

There are no easy answers to these questions. But there is one way to begin to look for them. And that is to recognize that energy problems will not be solved by technological sleight-of-hand, clever tax schemes, or patchwork legislation. The energy crisis and the knot of technological, economic, and social issues in which it is embedded call for a great national debate—to discover better alternatives to the deeply faulted institutions that govern how the nation's resources are used. And to begin that debate, we need to understand how the ecosystem captures energy, how the production system uses it, and how the economic system governs what is done with the resultant wealth.

To penetrate the chaos that surrounds the subject of energy, there is one essential, if difficult, tool available to us—the science of thermodynamics. The following chapter is an effort to make this tool more accessible, for all of us need to understand—and do something about—the energy crisis. Those who find this subject matter complicated will only be sharing an experience that most of us in the sciences have already had. But none of us can any longer indulge in the luxury of evading a science on which the future of the world has come to rest.

The First Law of Thermodynamics is simple enough: It states that energy can be neither created nor destroyed, so that, whatever happens to it, the amount must always remain the same. The Second Law is more important and more difficult to understand. It is important because it explains how work—which is the only value that energy has for us—is gotten out of the flow of energy from one place to another. It is difficult to understand because it relates this capability to several abstract and seemingly distant subjects, such as the meaning of order in the world, the nature of probability, and the one-way direction of time.

Once these unfamiliar concepts are grasped, we have a surprisingly clear path to follow. It begins with the *sources* of energy, the fossil and nuclear fuels on which we now depend, and the huge but still largely unused source—the sun. Here we need to learn why those energy sources on which we now rely are so poorly adapted to the purposes to which we put them; why they have begun to seriously disrupt both the environment and the economic system. Then we need to look at the *uses* of energy in the production system and discover why that system has been so designed as to waste energy so blatantly. Here we will find powerful links between the ways we use and misuse energy, capital, and labor. And only at that point will it become evident that our current crisis is a symptom of a deep and dangerous fault in the economic system.

This book is designed to trace this web of connections, in the conviction that the link between energy and the rest of our lives *can* be understood; that once it is understood, the origin of the crises can be identified; and that once this basic fault is identified, we can consider the painful but necessary steps that will, I am convinced, correct it.

2

THERMODYNAMICS, THE SCIENCE OF ENERGY

MOST PEOPLE HAVE a good deal of difficulty understanding energy problems. One reason is that the science of energy, thermodynamics, is a rather peculiar subject. In some strange, still poorly understood, and debatable ways, the laws of thermodynamics are different from most of the laws of physics. One distinguished physicist, P. W. Bridgman, put it this way:

> There can be no doubt, I think, that the average physicist is made a little uncomfortable by thermodynamics . . . the laws of thermodynamics have a different feel from most of the other laws of the physicist. There is something more palpably verbal about them . . . they smell more of their human origin.

Here Bridgman was reflecting upon a curious difference between thermodynamics and the rest of physics. Most basic physical laws were devised in order to explain a process that actually happens in nature: the apple falling to the ground, the rainbow forming in the sky. The laws of thermodynamics originated in the opposite way. They are based on the experience that something conceived by human beings *cannot* happen in nature; that a purely human conceit—perpetual motion—cannot be realized.

The search for perpetual motion was one of the liveliest enterprises of the seventeenth and eighteenth centuries. It gave rise to persistent, diverse, and often bizarre efforts to design a machine that could move and do work without using fuel or the effort of man or beast. For a long time these attempts were regarded as a legitimate part of science. But the inventions never worked. In a way, the laws of thermodynamics rationalize this human failure; that may be why "they smell more of their human origin."

Another way in which the laws of thermodynamics seem to differ from other scientific laws is that they are much easier to use than to understand. For many of us in scientific professions outside of physics—certainly myself—the effort to understand the energy laws is an unsettling, disconcerting experience. We know that these laws are extremely important and profoundly connected with every natural process. We have studied them in class and have used them in our work. We usually find it simple enough to apply them to the solution of a particular problem. This is based on the faith that the laws work. However, as faith gives way to questioning and we seek to explain to ourselves *why* the laws of thermodynamics work, we are often led into strange bypaths until, like a child wandering in the woods, we find ourselves in some totally unexpected, unfamiliar place—and suddenly know that we are lost.

In order to help the reader avoid, if possible, this bewildering experience, which is likely to confirm that energy is something too difficult for ordinary people to understand, I have chosen to start this discussion off in the deep woods of explanation. What I hope to do then is conduct us, step by step, from the unfamiliar but fundamental to the prosaic but practical. With this experience behind us, perhaps both reader and writer will be better prepared to confront the curiously convoluted but vitally relevant facts about energy, as they arise in the rest of this book and in our own experience.

The problem that is furthest removed from everyday practical energy questions (such as improving the gasoline mileage of a car)—and yet, as we shall see, intimately and fundamentally connected with them—is the distinction between the past and the future. The relevant observations are at once prosaic and profound: We know and remember the past; we can guess but do not know the future. We can hope to influence future events; we cannot change what has happened in the past. Our past life is done, our future life in doubt.

There is a way to turn these trenchant, vaguely disturbing ideas into a joke. Run a motion picture film backward. As the shattered fragments of a teacup leap off the floor and reassemble themselves until the cup rests whole in the waiter's hand, everyone laughs. They have seen something that never happens in real life: time running backward, so that the real future (the cup shattered on the floor) comes first and the real past (the cup whole in the waiter's hand) comes later. The joke is widely appreciated, evidence of the universal human experience that time flows in one direction, from then to now, from now to later.

It is disconcerting to discover that the one-way flow of time cannot be explained by the familiar principles of physics which, after all, are supposed to give us the deepest understanding of how the world works. The reason is that the basic laws of physics—for example, Newton's laws of motion—do not distinguish between past and future. Given a body's position in space, its direction and speed, a physicist can, with equal precision, tell us where it has been and where it is going. All of the equations of motion are reversible in time. A moving picture of billiard balls (or, for that matter, of molecules) colliding and recoiling in keeping with these equations would look the same running forward or backward; no one would know when to laugh. To quote the physicist Richard Feynman, who has written so clearly about this issue: ". . . in all the laws of physics that we have found so far there does not seem to be any distinction between the past and the future. The moving picture should work the same going both ways."

Perhaps the most important role of thermodynamics in the structure of science is that it establishes a link between the everyday awareness of the one-way passage of time and the time-reversible laws of physics. In establishing this link, the laws of thermodynamics also give us an enormously valuable means for determining how energy can be most effectively used to serve human needs.

How does energy relate to the direction of time? Let us go back to the falling teacup. Ignoring for the moment whether it is whole or broken, consider only its two alternative positions: resting on the floor, and several feet up in the waiter's hand. Now if we watch the cup (or its fragments) as they lie on the floor, even after a very long time nothing will happen. Certainly no fragment will fly up into the waiter's hand. In contrast, our experience tells us that the elevated cup, if released from the hand, will *spontaneously* fall to the floor. Of the two events, only one—the cup falling—can happen by itself; the reverse event does not, and the cup, once fallen, lies dormant on the floor.

A simple experiment shows that the downward flight of the cup—or of any other object—is in theory entirely reversible, and in practice nearly so. Let us attach a thread to the cup and, hooking it over a friction-free pulley (perhaps obligingly held by the waiter), attach a weight about equal to that of the cup to the other end. Now as the cup falls it will raise the weight, and with a little encouragement the raised weight can then be made to fall, and lift the cup. Carried out with more scientific sophistication, such an experiment tells us that as long as the cup is in motion there is nothing about its downward movement that cannot be undone—reversed. However, once it crashes against the floor and stops moving, the cup's condition is fixed and irreversible. It can no longer lift a counterbalancing weight and cannot leave its resting place on the floor unless some outside agency intervenes. There is such an agency—the application of energy, which can generate the force required to do the work of lifting the weight of the cup.

We can imagine various external agencies that might raise the teacup. A person could simply pick it up, using his muscles to do the work, the required energy coming from the combustion of the bodily fuel—sugar and other food substances. Or, if we wish to be more scientific about it, we could lift the cup on a little elevator, hoisted by a motor-driven reel, the requisite energy coming from a battery, or from the electric lines, and ultimately from a power station fueled by oil, coal, or perhaps uranium. This tells us that in the one-way world of real life, in which teacups and other objects cannot spontaneously move upward once they crash to the floor, this can be achieved, but only by doing work through the expenditure of energy. (Technically, *work* is defined as force exerted through distance, and the flow of energy is the agency that produces work. *Power* is the technical term for the rate at which work is done, the work accomplished per unit time.)

Or, at least, the energy *seems* to be expended. The muscular energy used to lift the teacup is certainly no longer available to do more work. (By lifting enough teacups a person could, after all, eventually exhaust his ability to work, if he failed to restore his metabolic energy by eating.) Or, if the teacup was hoisted by a battery-driven motor, it would certainly turn out, afterward, that the battery could do less work than it could have done originally—that some of its stored energy was gone.

But in fact the loss of energy is only apparent. This is the outcome of what was learned about energy in the seventeenth and eighteenth centuries. With the development of the first steam engines early in the eighteenth century, it became clear that heat could be converted into mechanical motion and made to do the work of lifting water out of a mine or of driving a train. Heat was at first regarded as a special kind of substance (*caloric*) which had no fixed relationship to the amount of mechanical work that it generated. However, by measuring the heat produced during the boring of a brass cannon, Count Rumford (originally the American Benjamin Thompson, later ennobled in the court of the Elector of Bavaria) showed that it resulted from the friction generated by the motion of the drill and was not—as widely believed at the time—due to *caloric* squeezed out of the brass as it was cut.

Such experiments suggested that both heat and mechanical motion are expressions of the same sort of thing—what we now call energy. Methods were developed to measure both, and it was found that the amount of energy involved in the mechanical motion of a machine (such as the cannon-boring machine) is quite precisely equal to the energy represented by the heat produced by the resultant friction. For example, in one experiment Rumford was able to bring about sixty pounds of water to a boil by immersing in it a brass cylinder within which a rod was turned by two horses over a period of two and a half hours. Knowing how much heat was needed to boil that much water, he concluded that one horse could generate the same amount of heat produced by burning nine wax candles.

This kind of experience was eventually embodied in the First Law of Thermodynamics: Energy can be neither created nor destroyed. When it is transferred from one form into another—in this case, motion into heat—no energy is lost or gained. Energy is conserved; the amount the world possesses is fixed.

If we now return to our teacup, we are confronted by a new problem: Where is the energy that is seemingly lost—for example, by the electric battery—when the cup is first lifted from the floor? If the law of energy conservation is obeyed, this energy cannot be "lost"; it must be somewhere. Initially the energy used to lift the cup off the floor must be somehow related to the teacup's new location. Any weighty object elevated above the earth contains a form of energy—gravitational potential energy—that can be gotten out of it by letting the weight fall. In falling, the weight exhibits this energy in the form of motion (technically, kinetic energy).

So far, so good. Our teacup experiment seems to obey the law of conservation of energy; the energy removed from the agency that lifted it is contained in the elevated cup. But in falling to the floor the cup loses both its kinetic and its potential energy. Now where has the energy gone?

From Rumford's experiment we know that as motion is countered by friction, its energy is converted to heat. And friction, on a magnified scale, can be regarded as a series of little collisions between the bumps on the surfaces of two objects rubbing against each other. We can suspect, then, that when the movement of the falling cup is halted by the collision with the floor, the kinetic energy of its motion is converted into an energetically equivalent amount of heat. After striking the floor, the cup—or its fragments—and the floor itself should be a little warmer than they were before.

While this measurement cannot readily be made on a

fallen teacup, it can and has been made on more massive objects falling a good deal farther. For example, at the bottom of Niagara Falls the water is about one-eighth of a degree (Centigrade) warmer than it is at the top. A computation shows that the energy represented by this extra heat is exactly equivalent to the potential energy of the water at the top of the falls. The energy is conserved.

All is well, then. We can assume that the energy used to lift the teacup is not destroyed and can be fully accounted for, after the fall, as heat. The First Law of Thermodynamics—the conservation of energy—works with a fallen teacup as well as it does with a bored cannon.

But this logical triumph is short-lived. With a little further thought a strange inconsistency appears. Since the energy needed to lift the teacup in the first place reappears as heat when it falls to the floor, why not use the energy represented by that heat to lift the teacup once more? But if that were possible, then the crash of the teacup would be a readily reversible process (teacups and floors easily containing, in their warmth, the needed energy) and we would have the experience of teacups falling and rising from the floor with equal ease. The backward movies would no longer be funny.

Clearly we are in some kind of logical trouble. The discovery of the First Law has solved one problem, but created another. While the First Law closes the door on perpetual motion by machines that purport to do work by "creating" energy, it appears to tolerate, and even to encourage, machines that are almost as miraculous in their freely given power. Consider this version of the teacup situation, for example: Here is a ship floating on the sea, which—like the floor—contains energy. The amount of heat energy in a given amount of sea water of known temperature, and its relation to the amount of energy needed to drive the ship, are easily calculated from the First Law. It turns out that the needed energy can be obtained from a four-inch layer of water around the ship's hull, by cooling it a little. A ship equipped with a device that extracted this heat from the surrounding water could, in cooling the water by one degree, obtain from it enough energy to sail through the sea, using no fuel, forever. The same marvelous device, sitting at the bottom of Niagara Falls and extracting enough heat from the water to cool it by one-eighth of a degree, could obtain sufficient energy to drive the water back to the top of the falls. Such a device would be a perpetual-motion machine which, far from being forbidden by the First Law, in a sense seems to be suggested by it.

If such a perpetual-motion machine could actually operate, it would not only levitate teacups and Niagara Falls. It would wipe out the passage of time. We can look at it this way. We are aware of the passage of time because events happen: The hands of a clock move; sand runs down the hourglass; water flows down Niagara Falls. Each of these events is a spontaneous, irreversible process in which the energy of motion is converted to heat. If a perpetual-motion device could indeed recapture the heat energy and, with no loss, use it to reverse the original process, the clock's hands would move backward as fast as they go forward; the sand and the Niagara would run upward as fast as downward. The forward and backward motions would cancel each other; nothing would happen; time would stand still.

Since none of these events actually happens, it would appear that this type of perpetual motion, in which (unlike perpetual motion of the first type) energy is not "created" but simply gathered up from the vast reservoirs of heat on the earth's surface, is also impossible. The relevant principle is that energy occurring only as heat stored in a single reservoir, no matter how plentiful in amount, cannot be used to do work. As we shall see, this is one way of stating the Second Law of Thermodynamics.

At this point in our journey from the disquieting profundities of time it would be useful to concern ourselves in a little more detail with the nature of heat—in particular, its intensity (temperature) and its relation to other forms of energy such as motion. Consider two objects that are made of the same material, water, but which may be quite different in their temperature—ice and liquid water. We know that both contain the same molecules, the familiar H_2O or H–O–H, formulas signifying that one atom of oxygen has attached to itself two atoms of hydrogen.

Common experience with water and ice can tell us a good deal about the behavior of these molecules, particularly as it relates to heat. For example, we are aware that liquid water has no form of its own; it flows freely and always takes the detailed shape of any vessel in which it is contained. Apparently, in liquid water the molecules must move about quite freely, and while they cling to each other with sufficient force to retain the identity of the mass of water, they are not so rigorously linked as to prevent their becoming arranged into whatever geometry is imposed by the container. In ice, the water molecules must be much less free to move about. Water frozen into ice will hold a singular shape —the angular form of an ice cube, or the lumpy one of a snowman. So long as they remain ice, the cube and the snowman retain their own distinctive forms. They lose their particular shapes and melt into the same puddle of water only when they are converted from ice into liquid water. This tells us that in ice the water molecules must be held together in a particular kind of geometrical arrangement, while in water their motion relative to each other must be freer. We also know that ice is converted into liquid water by the application of heat, and that the reverse takes place when heat is removed.

From all this we can deduce that heat intensity, or temperature, is associated with the freedom of motion of the water molecules. And this is indeed true. If we could turn a super-powerful microscope on ice, we would see that the H–O–H molecules are held together in a regular pattern (which turns up on a visible scale in the six-sided symmetries of ice crystals—snowflakes). Within this constraint each molecule moves slightly relative to its neighbors—but not much—as the bonds between them bend and stretch a little. Looking at cold liquid water, the super-microscope would show some of the molecules adhering to one another only in small, transient groups and the internal links between oxygen and hydrogen atoms stretching and bending much more than they did in the ice. Many molecules would be seen freely tumbling about, jostling one another, now adhering to each other for a time and then bouncing away. In hot water all these motions would be exaggerated, nearly all the molecules jiggling about (to use Feynman's descriptive term) quite energetically. The intensity of jiggling reflects the heat intensity, or temperature. The conclusion (supported by numerous experiments on many different materials) is a relatively simple one: Temperature, the intensity of heat, is represented by the intensity of molecular and atomic jiggling; heat is that form of energy which is associated with the small-scale, random motion of molecules and atoms.

We can now return to the earlier issue: Why is it that the conversion of the kinetic energy of bulk motion—the teacup smashing against the floor, or the water of the Niagara River crashing on the bottom of the falls—into heat makes that energy no longer available to reverse the spontaneous fall? This turns out to be an enormously meaningful question. In a sense, most of the science of thermodynamics is built around the efforts to answer it. To deal with it we need to wander further into the thicket of abstract thermodynamic ideas and consider two more subjects: order and probability.

The kinetic energy of the water falling down Niagara Falls is represented by the downward motion of huge numbers of H–O–H molecules. All these molecules fall together—as a random, jiggling crowd, it is true, but all progressing downward with the same overall direction and speed. In this respect the bulk downward motion of the water—its kinetic energy—involves a regular, coherent motion. Unless this were true on the microscopic, molecular level, the bulk of the water, as a whole, would not be falling. (In the same sense, a crowd of people dancing in random motion across the dance floor on the deck of a cruise ship are all in a coherent, ordered motion, let us say, along the line between New York and Bermuda.)

When the water hits bottom the energy represented by its bulk motion is converted into heat; the water molecules jiggle more fiercely, raising the temperature, as we have seen, by one-eighth of a degree. Their movements are random, on the average equally intense in all directions. As compared with their earlier coherent downward motion, the molecules' motion is now more disordered, in the sense that all possible directions of movement are equally expressed. Now, in bulk, the water as a whole goes nowhere; on the molecular scale, the motion has no recognizable pattern; it lacks the order of the falling water or the shipboard dance. Thus, in the conversion of the kinetic energy of the falling water into heat—an event which is crucially linked to the irreversibility of the process and to the one-way direction of time—order gives way to disorder.

Here is a fanciful but perhaps clearer way to picture this process. Imagine a billiard table divided down the middle by a removable barrier. On one side of the barrier are a dozen red balls and on the other side the same number of blue ones. These particular billiard balls are self-propelled (perhaps by installing in each of them some Mexican jumping beans) so that, like water molecules, all of them jiggle, move about, and bounce against each other in a constant jostling motion. Although within each group of balls the motion is random, the table as a whole exhibits a degree of order in that one side of the barrier is all red and the other all blue.

Now remove the barrier. As the jostling continues, the red and blue balls will gradually intermingle until both types are, on the average, evenly distributed across the entire expanse of the table. The intermingling, the decay of the original, ordered separation of the balls, is an inevitable, spontaneous, one-directional process. This can be seen by filming it and running the film backward. It would show the quite unreal process of a group of thoroughly mixed red and blue balls gradually separating themselves into two groups of pure red and pure blue. By this test, then, the real process of intermingling is spontaneous and irreversible—one of the many signs of the one-way direction of time. The reversible, time-independent bouncing of one ball (or one molecule) into another, of itself, creates disorder *if it is allowed to operate within an overall system which is, to begin with, ordered* (the dividend billiard table or the bulk of the falling water at Niagara Falls).

A sand castle provides a more prosaic example of the spontaneous, irreversible conversion of order into disorder. A sand castle is, of course, a more ordered arrangement of the grains of sand than an ordinary patch of beach. All the sand grains, whether or not part of the castle, are subject to the random motion imposed on them by the vagaries of wind and water. With time, these random motions will spontaneously reduce the ordered arrangement of the sand castle to the disorder of the rest of the beach sand. The sand castle will disappear. The reverse does not happen; sand castles do not spontaneously appear on the beach. An old barn is another common example. If the random effects of wind and weather are unopposed by human action, with time they will reduce the ordered arrangement of boards and timbers—the barn—into a disordered heap. And no one has seen such a heap become spontaneously assembled into a barn.

I have thus far used the words *order* and *disorder* in ways that fit their common usage, but in the process have done some violence to the strict thermodynamic meaning of these terms. Since the concept that governs the thermodynamic definition of order turns out to play a critical role in the practical value of the energetic laws, it is useful, at this point, to describe what is meant by order in these stricter terms.

In each of the above cases, disorder is represented by a situation in which the outward appearance of the object is consistent with a large number of different possible *internal* arrangements, and order is increased if the overall appearance will permit fewer of them. Thus, various heaps of lumber can have the same outward shape with the separate boards arranged internally in thousands of different ways. However, if the same pieces of lumber are to have the outward appearance of a barn, the number of possible internal arrangements is much reduced. In other words, the overall structure of a barn will tolerate fewer different internal arrangements of boards than will the structure of a heap.

Thus, in the thermodynamic sense, order is a measure of the degree to which the overall properties of a physical system dictate the selection of a particular internal arrangement of its constituent parts. Order expresses the relation of the properties of the whole (the barn) to the properties of its parts (the boards). Order signifies that the whole is not a simple summation of the properties of the parts and is strongly affected by the *relationships* among them, in particular how these relationships are limited or constrained. The whole, therefore, constitutes a *system,* the behavior of which is strongly affected by its internal design. (Architects are well aware that this is true of barns and other buildings.)

Let us now recall that spontaneous, irreversible processes are the events that signal the one-way passage of time, and the affected systems end up with less order than they had when they began. In each case, some random, reversible, time-independent processes (such as billiard balls or molecules bouncing against one another, or the random impact of wind currents on grains of sand) generate disorder in a system that began with some degree of order. Thus, we can account for the universal experience that, with the passage of time, more and more disorder is observed in the world if we assume that the world was once a more ordered system than it is now. It is the earlier existence of order that gives us a way to sense the passage of time. The barn can be seen to decay with time because it was once a perfectly formed barn. The clock tells time because it was once wound up.

This is the foundation of the Second Law of Thermodynamics, which, together with the First Law, governs the outcome of every energetic process. The Second Law asserts a single cosmic fact: that the universe is constantly, irreversibly becoming less ordered than it was. It is this behavior of the universe that accounts for the one-way direction of events and the irretrievable passage of time.

Probability also enters the picture because it is fundamentally connected with the occurrence of order in the world. Probability is a statement about the likelihood of encountering some particular event among all the possible events that can occur in a certain system. When a coin is flipped, there is a total of two possible outcomes and the probability of either one of them occurring in a given toss is one out of two, or one-half. Similarly, the probability of one of the six numbers on a die turning up in a single roll is one out of six. Thus, if the number of alternative possible arrangements is small (a coin has only two), the probability that one of them will occur is high (for coin-flipping, one-half). If, as in the die, there are six possible arrangements, then the probability of any one occurring is low, only one-sixth. The relationship of probability to order is then evident: A low probability reflects a singular choice among many possibilities, is synonymous with order, which in a system requires that its parts assume relatively few of their many possible internal arrangements.

Since we know that an ordered arrangement will, with time, spontaneously become more disordered, it follows that an improbable situation will tend to become transformed, with time, into a more probable one. This is yet another way of stating the Second Law of Thermodynamics: "Every system which is left to itself will, on the average, change toward a condition of maximum probability." Note that, stated this way, the Second Law does not claim that the system will certainly change into a more probable configuration. It claims only that this will happen *on the average*. Any particular change might go the other way, but with a low probability.

Returning to the teacup and the more obvious manifestations of energy, what this feature of the Second Law tells us is that we cannot be *absolutely certain* that the teacup (or its fragments) will not spontaneously leap upward. But the probability of this event is fantastically small. G. N. Lewis, a brilliantly iconoclastic chemist, who liked to be accurate about such things, once computed the actual probability that an object weighing ten billionths of a gram, if looked at repeatedly once a second, will ever be found 100 billionths of a centimeter or more above a supporting surface. On the average, the object will be found in this position 6.32 times every million years. For a more reasonably sized object, such as a teacup rising several inches off the floor, the probability of the event is so small that it would take a lifetime of writing zeros to record the number of years in which it might happen a few times. A reasonable estimate of this probability is "never." When we lift the teacup, this otherwise enormously improbable event does occur. Thus, work can powerfully increase the probability of an event. Work suitably done on a disordered heap of lumber can produce the more ordered, less probable state known as a barn.

In turn, probability is closely connected with information. Information theory is a relatively new aspect of science, which has now taken on a considerable practical importance as the basis for computer design. A computer generates information by operating a program which selects a certain pattern of choices from a series of optional ones. Each choice is usually determined by whether a switch is in the on or off position. The choice of one of the two optional switch positions represents one unit of information, technically a *bit*. The computer program specifies the position to be taken by each of a series of connected switches, and the total amount of information involved is the sum of the bits represented by the choices made at all the switches.

Thus, in general terms, information consists in the exclusion of some of the alternative possible arrangements of a system. For example, if, out of the huge number of optional arrangements of a pile of boards or of sand grains, we select only a certain restricted class of arrangements, we will acquire the information that the boards are in the form of a barn and the sand grains are in the form of a castle.

Information is thereby analogous to a decrease in probability and to an increase in order. As a result, the Second Law of Thermodynamics can also be written in this form: "Any spontaneous, irreversible process, acting on an isolated system, will result in a loss of information." If we come upon a jumbled heap of boards in a field, we may not know whether it once represented a barn or a house. The spontaneous effect of wind and weather has destroyed that information. Perhaps the most pointed comment about the relation between information and probability is Norbert Wiener's (one of the founders of information theory): "The more probable the message, the less information it gives. Clichés, for example, are less illuminating than great poems."

The framework of the Second Law of Thermodynamics binds together a very fundamental body of knowledge—about the spontaneity and irreversibility of natural processes, the degree of order and disorder in the universe, and the meaning of probability and information. The central assertion of the Second Law is that the spontaneous processes that are the actual events of the real world always lead to states that are less ordered, more probable, and represent less information than the states in which they began. This means that every spontaneous process irreversibly decreases the order of the universe and brings it to a more probable state that contains less information than before. Whatever happens in the world leads in this downhill direction. The Second Law also tells us that such a natural process can be reversed by the application of energy, but—as we shall see—this can be accomplished only at the expense of further decay in the overall order of the world.

In these ways the Second Law of Thermodynamics lays out the grand scheme of what happens in the world: what events (the teacup falling, the river crashing down the falls, the sand castle crumbling into anonymity) are likely to happen, spontaneously, on their own; what events (the cup or the river water raised to their original heights, the castle organized from the jumbled sand of the beach) are vanishingly improbable unless they are made to happen by doing work. Thus, every event, everything that happens in the world, is fundamentally connected with energy. And in this relationship we begin to see the strong links between the abstract, cosmic aspects of thermodynamics and its prosaic uses in industry and everyday life.

The chief practical purpose of thermodynamics is to learn how energy can best be harnessed to work-requiring tasks. These tasks—the work that people do—are all intended to, and usually do, generate order from disorder (building barns from heaps of lumber, or skyscrapers from piles of sand, cement, and metallic ores); to produce events that, in nature, are enormously improbable (teacups lifted from the floor; rockets shot toward the moon); to create new information (the designs of the barns, skyscrapers, and rockets). What people do, then, is to use energy to reverse, in highly specific, localized ways, the overall decay of the universe toward disorder, increased probability, and loss of information.

We cannot, of course, change the fate of the universe; overall, the spontaneous, downhill process continues. But human activity does create, for a time, local islands of order, improbability, and information—barns, skyscrapers, rockets, and all the other trappings of civilization. This takes work, which is available to us from the very spontaneous processes that mark the downhill course of the universe. The practical value of thermodynamics is that it can teach us how to mobilize this energy and most effectively use it to generate the activities of civilized life.

The junction point between the splendid, arching abstractions of thermodynamics and its powerful, concrete achievements is the work of a young French engineer and economist, Nicolas Léonard Sadi Carnot. This is contained in a single 128-page pamphlet published by Carnot in 1824, when he was twenty-eight (he died in a cholera epidemic eight years later), under the title *Reflections on the Motive Power of Fire and on the Machines Necessary to Develop This Power*. Carnot was interested in improving the efficiency of steam engines. The engines of the time had very low efficiencies; only a small percentage of the energy applied to them as heat was recovered in the form of mechanical work. Carnot discovered that there is a theoretical limit to this efficiency. He worked out general principles which govern the operation not only of steam engines, but of "all imaginable heat engines" as well.

Such a heat engine can operate in two opposite ways. Operating in the conventional direction (as, for example, a steam engine), energy enters the engine as heat (in the steam engine, at the boiler), flows through the machinery, and emerges in two forms: the engine's mechanical motion and leftover "waste" heat, which is always at a lower temperature than the entering energy.

Running in reverse, mechanical work is applied to the engine, which causes heat to flow from the cooler reservoir of energy to the hotter one. It is then a refrigerator (in which an electric motor, doing work, causes heat to flow from the colder interior to the warmer exterior—the kitchen).

Carnot's analysis showed that the efficiency of such an idealized heat engine—that is, the fraction of the energy which enters it as heat that is converted to mechanical work—is affected only by the difference between the temperature at which the energy enters the engine (in the steam engine, the steam temperature) and the temperature at which it leaves (in the steam engine, the temperature of the water that is used to cool the exhausted steam). The efficiency increases with the difference between the two temperatures. He also showed that there is an absolute limit to the efficiency of an ideal heat engine, because it inevitably rejects part of the entering energy into the surroundings as heat. In this sense, some wasteful loss of heat to the environment is inherent in the operation of any heat engine. (This explains why "thermal pollution" of the environment is always associated with the operation of a power plant.)

Carnot proved this point not by reasoning from the laws of physics, but by the testimony of the human failure to build a perpetual-motion machine that would "create" energy. He argued that if a heat engine were more efficient than the ideal one, it would yield some work beyond his calculated limit. With the heat engine running in reverse (that is, as a refrigerator), this extra work (if it really existed) could be used to transfer heat from the colder reservoir to the hotter heat source. This would cool the cold reservoir and heat up the hot one, and at the same time restore the engine to its initial condition. The engine would then be able to operate in the forward direction and the cycle could be repeated indefinitely, producing work *without any further addition of energy*. This would constitute perpetual motion, which, Carnot said, ". . . is entirely contrary to ideas now accepted, to the laws of mechanics and of sound physics. It is inadmissible."

By transforming the human failure to create perpetual motion into a subtle instrument of scientific analysis, Carnot established a principle that in turn set a new limit on this human conceit. Any heat engine that could run above the limit of efficiency deduced by Carnot would become a device capable of doing work by extracting energy from a heat reservoir and cooling it. This is precisely the sort of perpetual-motion machine (of the "second kind") that—if it worked—would allow ships to sail the seas forever, reverse the flow of Niagara Falls, and halt the passage of time. By arguing from the human failure to build perpetual-motion machines of the "first kind," Carnot predicted that no one could build a perpetual-motion machine of the "second kind."

Clearly Carnot's ideas, in Bridgman's words, "smell more of their human origin." Nevertheless, they have become the foundation of a realm of science of enormous theoretical power and relevance to the practical world. The specific outcome of Carnot's work was the establishment of the Second Law of Thermodynamics. One of the forms of this law emerges directly from his reasoning about efficiency:

"A process whose *only* net result is to take heat from a reservoir and convert it to work is impossible."

Carnot's formula for efficiency also establishes the basic thermodynamic meaning of temperature: It is a measure of the *availability of heat energy for conversion to work*. Temperature measures not the amount of heat energy, but rather the special quality of energy that tells us how well it can yield its valuable product —work.

The basic outcome of Carnot's thinking was the idea that any engine that can absorb heat to do work, and can use work to do the reverse, must be hot in one place and cold in another. The amount of work that can be gotten out of a given amount of heat, as it flows from the engine's hot place to the cold reservoir, depends on the difference between their temperatures. Although the energy content of the whole system is constant (in keeping with the First Law), a particular quality of the energy—its availability to do work—is diminished as the energy flows from its hot, entering status to its cooler, final status. The work that can be produced by the operation of the engine is equivalent to the loss of the energy's work-capability as it flows through the engine. Thus, although no energy is lost in the operation of a heat engine, something associated with that energy—its ability to do work—*is* irretrievably lost.

Carnot's little pamphlet became the starting point of thermodynamics, which created a series of mathematical relations that connected the efficiency of heat engines to measures of the work available from energy, of disorder, probability, and information. There emerged a new concept, *entropy,* which was mathematically related to all of these thermodynamic properties. Entropy is a measure of the *un*availability of energy for work, of *dis*order, of a *high* degree of probability, of a *loss* of information. When the entropy of a system increases, its energy is less able to do work. Thus, in any real irreversible process, in which entropy necessarily becomes larger, the total energy is conserved, but some of the work that can be gotten out of it is irretrievably lost.

The broad reach of thermodynamics has been compressed into two aphorisms:

> FIRST LAW: The energy of the universe is constant.
> SECOND LAW: The entropy of the universe is constantly increasing.

Here, we arrive at a kind of paradox which seems to lie at the heart of a good deal of the confusion about the theoretical and practical meaning of the energy laws. The laws of thermodynamics tell us that while energy cannot be lost, merely possessing it is of no value. Energy is valuable only insofar as it is used to generate work, to produce power. But in that process some of its ability to do work is necessarily lost. What inevitably diminishes is not the world's constant stock of energy, but its ability to do what we value—work.

The scientific knowledge that is symbolized by the laws of thermodynamics gives us the capability of measuring *both* of the basic attributes of energy—its amount and its ability to do work. The First Law gives us the means of measuring amounts of energy, regardless of their form or their availability to do work. It enables us to count up our stores of energy, the amounts represented by a tank of gasoline or by the huge beds of coal in the Western states. Using these measures, we have begun to worry about budgeting the use of these stores. We have begun to think about "conserving" energy—saving so many BTU (British thermal units) of energy by home insulation and so many by driving at fifty-five miles per hour.

But the Second Law tells us that it is not energy which needs to be conserved, because in fact energy is never consumed. What does need to be conserved is a certain quality that is associated with energy, but which it may possess in differing degrees. This quality—the available work that can be obtained from the energy— is *not* conserved; it is irretrievably lost whenever energy is used to produce work. The science encompassed in the Second Law, if we would use it, is specifically designed to show how we can maximize the amount of work, the power, the value, that can be gotten out of using a given amount of energy. It is not the First Law, but the Second that ought to govern the campaign to conserve energy.

Yet, all of the present measures of energetic efficiency and the resultant conservation efforts are based only on the First Law. Indeed, the first comprehensive effort to show how the Second Law might be used to measure and maximize the work yielded by energy in transportation, industrial processes, and home heating was made by a group of U.S. physicists in the summer of 1974. Their analysis showed that in many instances the efficiencies measured according to the precepts of the Second Law are about ten times lower than the efficiencies measured by applying the First Law. Because we have thus far failed to use the appropriate (Second) law of thermodynamics to judge the efficiency with which the limited stores of fuel that drive the production system are used, we have been misled into the illusory belief that we are many times better off than we really are.

The Second Law of Thermodynamics is perhaps our most powerful scientific insight into how nature works. Now that 150 years have elapsed since the law was discovered, it is perhaps time that we should begin using it to govern the ways in which energy is employed.

Science has social value because it can provide useful answers to important questions. But science also has the more basic capability of *asking* the right questions. The science of thermodynamics is a rich source of both answers and questions, but we have used it chiefly to find answers rather than to propound questions. Thermodynamics has given us numerous valuable answers; it is the foundation of the design and construction of every modern instrument of agricultural and industrial production, of transportation and communication. But the energy crisis and its attendant environmental and economic problems tell us that there is something seriously wrong with the ways in which the automobiles, power plants, and factories that are the practical fruits of this science meet human needs. Yet, among these devices there are relatively few that are purely technological mistakes; most of them work fairly well.

What, then, has gone so wrong? What has gone wrong, I believe, is that we have failed to use thermodynamics to ask the right questions. As a result, we are burdened by powerful and overbearing answers to the wrong questions, or to questions that no one has bothered to ask. For example, one reason some people are so enthusiastic about nuclear power is that they assume that its sole product, electricity, is an essential and unquestioned good. However, behind this assumption lies an unasked question: What is electricity good for?

Thermodynamics can answer that question; but even more important, thermodynamics requires that the question be asked. As we have seen, there is a limit to the efficiency with which heat energy can be transformed into mechanical motion. However, motion can be converted to electricity with an efficiency of nearly

100 percent. Moreover, electricity is readily transformed into mechanical motion, with the same high efficiency, by means of electric motors which can be used to perform an enormous variety of work-requiring mechanical tasks. Thus, electricity is a maximally efficient, extremely convenient way to transform the energy of heat into the work needed to perform mechanical tasks.

Thermodynamics teaches us to think of available work as the quality of energy that gives it value, and it is useful to classify both energy sources and energy-requiring tasks in these terms. Generally, energy that is transferable at high temperature is readily available for mechanical work, and is, so to speak, of high quality. And, conversely, a process that involves mechanical work (motion) requires such high-quality energy. Energy is efficiently used when the quality of the source is matched to the quality demanded by the task. Thus, electricity is a thermodynamically efficient way to drive the motor that agitates the clothes in a washing machine. It is not a thermodynamically sound way to heat up the washing machine's water. The requisite heat energy can be obtained much more efficiently from fuel burned directly in a water heater than from fuel used to drive a power plant. This emerges from Carnot's teaching that a heat engine can convert only a part of the energy which it uses into mechanical motion. As a result of this limit and transmission-line losses, a power plant converts only about one-third of the fuel energy that it uses into delivered electricity. Therefore, if electricity is used to provide heat, two-thirds of the original fuel energy has been wasted.

Clearly, no one has bothered to ask this question about electricity, as power plants have been sprouting across the land like mushrooms, for an increasing portion of their output is being devoted to the wasteful purpose of generating heat. Yet, the need to *ask* this question is just as much a part of thermodynamics as the ability to answer it. Thermodynamics is concerned with the properties not of separate things, but of things organized into a *system,* the behavior of which is determined by relationships among its parts. The thermodynamic consequences of using electric energy are not inherent in the electricity, but are determined by the process that links it to a particular energy-requiring task. Thermodynamics tells us, quite pointedly, that the value of electricity depends on the task toward which it is applied and the process in which it is used. The proper answer to the question "What is electricity good for?" is "It depends on what it is used for."

Thus, properly perceived, thermodynamics calls upon us to base the use of energy on a definition of the tasks that we wish it to perform. The characteristics of these tasks can then determine the thermodynamic quality of the energy that can best be applied to them—as electricity, fuel, or solar heat. By thermodynamically matching sources to tasks, we can avoid the enormous waste of using high-quality energy for low-quality tasks, and minimize the growing economic and social costs of energy production. Thermodynamics, the science of systems, demands this kind of systematic approach to the use of energy.

These are the imperatives of thermodynamics. How well have we responded to them in the massive production and use of energy that is the cardinal sign of modern civilization? How well does the economic system, which is so closely dependent on the prodigious use of energy, reflect the simple arithmetic of the First Law and the powerful subtleties of the Second Law? We must answer these questions if we hope to solve the intricate knot of problems that threatens to turn our age into the Century of Crises.

3

THE FOSSIL FUELS: OIL

OIL EPITOMIZES the energy crisis. It is the dominant source of energy for most of the world. In the United States, together with the closely related fuel, natural gas, it provides three-fourths of the national energy budget. Oil is the basis of the two industries—automotive and petrochemical—which, together with the petroleum industry itself, make up nearly one-fifth of the total U.S. economy. And apart from their economic effects, the oil-based industries have powerfully molded the pattern of national life. Oil powers the horde of cars, the vehicles of the urban diaspora that has scattered people's homes and the places where they work and shop over wide, once-rural areas. The intensive use of petroleum-based fertilizers and pesticides has nearly transformed the farm from an outpost of nature into a branch of the chemical industry.

Because of the enormous importance of petroleum in the U.S. economy, an ensured supply of oil ought to be among the highest of national priorities. Many people were shocked, therefore, in the fall of 1973 to find that the petroleum supply was far from assured; that nearly half of it came from abroad; and that the embargo imposed by Saudi Arabia and other Mideast oil producers —presumably to express their displeasure with the U.S. attitude toward their conflict with Israel—appeared to create serious shortages of gasoline and fuel oil. On the East Coast, gasoline was so hard to find that motorists spent hours in long lines of cars (their idling engines uselessly burning gasoline) waiting to buy a few days' supply. Heating oil was also scarce, and farmers were forced to pay premium prices for the propane that they needed in order to dry harvested grain before it would rot.

The 1973 oil embargo set off a sharp rise in the price of gasoline, heating oil, propane, and the numerous chemicals—especially fertilizers and pesticides—that are made from petroleum products. The gasoline shortage depressed the sale of cars, and the automotive industry went into a steep decline; within a year about 20 percent of its plant capacity and over 100,000 of its workers were idle. The increased fuel costs raised rents, and the rising cost of agricultural chemicals contributed to inflated food prices. Suddenly energy problems were problems of inflation and unemployment; energy had become firmly enmeshed in the deepening economic crisis.

The oil companies were quick to respond to the nation's ordeal: They sharply stepped up their advertising campaigns. Oil-company advertisements sought to explain the sudden onset of the energy crisis. They blamed the environmentalists for delaying the construction of offshore wells, refineries, and power plants; Congress for its failure to enact tax concessions that would give the industry the "incentive" to produce more domestic oil; the Arabs for imposing the embargo; and Israel for confronting the Arabs. Yet, despite the advertisements —or perhaps because of them—public-opinion polls showed that most people blamed the energy crisis on the oil companies.

The ensuing debates and discussions—including the interminable and largely fruitless haggling by the Congress and President Ford over the control, or lack of control, of the price of oil and natural gas—have been seriously hampered by the shortage of an essential ingredient: the facts. During the 1973 oil crisis no one knew exactly how much oil the country had or needed. The oil companies explained the long gasoline-station lines by a severe shortage of crude oil due to the embargo. However, when all the data were in, it was learned that even during the worst part of the embargo the available amounts of most petroleum products were only about 1.5 percent or less below the amounts

available a year earlier. When Congressional commit-
tees tried to investigate such discrepancies, they discovered that nearly all the original information about
the production and availability of petroleum was in the
hands of the oil companies and their organizations. Few
hard facts about the oil situation reached the arena of
public debate in a form that could be understood by
the participants. In their absence, sharp disagreements
broke out and suspicions flourished.

Was the country really "running out of oil," or were
the oil companies promoting that idea in order to justify
a price rise? Was the recent decline in domestic oil production the natural depletion of a limited resource or
the result of deliberate oil-company policies? Where
were the missing facts?

Ironically, the sought-for data were hidden, perhaps
unintentionally but nevertheless effectively, by a modern bureaucratic version of the wonderfully simple
method made famous by "The Purloined Letter." The
facts needed to delineate, in stark and frequently em-
barrassing terms, the role of the oil companies in the oil
crisis are available. They are laid out in great detail in
reports published by the Federal Energy Administration and other government agencies, and by an official
arm of both the oil companies and the U.S. Department
of Interior, the National Petroleum Council. These reports make up thousands of heavily documented pages;
one report on the availability of oil in the next decade
contains 688 tables and 114 illustrations and graphs.
Nearly all of the data described in this chapter are tak-
en from these informative but rarely discussed reports.

THE PHYSICAL FACTS about petroleum (crude oil)
and the closely related fuel, natural gas, are well known.
Crude oil and natural gas consist almost entirely of a
mixture of hydrocarbons, a class of compounds made
up of carbon and hydrogen atoms. The carbon atoms
are linked in straight and variously branched chains,
or rings, of different sizes. The carbon-to-carbon bonds
that make up the skeletons of such compounds leave
each of the carbon atoms free to form additional bonds

with other atoms. In a hydrocarbon nearly all these extra bonds are taken up by attachments to hydrogen atoms, and the molecule can be visualized as a linear, branched, or ring-shaped core of carbon atoms surrounded by a layer of hydrogen atoms.

Hydrocarbon molecules are good stores of energy, which is readily released, as heat, when they react chemically with oxygen. This is characteristic of a fuel —a substance which, sufficiently supplied with air, burns and generates heat. In thermodynamic terms, burning is a spontaneous, irreversible process. The spontaneity is somewhat obscured by the fact that a fuel usually will not burn unless heat is applied to ignite it. Once started, burning proceeds spontaneously, the heat of the flame itself thereafter maintaining the necessary temperature. Burning is a self-propagating chain reaction in which the heat that the process itself produces keeps it going until fuel or oxygen is exhausted.

If a hydrocarbon fuel is well exposed to air (typically by being impregnated into cloth or paper) and insulated from heat loss (for example, by being enclosed in a sufficiently large pile of the same material), it is likely to become hot enough, after a time, to catch fire by itself. In this process—spontaneous combustion— the slow reaction of the fuel with oxygen releases heat. The heat accumulates in the insulated pile until it reaches the temperature that ignites a flame, and finally a fire breaks out. Thus, like the water at the top of Niagara Falls, a hydrocarbon fuel is poised to release its potential energy spontaneously; the match is needed only to push it over the edge.

When a hydrocarbon burns, its carbon and hydrogen atoms combine with oxygen to form oxides: in the case of carbon, usually carbon monoxide and carbon dioxide; in the case of hydrogen, the oxide of hydrogen more commonly known as water. The principles of thermodynamics, extended into the field of chemistry, describe the changes in energy and entropy that occur in such chemical reactions. Standard tables of the heat content of different fuels are now available. These are given as the amount of heat that can be obtained from the fuel when a unit amount is burned, usually expressed as the number of BTU. Computations of the entropy levels of hydrocarbon fuels—that is, the availability of their potential energy for work—show that they lie somewhere between the very high-quality level of mechanical motion (and its products such as electricity) and low-temperature heat.

Thus, like a teacup smashing on the floor, or the Niagara River crashing to the bottom of the falls, the burning of a hydrocarbon fuel is a spontaneous, irreversible process. It converts the fuel's potential energy into heat or work, forms of energy that can be usefully applied to many tasks. To accomplish these tasks, the world now consumes a huge amount of petroleum—an average of about two-thirds of a gallon per day, per capita. In the United States, the per-capita consumption is about 3.5 gallons per day.

In the United States, petroleum fuels are used in the main for two energy-requiring tasks. About 54 percent is used to drive transportation vehicles, and about 21 percent is used to warm up the places where people live and work (space heat) and to heat water for washing. In view of the enormous amount of petroleum used for these purposes, and the considerable trouble resulting from consuming more petroleum than we produce, it is useful to realize how much of it is wasted.

Waste—or its converse, efficiency—can be looked at in several ways. The most obvious way to waste a resource such as petroleum or natural gas is to lose it before it can be used. Oil spills and pipeline fires fall into this category; but the amount of petroleum lost in such events is vanishingly small compared to the amount used, and can reasonably be neglected.

A resource can also be wasted when it is used, in the sense that some of it is frittered away in the process and does not end up where it is wanted. In the case of petroleum, this kind of waste is moderately large but not overwhelming.

Consider a familiar example: the amount of heat that is wasted as an oil-burning furnace system delivers heat to the rooms that it is supposed to warm. One way to compute this efficiency is based on the First Law of Thermodynamics. This tells us that the energy produced by burning a given amount of fuel must be conserved as it flows from the furnace to the rooms. Therefore the amount of energy wasted is equal to the amount produced in the furnace less the amount that reaches the rooms. (The difference might represent heat that goes up the smokestack or leaks out of the house as it is transferred.) This "First Law efficiency" can then be expressed by the ratio of the amount of heat delivered to the rooms to the amount that is generated when the oil is burned.

Measurements of such efficiencies were for a long time ignored by everyone but heating engineers. But in the last few years, as the need for conserving fuel has become painfully apparent, such data have been reported in the growing literature of energy technology. By all accounts, the efficiency of furnaces *computed in this way* is moderately good. A typical efficiency for an oil burner supplying warm air to a home at 110° F. when the outside temperature is 32° F. is about 60–65 percent. This would suggest that there is some room for improvement, but not a great deal. Even if the oil-burner system were made 100 percent efficient (impossible in practice) by this measure, the amount of fuel used would be reduced by less than 40 percent.

Nearly all of the current estimates of possible energy savings are made in this way, using the First Law to find out where energy is lost, and how to stop some of the losses. The general outcome is a possible saving of no more than 30–35 percent.

However, the First Law, as we have seen, is only the initial building block of the science of thermodynamics, which in the subtleties of the Second Law becomes a vastly more revealing instrument. The Second Law reminds us that energy in itself has no value unless it can be used to produce work by flowing from one place to another; that every human activity, such as heating a home, requires work; that the *value* of energy is measured by the work it can do; and that the efficiency with which energy is used ought to be measured by how closely the amount of available work used to accomplish a task corresponds to the minimum amount that the task requires.

These basic precepts define the "Second Law efficiency" proposed by the American Physical Society study referred to earlier. To compute this efficiency, one begins by determining the minimum amount of work that needs to be done to accomplish a particular task—in this case, to warm a home by delivering air at 110° F. while the outside is at 32°. The next step is to compute the work that is available from the amount of energy that is actually used to accomplish the task—in this case, the available work that is consumed when the oil is burned and the heat transferred to the rooms. The Second Law efficiency is the ratio between these two measurements, or (to quote the APS study) ". . . the efficiency is equal to the ratio of the least available work that could have done the job to the actual available work used to do the job."

When such a Second Law efficiency is computed for the oil-burner system, it turns out to be 8.2 percent. According to the First Law, the oil-burner system wastes a little less than half of the energy that it uses; according to the Second Law, it wastes all but about 8 percent of the work available from the energy that it uses. The Second Law efficiency tells us that there is much more room for improvement than the First Law would suggest.

In a sense, the two procedures take an opposite approach to the efficiency problem. The First Law approach focuses on the energy content of the *fuel* and computes how much of it fails to get where it is supposed to go—the rooms; it ignores alternative ways to heat the home and is concerned only with how well a particular method works. The Second Law approach focuses on the *task* and determines how much work is needed to get it done. It then seeks out whatever method of doing the job comes closest to doing it with the least amount of work. The Second Law approach makes the most out of that quality of an energy source that gives it its value—the work available from it. This is the quality which, unlike energy itself, is *always* consumed, and the Second Law efficiency aims to find a way of using as little of it as possible in getting the task done.

It turns out that the most efficient way to warm a house is usually not by burning the fuel, but by employing it to run a kind of refrigerator. In its familiar usage a refrigerator is a heat engine that uses mechanical work (the motion of a pump, driven by a motor, acting on a compressible gas) to cause heat to flow from a colder place (inside the refrigerator) to a warmer place (the kitchen). The same kind of device (now called a heat pump) can be used to bring heat into a warm house by extracting it from the colder out-of-doors. The heat pump cools the out-of-doors in order to warm the house, just as the refrigerator warms the kitchen in order to cool its own interior. But Carnot's work reminds us that the engine used to drive the heat pump—for example, a diesel engine—cannot possibly convert all of the energy of its fuel into such mechanical work. Some of it must be rejected into the environment as waste heat. Since this waste heat is at a suitably low temperature, it can readily be used to help warm the home (through an appropriate heat exchanger). According to the APS study, with this sort of arrangement a diesel-driven heat-pump home-heating system can readily operate with a Second Law efficiency of about 20 percent. This is a more than twofold improvement over the conventional furnace—something that would appear to be impossible if the efficiency were computed, by the First Law, at 65 percent.

As we shall see later on, the same sort of considerations can be used to improve noticeably the Second Law efficiency of transportation, which is only about 10 percent. Since transportation accounts for most of the petroleum that is consumed, such an improvement could to a great extent reduce the enormous waste of petroleum that is revealed by thermodynamic analysis.

What is so shocking about this waste is that petroleum is an irreplaceable resource, as is evident from what we know about its origin. There is persuasive geological evidence that underground deposits of petroleum, natural gas, and coal are the residues of fossil plants; hence the term *fossil fuels*. As the plant remains were buried, their organic compounds were subjected to variable pressures and temperatures. Depending on local conditions, the ensuing chemical reactions produced the hydrocarbons of petroleum and natural gas, or the nearly pure carbon of coal. All of these fossil-fuel deposits represent energy originally delivered to the earth as sunshine and converted into chemical form by photosynthesis.

Photosynthesis occurs whenever a green plant is exposed to light. The radiant energy of the light is absorbed by the plant's green pigment, chlorophyll, and through an intricate series of chemical changes the absorbed energy drives the combination of hydrogen with carbon dioxide to form a series of organic molecules. Many of these are made of carbon, hydrogen, and oxygen—the carbohydrates, of which sugar is the best-known example. Part of the light energy absorbed in photosynthesis is also used to split water molecules. This produces the hydrogen that combines with carbon dioxide to yield organic compounds; it also releases oxygen—the other main product of photosynthesis—into the air.

As the earth's ecosystem is now organized, the global photosynthetic reaction is perfectly counterbalanced by a reverse process in which the organic matter and oxygen that it produces react to form water and carbon dioxide. This is the metabolic reaction that yields energy for most living things. Because of the balance between photosynthesis and metabolic oxidation, neither organic matter nor oxygen accumulates.

When the earth was first formed, its atmosphere was devoid of oxygen, which appeared only after the first photosynthetic green plants were evolved. As the plants proliferated, the oxygen content of the atmosphere gradually increased until some 500 million years later it reached the 20-percent level that has since then been maintained. Oxygen-using organisms could evolve only toward the end of this time, so that during this period both oxygen and the organic products of photosynthesis were produced more rapidly than they were destroyed by metabolic combustion. The organic products accumulated as fossil plant remains that were eventually converted into oil, natural gas, and coal. At the same time the oxygen accumulated in the atmosphere. This period in the earth's history—a unique, never-to-be-repeated event—produced both the earth's store of fossil fuels and the oxygen needed to burn it.

Against this theoretical background we can turn to the exceedingly practical and highly controversial question of the amount of fossil fuel that we can actually hope to find and use. There is a widely circulated, portentous diagram that plots the past and anticipated rates of world fossil-fuel consumption over an extended time scale. It shows fossil-fuel consumption spanning only a very short transitory period in human history, from about 1800 to 2800. According to this estimate, in that 1000-year period human society is expected to consume all the fossil fuel available on the earth, an estimate that involves only about 4 percent of the total amount of carbon that, in theory, must have accumulated on the earth during the photosynthetic build-up about a billion years ago.

The very considerable disparity between the total amount of fossil fuel that must have been laid down on the earth and even the most optimistic estimates of the *accessible* deposits emphasizes the overriding importance of the effort to find them. This issue—the expected ultimate success of exploration for fossil fuel —is the source of much of the present confusion about energy resources.

Finding coal is not a very difficult problem. Most of it lies at fairly shallow depths (ranging from less than 100 feet to about 5000 feet) and fairly simple, inexpensive test drilling can readily locate and estimate the size of coal beds. Present estimates of the amount of coal available from such known deposits are about 16.8 trillion tons in the world. This would supply the world's total energy needs, at the present rate of annual consumption, for some 400–600 years.

The estimates of known and potential deposits of oil and gas are far more difficult and uncertain. Nevertheless, because of the importance of these fuels, the problem of estimating the resources as accurately as

possible is an immediate and urgent one. I shall restrict
this discussion to petroleum, since gas deposits are often
closely associated with oil and since, in any case, the
principles involved are essentially the same in both.

Oil deposits are now generally found at depths of a
few hundred feet to about 20,000 feet. The only way
to know that oil lies below a particular point on the
earth's surface is to drill down and find it. The amount
of oil in a given geological area, or field, can be estimated by drilling enough exploratory wells into it.
Since drilling to such depths is expensive, an effort must
be made, in advance, to locate the places where oil
might occur. This is done by geophysical exploration
—for example, by monitoring the echoes of shocks
from explosive charges in order to map the reflecting
contours of underlying structures. By examining such
an underground-contour map, an experienced geologist can judge which areas are most likely to contain oil.
The judgment involves a certain amount of guesswork
and the results are unreliable. In any case, the most
promising sites are chosen and exploratory wells are
drilled. These usually fail to find oil. In the United
States at present, even after the best available geophysical exploration, about eight out of every ten exploratory
wells are "dry holes." Finding oil is very much a hit-
or-miss geological proposition, and a risky economic
one.

Once an oil field is located, production can begin.
This involves drilling a number of producing wells,
suitably spaced across the field. Oil is then pumped
from the wells (or, less often, driven out under the
well's own gas pressure) until the field is exhausted and
the wells run dry. The total amount of oil that can be
taken out of a field depends not only on its size, but
also on the rate of pumping. The oil is contained in
porous rock through which it flows rather slowly. If
the pumping is too fast, the flow of oil toward the well
cannot keep up with it; this may break the continuity of
flow, leaving a good deal of the oil inaccessible. Even
after a field runs dry, more oil can often be taken out
of it by using additional procedures (secondary and
tertiary production), such as forcing water or gas into

some wells in order to push the remaining oil toward others.

Oil operations have been under way in the United States since 1859, when the first successful well was drilled in Pennsylvania. Since then the industry has expanded rapidly, and the United States has become one of the major sources of petroleum in the world. The records of the U.S. petroleum industry contain a large amount of information about where oil has and has not been found. Properly analyzed, this information can be used to estimate the amount of oil that we can expect to find in the future, and so to determine how long the supply of domestic petroleum will last.

The immediate outcome of a successful exploratory effort is the discovery of a certain amount of crude oil "in place." This represents the size of the underground deposit of oil that has been discovered. However, only part of the oil actually located can be brought to the surface, or "produced." As of 1970, an average of about 30 percent of the oil "in place" was actually produced, although this is expected to increase to about 42 percent or more over the next twenty-five years. The amount of oil discovered, corrected for the recovery rate, constitutes what is called the crude-oil reserve—that is, the amount of oil that is known to exist underground and that can actually be brought to the surface. It represents the nation's stock of available oil as it is known at the time. Two processes affect the size of this stock. One of them is discovery of new oil "in place," which gradually adds to the reserve. The other process is the rate of production of oil, which of course diminishes the reserve.

Until 1959 the size of the U.S. crude-oil reserve gradually increased, as the rate of new discoveries each year exceeded the annual rate of production. For several years after 1959 the reserve remained about constant in size. Then in 1967, for the first time in history, it began to decline progressively. We were then consuming more oil each year than was found, suggesting the notion that we were beginning to "run out of oil." This idea plays a powerful role in the current arguments over oil policy and needs to be closely scrutinized.

One reason for the falling reserve in recent years is that the rate of petroleum production has increased in response to a rapidly growing demand. The annual rate of production of domestic oil increased by 43 percent between 1953 and 1969, reaching a peak of about 9.0 million barrels a day in 1970. Over the same period of time the rate of finding new oil—the amount found each year—*decreased* by some 35 percent of its 1953 value.

The decline in the oil discovery rate that began rather abruptly in 1957 has continued. It has brought on an equally abrupt decline in the petroleum industry's ability to meet increasing domestic demand and led to the now lamented dependence on imported oil. Between the years 1954 and 1957 oil imports increased from 14 percent of total domestic consumption to 19 percent. Imported oil amounted to 22 percent in 1965 and 40 percent in November 1974. Thus, the gap between U.S. oil consumption and domestic oil production, and its grave economic and political consequences, can be traced back to a rather sudden decline after 1957 in the rate at which oil was discovered in the United States. If we are to make any sense out of the confused debate over oil policy, we need to find out why this decline occurred and whether there is any hope of reversing it.

An analogy may be helpful here in order to specify what we need to know to answer such questions. Consider foreign-car imports. No one regards the substantial dependence of U.S. car sales on such imports as a sign that we are "running out" of our ability to produce cars in the United States. The real reason is a simple economic one: U.S. manufacturers are unwilling, or unable, to undersell foreign cars of comparable quality. They have therefore decided to limit their rate of production, and match it as closely as possible to the rate at which they expect to sell cars in the face of foreign competition. No one is worried that some foreign country will—to paraphrase Mr. Kissinger's belligerent comment about the oil embargo—"get a stranglehold" on the United States by cutting off our supply of foreign cars. That would hardly be a disaster for the U.S. automotive industry, which would be delighted to use some of its idle capacity to take up the slack. No one would be impelled to threaten military action against Japan or Germany in the event of a "car embargo."

This makes a point which is obvious in the case of car production but much less so in the case of oil production: One's attitude toward a shortage of needed goods will depend heavily on whether it signifies the irremediable exhaustion of a natural resource or voluntary action by some human agency. In the first case, policy makers must accept the inevitable and try to find alternative sources of the needed goods, such as imports. In the second case, policy can be directed toward changing the governing decisions, which are, after all, made by human beings and can therefore be changed by them—or by others.

The issue that we must examine, then, is whether the falling rate of new oil discovery in the United States is due to the physical depletion of accessible oil deposits (and is therefore irremediable) or to conscious decisions on the part of those engaged in the search for oil to search less diligently. As it turns out, the records of both the physical process of oil exploration and the relevant policy decisions are available. They tell us a good deal about why we now depend on imports for nearly half of our oil.

Suppose it were actually true that the rate of finding new oil in the United States is declining because we are really running out of oil. Then, as new oil fields are found, and the number remaining to be found is thereby reduced, each additional new field would become progressively more difficult to locate. A more familiar analogy might be trying to find all the beads scattered from a broken necklace. The first few beads are easy to find, but the task becomes increasingly difficult as there are progressively fewer beads to be located in widely dispersed places. In the beginning, the ease of finding beads (as measured, for example, by the number found per minute) would not diminish; but when only a few beads remained to be found, the rate of finding them would begin to decline.

Now, suppose that you were unaware of the number

of beads originally on the string, and wished to know, nevertheless, when during the progress of the search you had found all or nearly all of them. This could be done by keeping a record of the number of beads found per interval of time. As long as the rate of finding beads increased or remained constant, you could be sure that a significant number of them were still to be found. After a time, when the rate of discovering new beads began to decline, you could expect that there were only a few remaining ones. When a long time passed and no new bead was found, you could assume that you had run out of findable beads, and probably had the entire necklace in hand.

In the same way, if the number of accessible but as yet undetected oil fields in the United States were now being appreciably reduced by current discoveries, then the effort needed to find each new field should be increasing. If we chose not to increase the exploratory effort, then the amount of oil found per year would decrease. On the other hand, if the amount of oil discovered *per unit of exploratory effort* remained constant with time it might be concluded that there was still a good deal of oil left to be found. Thus, as in the hunt for scattered beads, the rate of discovery of new oil can be used as an indicator of the phase of the discovery process. A year-by-year record of the rate at which oil is found and *of the effort made to find it* can tell us where we are, at the moment, in the inevitable process of exhausting the discoverable fields of oil.

Much of the controversy among oil experts regarding the potential oil reserve in the United States, and what fraction of it we have consumed thus far, results from the different ways in which they obtain and analyze this record. Depending on the method used, geologists can arrive at very different estimates of potential oil reserves. Unfortunately, the way in which the analytical method influences the results is not usually made clear. This is one reason why policy makers and the public are confused by the disagreements on how much oil remains to be found in the United States, and the unexplained disagreements have seriously hindered the effort to develop a sensible petroleum policy.

One of the curious aspects of these disagreements is how sharply they divide oil companies and government agencies. A recent Department of Interior summary lists five oil-company estimates of the amount of recoverable oil, as yet undiscovered, which future explorations expected to locate: 168, 90, 89, 55, and 24–64 billion barrels. Also listed are four U.S. Geological Survey estimates: 458, 400, 200–400, and 72 billion barrels. (The last and much the lowest of these estimates was made by the same geologist, M. King Hubbert, who reported the figure of 24–64 billion barrels while working for an oil company.) Even more curious are the separate estimates of onshore and offshore reserves made by the U.S. Geological Survey and the Mobil Oil Company. For onshore reserves the USGS estimate is 135–270 billion barrels of oil. The Mobil Company estimate is much lower: 34 billion barrels, or 13–25 percent of the USGS estimate. However, the offshore estimates are in much better agreement; the oil company's estimate (54 billion barrels) is within 42–84 percent of the government's (64–130 billion barrels). Perhaps by coincidence, the disparities between the two sets of estimates parallel the interest of oil companies in developing offshore deposits rather than onshore ones.

Such disagreements—and the resulting confusion—can be considerably reduced by sorting out the factors that influence the rate of finding oil. As already indicated, oil exploration depends on two general methods: geophysical exploration, which seeks to locate geological deposits that may, it is hoped, contain oil; and the drilling of exploratory wells. Both of these activities are carried out by people—geologists, geophysicists, drillers—who are in the hire of oil companies (the U.S. government does little or no exploration itself). The decision to employ these people and to direct them to look for oil is, of course, made by the oil-company management. Thus, one element in the effort to find oil that will affect the rate of discovery is simply the company's policy on how hard to look for it. Of course, apart from these administrative decisions, physical factors arising from the actual depletion of deposits will also affect the discovery rate.

The total effect of the administrative and physical factors together can be measured by the rate of discovery—the amount of new oil found per year. Such a measurement does not distinguish between the influence of the two factors. The main practitioner of this type of measurement is the aforementioned oil geologist M. King Hubbert, formerly with the Shell Oil Company and later with the U.S. Geological Survey. Hubbert's estimates are based on the yearly variations in the amount of oil discovered per year, starting in 1860, when record keeping began. Despite the dual factors involved in these measurements, this estimate leads him to conclude that "the discovery of crude oil in the coterminous part of the United States and its adjacent offshore areas has passed its culmination and is well advanced in its decline." He reaches the pessimistic conclusion that the ultimate amount of recoverable oil available in the United States is about 175 billion barrels. Since about 110 billion barrels had already been consumed by 1974, this would leave only about 65 billion barrels available for future use. With oil now being consumed at the rate of about six billion barrels a year, we would indeed be "running out of oil."

Hubbert acknowledges that this estimate includes the influence of company decisions on how hard to look for oil, for he states that "When a *given amount of exploratory effort per year* in a given area yields over a long period of time continuously diminishing returns in the amount of oil discovered, the inference can hardly be avoided that the pond is fished out." The phrase that I have emphasized is critical, as can be seen by going back to the bead analogy. It is certainly true that for "a given amount of exploratory effort" a declining rate of finding beads would mean that there are few remaining ones to be found. But if you stop looking for a while, the amount of exploratory effort is no longer "given" and the resultant slow rate of finding beads means not that most of the beads have been found, but that you have become less interested in finding them.

✳ Another geologist, A. D. Zapp, proposed a different way to measure the trend in the rate of oil discovery. His method sharply diverges from Hubbert's, both in its assumptions and in its results. Zapp's measure neatly eliminates the influence of company decisions. This is done by comparing the amount of new oil discovered with the amount of exploratory drilling actually carried out (as given by the total length, in feet, of the exploratory wells). Thus, where Hubbert plots the amount of oil discovered per year, for successive years, Zapp plots the amount of oil discovered per foot of exploratory well drilled, for successive cumulative lengths of wells drilled. In this way Zapp's method, unlike Hubbert's, measures the amount of oil found for "a given amount of exploratory effort." It excludes the effect of oil-company decisions and reflects only the frequency with which a purely physical effort—the probing of the earth by a given length of exploratory well—manages to hit upon an oil deposit, and the amount of oil in it. Again, Hubbert acknowledges this difference in methods, stating that Zapp's results are "less subject to economic and administrative influences."

To go back to the bead analogy once more, Zapp would record how many beads are found *per unit effort,* as perhaps measured by the amount of floor space covered in order to find one bead. In contrast, Hubbert would measure the number of beads found *per minute*. This measure would include the effects of "administrative," decisions, such as deciding to hurry the search for a time, or giving it up temporarily in favor of some more attractive pursuit.

Using his method, Zapp estimated that the total potential deposits of recoverable oil in the United States amounted to about 600 billion barrels. As noted earlier, other estimates by government geologists, also based on the Zapp method, yielded values in the range of 400 to 450 billion barrels of recoverable oil, all of them well in excess of the estimates made by Hubbert and the oil companies.

Hubbert's rejoinder to these estimates, which is supported by a recent National Academy of Sciences report, has been to re-analyze Zapp's data in an effort to

show that the amount of oil found per foot of exploratory well has actually been decreasing with the total
length of wells drilled, as one would expect if oil deposits were becoming scarcer. Some evidence of such a
decline can be seen in the data, but it is very sporadic
and, rather than following a smooth curve, as Hubbert's hypothesis would require, the decline actually occurs in two rather abrupt drops, one around 1945 and
the other around 1953. This suggests that the decline is
the result not of some gradual process, such as the progressive depletion of accessible oil deposits, but of some
more abrupt event, such as a change in drilling procedures.

In any case, since 1953 there is no sign at all that the
Zapp finding ratio has fallen as more exploratory drilling has been done. Indeed, the ratio has actually increased slightly. This is a crucial fact, for it is precisely
in the post-1955 period that the amount of oil found
per year (that is, the Hubbert type of measurement)
has progressively decreased: Between 1956 and 1969
the amount of oil newly discovered per year decreased
nearly 30 percent. Thus, in this critical period Zapp's
measure shows that there has been no decrease in the
physical efficiency of discovery (as measured by the
amount of oil found per foot of well drilled), while
Hubbert's measure of discovery rate—which includes
policy decisions as well as the physical efficiency factor
—has declined sharply. It follows, then, that the reason for the decreased rate of oil discovery per year is
not the diminishing returns to be expected as the stock
of oil is depleted, but that the oil companies were making progressively less effort to look for it.

This is confirmed by the records of the exploratory
wells drilled annually between 1950 and 1973. In 1950
about 10,000 wells were drilled; the number increased
to a peak of about 16,000 in 1956 and then dropped
sharply, reaching about 7000 in 1971. The number of
crew-months spent in the field by geophysical crews
also dropped from about 8000 in 1956 to 2700 in
1971.

Thus, there is in fact no discrepancy between Hubbert's results and Zapp's. Indeed, with respect to the

crucial events since 1957, which have led to the heavy
foreign-oil imports, the two sets of results lead to the
same conclusion: The declining rate of oil discovery per
year is a result of company decisions to cut back on
exploration efforts rather than of the depletion of accessible oil deposits. We are not so much running out
of domestic oil as running out of the oil companies'
interest in looking for it.

Why should U.S. companies that have been organized to produce oil decide, after 1957, to reduce their
effort to find it in the United States? Once more, the
officially published reports provide the answer. In July
1970 a committee of the National Petroleum Council,
in response to an earlier request from the Assistant
Secretary of the Interior, published a detailed study of
the nation's potential oil reserves. The study committee
was headed by the chairman of the board of the Standard Oil Company of California; members included
officers of every major and a number of minor oil companies. Leading geologists from universities, government agencies, and industry served as advisors. The
actual work was done by eleven regional subcommittees
comprising a total of 141 geologists drawn from oil
companies and the U.S. and state geological surveys.
Obviously the group was in an excellent position to
consider both the geological and the business aspects of
the problem of finding new oil in the United States, of
estimating the potential size of the resource, and of determining the reason for the reduced rate of discovery.

The report completely supports the conclusion which
I have drawn from the Hubbert/Zapp controversy: that
the recent decline in the oil discovery rate was due to
deliberate oil-company decisions. The reasons for the
abrupt change in the oil companies' exploration policy
are spelled out quite explicitly. A sharp distinction is
made between oil-company practices before and after
1957. Before 1957, company expenditures for exploration and development of new oil fields, per barrel of oil
produced, increased steadily, rising about 200 percent
between 1942 and 1957. After 1957, there was an
abrupt change: Instead of increasing, the exploratory
expenditures per barrel of oil produced fell by some 25

percent in the next ten years. This trend is in keeping with the post-1957 decline, noted earlier, in the footage of exploratory wells drilled and in the rate of geophysical exploration.

The report showed that this abrupt reversal in the trend of exploration expenditures was foreshadowed by changes in the oil companies' income. While the price of a barrel of oil increased by more than 100 percent between 1942 and 1952, in the next five years it increased by only 11 percent, and after 1957 it remained essentially constant (until, of course, the recent sharp rise beginning with the 1973 embargo).

Summarizing the analyses of potential oil reserves in the country's geological regions, the report remarks that "None of the 11 regions has been adequately explored" and concludes that the potential recoverable oil reserves of the United States "may exceed 432 billion barrels." With about 110 billion barrels already consumed by 1974, according to this estimate there would remain some 320 billion barrels available for future use. This is more than four times Hubbert's estimate. Finally, the report reaches an unmistakable conclusion about the cause and the consequences of the declining rate of oil discovery:

> The trend in the last decade of devoting a declining percentage of producing revenue to finding and developing production of crude oil and natural gas has resulted in a drastic decline in exploratory and development drilling which together with de-emphasis of the onshore of the coterminous United States is inimical to the development of the country's enormous petroleum resources. To the extent that policies of industry and government militate against accelerated exploration, particularly drilling, a high percentage of the petroleum resources of the United States is immobilized.

The evidence provided by this distinguished group, which was in a unique position to estimate the effect of both geological and economic factors on discovery rate, appears to be conclusive: The oil companies' failure to keep up with increased domestic demand is the result of oil-company decisions to reduce exploratory efforts following a period of disappointing economic returns on the oil produced. It was this decision that led to lower production of domestic oil, to the growing gap between domestic production and demand, to the increased importation of oil to make up the difference, to the nation's vulnerability to an oil embargo—and to all the ensuing economic troubles.

The motivation for this historic shift in the status of the nation's oil supply is not hard to find. Between 1947 and 1956 the profitability of the domestic petroleum industry dropped from a return of about 15 percent on equity to 14 percent. In that same period the profitability of foreign operations by U.S. petroleum companies *increased* from a return of about 15 percent on equity in 1947 to a 28-percent return in 1956.

The lesson was not lost on the oil companies. This is made clear by the explanation given by H. W. Blauvelt, then vice-president (and now chairman) of the Continental Oil Company, as to why his company, which in 1950 operated only within the United States, "decided to go abroad." In a paper published under the refreshingly frank title "How to Become a Foreign Oil Company," he gives three reasons for this move:

First, there was the need to maintain and increase our sources of low-cost oil . . . only the low-cost operator can survive and earn a reasonable profit. The cost of finding and developing a barrel of crude oil in the U.S. was revealing a stubborn upward trend . . . the discovery of prolific reserves in the Middle East, beginning prior to World War II . . . had made it evident where the large fields of low-cost oil could be found.

A second consideration was the simple fact of economic competition: that a producer of purely domestic oil would find it hard to compete with companies which, through foreign operations, could sell oil in the United States at a lower price.

Finally, Mr. Blauvelt tells us:

A third consideration important in our decision was the apparent profitability of foreign oil operations. As overseas crude output rose, profits also grew rapidly, and the rates of return earned by U.S. companies from their international operations proved considerably higher than the returns from their U.S. operations alone.

We also have Mr. Blauvelt's word that his own company's actions were not unique:

The decision taken by Continental in the fifties to go abroad was in line with similar decisions by other U.S. oil companies to the number [sic] of U.S. oil companies operating abroad rose from 13 in 1945 to over 200 at present [1966]. . . .

Thus we have the direct testimony of an officer of a major U.S. oil company as to *why* the decision was made in the 1950s that the effort to find and produce oil should be diverted from the United States to foreign countries. It can fairly be summed up in one word: profit.

But all this is past. If we are to benefit from an understanding of the recent history of U.S. oil resources, that knowledge must be used to develop a more rational oil policy. We now know that there is no *physical* reason for the sharp decline in the rate of domestic oil production that made the country dependent on foreign oil and set the scene for the 1973 oil crisis and the ensuing economic troubles. Despite confusing disagreements among oil geologists, it is now clear that, in round numbers, some 350 billion barrels of domestic crude oil are available to us. (This consists of the existing reserve of 35 billion barrels plus about 320 billion barrels available from anticipated future discoveries.) At the present rate of oil consumption (slightly more than six billion barrels per year), this amount would take care of the *total* national demand for oil, without any imports, for a period of fifty to sixty years. The last figure is an important one, for, as we shall see, there is good reason to believe that in that time nearly all of our present reliance on oil could be replaced by alternative, *renewable* sources of energy.

What would be a rational, prudent response to these facts? Clearly there is no need to act as though we are now running out of oil, for we are not. On the other hand, there *is* a limit to the accessible supply of domestic oil, and, if this limit is not approached in fifty years, it is very likely to confront us in the following half-century. This physical fact alone is a persuasive reason to plan for a transition from our present heavy dependence on petroleum to renewable sources of energy. As we shall see, there are strong economic reasons as well. And it is essential that the transition should be an orderly one; this is clear from the disastrous economic consequences of the chaotic response to the 1973 embargo.

Given that there is enough domestic oil to support us during the expected development of renewable resources, the basic problem is to discover what it will cost to produce the available oil and how these costs can be met. A task force, "Project Independence Blueprint" (an effort by the Federal Energy Administration to discover how the United States might become independent of imported oil), has made a detailed study of this problem, based on an earlier one conducted by the National Petroleum Council (NPC). The task force concluded that it should be possible to reach an annual production of total petroleum liquids (crude oil plus a small amount of liquid petroleum derived from natural-gas production) of 8.1 billion barrels per year. This is larger than the *total consumption* of petroleum liquids (including imports) in 1974, which was about 6 billion barrels. Thus, with some steps to control the rate of increase in petroleum consumption, it should be possible —if we wished—to produce all, or nearly all, of our needed oil from domestic sources in the next decade. We could then readily sustain our energy needs during an orderly transition to renewable sources, without shortages, rationing, or panic over future energy supplies.

The task force also computed the capital that would be needed to meet the cost of reversing the present trend toward reduced exploration and production. In 1974, in order to produce about 3.8 billion barrels of domestic petroleum liquids, the industry invested about $1.3 billion of capital. In order to increase domestic production from the present level to about 7.3 billion barrels in 1985 and to 8.1 billion barrels in 1988, annual capital expenditures would need to rise to about $9.1 billion in 1980 and remain at a level of about $8 billion per year thereafter. (These and the following dollar values are cited in 1973 dollars to eliminate the effect of inflation.) The productivity of the invested capital (that is, the amount of oil produced per dollar invested) was about 3 barrels per dollar of capital invested in 1974. In contrast, to produce a total of about 80 billion barrels between 1975 and 1988, about $100 billion of capital would be needed, representing a capital productivity of about 0.8 barrel per dollar. In increasing the annual rate of oil production, the productivity of invested capital—the efficiency with which capital is converted into oil production—would fall by 70 percent.

This considerable increase in the cost of producing the extra oil must be met in some way. The task force has computed that in order to provide the capital needed to support such a high rate of production, a barrel of oil would have to be sold at a minimum price of $11 (in 1973 dollars). The price early in 1975, also in 1973 dollars, averaged about $7 per barrel. Thus, the United States could become essentially independent of imported oil—*if* there were a sharp increase in the price of oil.

This is, of course, nothing more than the oil companies' demand for higher returns, to provide "incentives" to invest enough capital to produce more oil. If we meet this demand, how much more oil can we expect to get in return for paying such a high price for it? According to the task force, if the price were held to $7 per barrel, total production between 1975 and 1988 would amount to only about 70 billion barrels. To finance the production of that much oil, the public would have to pay a total of $490 billion for crude oil. If the price were allowed to reach a minimum of $11 per barrel, the industry would produce about 80 billion barrels of oil, and the total cost to the public would be $880 billion. Thus, in order to finance an increase of about 10 billion barrels in national oil production, an additional $390 billion would be paid for the oil, representing an incremental price of about $39 per barrel for the additional oil. In other words, the price of oil must rise disproportionately more than the increase in production that it is supposed to finance. For each additional dollar spent to meet the oil industry's demand for higher prices, the nation would receive progressively less return in the amount of oil produced. The law of diminishing returns is at work.

It becomes apparent, then, that although we have the *physical* resources to satisfy the total demand for oil from domestic production over the next few decades, actually producing oil from these resources will involve a considerable *economic* stress. As we already know from recent experience, any appreciable increase in the price of oil carries serious economic problems in its train.

Why is increased oil production so closely linked to higher prices? Here we can turn to the NPC report that provided the methodology used by the FEA task force. The NPC report determined the price of oil required to support various levels of domestic oil production by computing what income the oil companies would need in order to sustain a specified rate of return on their investment. The report shows that the price of crude oil in 1970 was equivalent to a 15-percent return on net oil-company assets. However, if the price of oil were to remain constant, "In 1985, the rate of return on net fixed assets would decline to a completely unacceptable level of about 2 percent." Accordingly, the report explains that "the projections indicate the need for significant 'price' increases, a strong reversal of 'prices' being required if the industry is to attract the venture capital required."

This study, which was completed in 1972, shows that to maintain the current rate of oil production from the continental United States, the price, which had remained essentially constant in real dollars between 1955 and 1970, would need to increase, slightly at first but rather sharply beginning in 1973–75. This is a very impressive demonstration of the accuracy of the NPC computations. In advance of the oil embargo of 1973 they predicted, from the requirements of the oil industry for a satisfactory rate of profit, that in 1973 the price of oil, which had been constant for so long, would need to rise. And it did. This reflects either a remarkable gift of economic prophecy or, perhaps, that the industry's prophecy was somehow self-fulfilling.

Again it would seem that the factors which govern the price that the oil industry demands in return for producing, from existing oil reserves, the amount of oil that the nation needs can quite fairly be summed up in a single word: profit.

Profit is a highly contentious word in the lexicon of public affairs. It is such a sacrosanct emblem of the ideology which is supposed to guide the private-enterprise economic system that discussions of business profit tend to be rather muted. In newspapers such discussion is usually relegated to the pages of the financial section. The oil crisis has considerably eroded this restraint. Following the 1973 embargo, as oil prices escalated and carried company profits to new records, their upward march was periodically reported in graphs published on the front page of the *New York Times* and other newspapers. There followed considerable public discussion and innumerable newspaper editorials, generally criticizing the oil companies for deriving high profits from the nation's energy troubles. And once the sanctity of the subject had been fatally compromised, the oil companies, for their part, commented somewhat caustically on the concurrent increase in the profits of the *New York Times* Company.

Nearly all these discussions of oil-company profits have been cast in terms of a kind of quantitative morality: How large a profit should the companies be allowed to enjoy? How much profit is "excessive"? (As we shall see in a moment, oil-company profits, which of course fluctuate from year to year depending on current economic conditions, have not really been appreciably different from those of other industries over the years.)

Here we are concerned with a quite different aspect of the profit issue: How does the expected rate of profit influence the companies' decision to find and produce domestic oil? Despite the apparent complexity of this question, the answer turns out to be readily at hand—in the deliberations of the FEA task force which studied the factors that might influence future production of domestic oil. The report states:

> Future oil production is mainly a function of its antici-pated profitability compared to other opportunities for investment, the amount of exploratory drilling undertaken and its success, and the extent of constraining policies that limit profitability or the availability of land favorable for exploration and production.

Of these operative factors, the only directly economic one is the *relative* profitability of producing oil—that is, the profit it is expected to yield, compared to any other investment which can be made with the available cap-ital. This is, of course, precisely why, according to Mr. Blauvelt, the U.S. oil industry hastened to take the profits that it had earned in the United States in the 1950s and invest most of them in the development of foreign oil business. This decision was mandated not by the *absolute* size of the industry's profit rate (which at the time was not very different from the rest of U.S. industry), but by the *difference* between that rate and the profit that might be had elsewhere—in this case, the Mideast. It is this principle—that the profit differential will determine where investments are made—which also accounts for the purchase of the Montgomery Ward mail-order business by the Mobil Oil Company out of its huge 1973 oil profits, and for the current tendency of oil companies to invest their capital in chemicals.

Apparently, then, the oil companies' interest in pro-ducing domestic oil is not governed by devotion to the national need for oil, or even by an insistence that their effort to meet that need should be rewarded by an equitable rate of profit. Rather, the oil companies' decisions are governed by their insistence on being free to invest their capital in any activity that promises the *greatest* profit. This position is explicitly confirmed by statements from oil-company officers, of which the following recent example is typical:

It doesn't mean a thing to say to a private company that
there's a great need for oil. You have to have incentive. If
it turns out that phosphate rock is more profitable, we'll
put our money there. [John J. Dorgan, executive vice-
president, Occidental Oil Corporation]

It would appear, then, that the oil companies are not
a reliable vehicle for the production of U.S. oil, for they
seem to be interested less in producing oil than in producing profit. Like a poorly trained bird dog distracted
by the appearance of a stray rabbit, an oil company is
likely to drop one project for another whenever there is
a hint of larger profits. The oil companies seem to be
poorly prepared to pursue the orderly, long-term development of a particular resource—such as the onshore U.S. oil deposits—and to resist the distracting
allure of more profitable investment opportunities elsewhere. Once more, we can rely on an oil-company
official (G. C. Hardin, vice-president of the exploration
subsidiary of the Kerr-McGee Corporation) to confirm
this inference, as it affects the direction taken by oil
exploration efforts: "Although modern oil and gas exploration is based on geology and related sciences, the
goal is economic. . . . The goal of any exploration program should be to find oil and gas *at a profit*" (em-
phasis added).

Apart from their unreliability as orderly vehicles for
the development of the nation's oil resource, the oil
companies suffer from another serious disability. Like
the rest of the U.S. economic system, the oil companies
operate on the principles of private enterprise. Therefore, not only their willingness to undertake a new
productive operation, but also their *ability* to do so depends entirely on whether or not their own private
efforts are sufficient to produce the requisite amount of
capital. From the data described earlier it is evident
that the productivity of capital will decline sharply in
future efforts to find and produce more domestic oil, so
that very large and rapidly increasing amounts of capital will be needed if the expansion is to take place.
The question arises, therefore, as to whether the
industry will be able to raise these large amounts of

capital by its own efforts, out of accumulated profits and borrowing power.

A recent article in the *Oil and Gas Journal* carries the headline "U.S. Oil Industry Falling Far Shy of Capital Needs" and opens with the following statement: "Will the U.S. oil industry be able to raise enough money to make the investments required to meet future energy demand? That's a question causing increasing worry among oil executives." Current (1974–75) earnings of U.S oil companies are at or close to their highest rates in history (an average of about 15.5 percent, after taxes). Nevertheless, the senior vice-president of the Exxon Company is quoted as saying: "Current earnings aren't adequate to generate the necessary capital."

In fact the annual earnings of the eight largest U.S. petroleum companies over the period 1951–71 were not very different from those of all manufacturing companies. Petroleum companies earned about 12 percent and all manufacturing companies about 11 percent on stockholders' equity, after taxes. But apparently this rate of return, or even the present rate of 15.5 percent, may be insufficient to raise the industry's needed capital, for a Gulf Oil official is quoted as saying: "Unless the industry can earn a 15–20 percent rate of return after taxes, it will neither be able to generate the needed funds internally [i.e., out of profits] nor will it be able to borrow them at attractive rates."

This appears to be a worldwide problem in the petroleum industry, for a recent survey by the Chase Manhattan Bank reports that, of the capital needed for world petroleum production between 1970 and 1985, only 7 percent had been accumulated by 1974.

This makes the situation quite plain: Unless the oil companies are allowed to earn a rate of profit that considerably exceeds the rate of profit of corporations generally—and of their own average rate of profit in the post-war period—the industry will not be able to generate, from its own productive activities, the capital needed to maintain, let alone expand, domestic production of oil in the United States.

In sum, there is considerable doubt that the oil industry, even if it were willing, has the capital-generating capability needed to sustain domestic oil production —unless, of course, it is allowed to earn an extraordinary rate of profit. This would mean a sharp increase in the already high price of oil, which even now seriously threatens the economic system. This disability, and the oil companies' firmer devotion to producing profits rather than to producing petroleum, challenge the wisdom of relying on these companies to find and produce the nation's oil.

4

THE FOSSIL FUELS: COAL

LIKE OIL, coal is the product of the singular burst of photosynthetic activity which, some billion years ago, produced all the fossil fuels—and the oxygen needed to burn them—that the earth now possesses. But there are striking differences between the problems of using hydrocarbon fuels—oil and natural gas—and coal. The known reserves of coal are about ten times larger (as measured by their energy content) than oil and gas reserves. There seems to be quite general agreement among geologists that the accessible deposits of coal, both in the United States and worldwide, would last about 400–600 years at the present rate of use. There is therefore no short-term problem of "running out of coal"; the United States exports rather than imports coal; there is no threat of a "coal embargo." All of these issues, which loom so large in the case of oil and natural gas, can therefore be set aside as we consider how coal fits into the energy problem.

While there are huge reserves of coal, using them (for example, during a transition to renewable energy sources) involves two difficult problems. One problem is how to use coal for transportation, which represents about one-quarter of the national energy budget. The second difficulty is the effect of coal production and use on environmental quality and health.

Coal was once the main source of energy for transportation; until the 1920s, coal-fired railroads and shipping carried most of the freight and passengers. Since then, petroleum-driven cars, trucks, and airplanes have been displacing the railroads. And after World War II the U.S. railroads themselves gave up coal; the coal-driven steam locomotive has become a museum piece, displaced by diesel engines. One reason for these shifts is that, weight for weight, hydrocarbon fuels contain nearly 50 percent more energy than coal. Another reason is that hydrocarbon fuels can be used in internal-combustion engines, while coal is restricted to externally heated devices such as steam engines. The most efficient internal-combustion engine, the diesel, has a thermal efficiency in the Carnot sense—that is, the efficiency with which heat is converted to mechanical work—which is about 40 percent greater than that of a steam engine. In addition, internal-combustion engines have a considerable weight advantage over steam engines. The weight of a diesel engine is significantly less than that of an equally powerful steam engine, and the weight advantages of gasoline and jet engines are even greater.

For these reasons, coal cannot directly meet the enormous needs for energy to fuel vehicles. There is one outstanding exception (to be discussed later on): electrified railroads, which can be operated very efficiently on electric power produced by a coal-fired power plant.

However, coal can be chemically converted into either liquid or gaseous hydrocarbon fuels that can be used in engines that are now run on petroleum products. A rather similar process produces oil from certain shale deposits. The problems of producing and using synthetic hydrocarbon fuels made from coal and shale are similar and will be considered together in this chapter.

Under the impetus of the notion that we are "running out of oil," there has been a recent upsurge of interest in the production of such synthetic fuels. The latest manifestation is the $100-billion corporation, originally proposed by Vice-President Rockefeller and later embraced by President Ford, that would use public funds to finance the development, by private corporations, of synthethic fuel processes and other, unspecified energy sources.

However, as indicated in Chapter 3, the existing reserves of natural petroleum could readily take care of our total needs for such fuels for a period of fifty years or more, a time in which they could be replaced by renewable energy sources. There would then be no need to develop coal conversion or shale-oil production. Nevertheless, in the absence of such a rational energy program, the production of synthetic fuels from coal and shale is often put forward as a viable substitute for imported oil, and we need to consider how well it might serve that purpose.

COAL IS LARGELY COMPOSED of carbon. Like oil, it can be burned at high temperatures and is therefore a source of high-quality energy. Coal now provides nearly one-fourth of the total energy consumed in the United States. As we have seen, in order to determine how efficiently it is used we need to look at the tasks to which coal is applied. A 1968 survey showed that 54 percent of the coal was used to generate electricity, about 24 percent to provide heat for industrial processes, and about 18 percent to provide industrial steam. Thermodynamically, coal is well suited to each of these tasks, since they all need relatively high temperatures (ranging up to about 3000° F.) and therefore a high-quality energy source. The Second Law efficiencies for these tasks, computed on a national average by the APS study, are about 25–30 percent—much higher than the efficiencies for the main uses of petroleum: transportation, space heat, and hot water. Thus, in sharp contrast with petroleum, the use of coal in the United States is fairly well matched, thermodynamically, to appropriate energy-requiring tasks.

However, if we look more closely at the _end-use_ of the electricity that is produced by coal-fired power plants, at least one very wasteful practice turns up—the use of electricity for space heat and hot water. As pointed out in the last chapter, when high-quality electric energy is used to provide such low-quality heat, even by First Law computations about two-thirds of the energy content of the ultimate source of the energy— the fuel burned by the power plant—is wasted. The Second Law efficiencies are very much lower—1.5 percent for hot water produced from electricity; electric space heating is almost as inefficient.

Of the electricity generated by coal-burning power

plants, about 10 percent is devoted to such thermodynamically mismatched uses. Almost all of the energy
used in this wasteful way could be saved by using
other, low-quality energy sources instead.

⚹ One obvious way to do this is to recognize that a
home using electricity for space heat or hot water is
linked to the wrong energy output of the power plant.
As we know from Carnot's teachings, every power
plant produces two kinds of energy which are very different in quality: electricity (high-quality) and rejected
heat (low-quality). For maximum efficiency these two
sources should be matched to thermodynamically appropriate tasks. Electricity should be used for tasks that
do mechanical work (driving a train or a washing
machine)—and which therefore demand high-quality
energy. The rejected low-temperature heat should be
used for low-temperature heating (of a home or the
washing machine's hot water)—for tasks that can be
done with precisely that kind of low-quality energy.
(Air-conditioning offers an interesting option. Common
air-conditioners are driven mechanically by a com-
pressor and are therefore efficiently run by electricity.
However, the less common heat-operated air-conditioners could be run by the power plant's rejected heat,
saving the electricity for tasks which *must* use it.)

To achieve such a thermodynamically efficient match
between energy sources and energy-requiring tasks,
the power plant and the homes (or commercial buildings) that it suppies must be linked into an integrated
system—via wires to conduct electricity and steam or
hot-water lines to conduct low-temperature heat. The
Second Law efficiencies of such combined electric/
heat systems are very high, ranging from 44 to 49 percent. If the same fuel were used to provide electricity
and heat (and heat-operated air-conditioning) separately, about 30 to 70 percent more fuel would be
needed to obtain the same output as the combined system. Such "total energy systems" have been installed in
apartment and commercial building complexes. Some
buildings in New York and many in Moscow are supplied with waste heat from local power plants.

From thermodynamic considerations it would appear that the task to which coal can be applied most efficiently, apart from producing electricity to drive domestic appliances and industrial equipment, is the one for which it is now least used—ground transportation. (Only about 0.2 percent of coal is now used for that purpose.) Electricity can be converted with nearly 100-percent efficiency to the motion of a train. What is more, an electric train can neatly prevent one of the main energy losses in transportation—the heat dissipated when friction is used to brake a vehicle to a stop. Suitably equipped, an electric train can be stopped by a switching arrangement that converts its motor into an electric generator, which transforms the train's forward motion into electricity that can be fed back into the power system while the train slows down. A large power network receiving electricity from a number of coal-fired plants, whose low-temperature output is integrated into local communities, that is employed to run electrified railroads would be an ideal way to make thermodynamically efficient use of coal. While transportation now accounts for about one-fourth of the U.S. energy budget, only about one percent of the required energy is obtained in this thermodynamically sensible way.

In contrast, the notion of converting coal to a liquid fuel to run vehicles flies in the face of thermodynamics. For one thing, by the time the fuel has been produced, about a third of the coal's original energy content has been used up to run the liquefaction process. Then, when the fuel is used to run cars and trucks, most of it is wasted because these vehicles operate with a Second Law efficiency of about 10 percent. The waste heat that their engines produce is spewed into the environment, and cannot possibly be applied to any practical task.

Thus, while the present uses of coal are well matched to thermodynamically suitable tasks (production of electricity and industrial heat), there is an as yet unexploited opportunity to extend its use to transportation and to combined electricity/heat systems.

COAL EXISTS in several forms: anthracite (hard); bituminous (soft); lignite and other low-quality coals (in descending order of their heat content). Coals also vary a good deal in sulfur content and therefore in their contribution to the environmental problems due to sulfur dioxide (which will be considered later on).

Coal beds are found at various depths. Some lie at depths that require underground operations; others are so close to the surface that they can be mined by stripping away the overlying layers and digging out the coal with huge power shovels and bulldozers. Until recently, underground mines produced considerably more coal than strip mines, but the two kinds are now about equal in production.

This shift was a response to economic factors. The labor productivity of strip mining (that is, the amount of coal produced per man-hour) is about three times that of underground mining. The types of skills—and the labor unions—involved in the two types of mining are also different. The current tendency to shift from Eastern underground mines to Western strip mines reflects these economic factors. As we shall see, the two types of operations also create different kinds of environmental and health problems. About 70–80 percent of the Western coal reserves are Federally owned.

The two types of mines have different capital requirements. In 1970 an average strip mine produced .09 ton of coal per year per dollar of capital invested, while underground mines produced only .05 ton per year per dollar of capital invested. About two-thirds of the known U.S. coal reserves are at depths that require underground mining, and the rest are amenable to strip mining. The advantage in capital productivity of surface mines is more or less counterbalanced by the greater prevalence of underground reserves. In contrast with oil and gas, further extension of coal production can probably be carried out without any significant reduction in the productivity of the invested capital, simply by extending operations into new areas that have about the same capital requirements as the older ones.

Underground coal mining involves some well-recognized environmental hazards—in particular, water pollution due to acid seepage from the mines. The environmental consequences of strip mining are more serious. The gross disruption due to present strip-mining practices has been fully aired in connection with the recent bill that forbids most of these practices— and which was successfully vetoed by Mr. Ford. The problems arise from the practice of more or less abandoning the mine once the coal is exhausted, with only a minimum effort to fill the huge holes, or to cover the enormous piles of waste with fertile soil that will sustain plant growth. The general outcome is that an area that was once a wooded hillside ends up looking like a scene televised on the moon. Some idea of the environmental impact can also be gained from the estimated costs of properly reclaiming land damaged by strip mining—that is, returning it to some sort of stable, vegetated condition. The estimated costs range from about $1000 to $8000 per acre. This makes the reclaimed land more costly than highly productive Corn Belt farm land (which sells for about $1500 per acre), once the income from coal is discounted. It has been estimated that proper reclamation and other environmental control of strip-mined land would add about $1 per ton to the cost of strip-mined coal, which now sells at about $20 per ton.

Another well-known social cost of mining is the damage to the health of miners who work in underground coal mines. After a long and bitter battle, the government has been forced to recognize the devastating work-related effects of black lung, the disease so common among underground coal miners. The dollar costs give an "objective" but inadequate picture of the human costs of this disease. As of May 1973, compensatory payments to miners suffering from black lung (or to their widows) amounted to about $1 billion, and the sum is expected to reach $8 billion by 1980.

Proposals to expand coal production are closely linked to plans for converting coal to gaseous and liquid fuels; most of the justification for expanding strip mining in the Western states is that it would supply low-priced coal for conversion plants to be located in that area.

Coal conversion—and shale-oil production as well —makes heavy demands on another vital environmental resource: water. Whereas strip mining itself uses about 0.7–1.6 gallons of water per million BTU of coal-heat energy, shale-oil production uses about 30 gallons per million BTU and coal conversion uses between 30 and 200 gallons per million BTU. The main impact of this demand for water would be in the Western states, where most of these new processes are to be located, according to present plans. A recent survey shows that these plans for coal conversion and shale-oil operations in the Western states would use more water than is available in that region, if existing allotments, which are chiefly for agriculture, are maintained. Thus, for the sake of developing coal- and shale-based substitutes for natural petroleum—*non*-renewable resources—we would destroy land and water, both of which are vital, renewable resources that can produce food indefinitely, if they are properly conserved.

Apart from these well-known environmental and health effects of the production of coal and of synthetic coal and shale fuels, there is another very poorly perceived danger in these operations—cancer. In an industrialized country such as the United States, cancer is mainly an environmental disease; about 75–80 percent of the cancer incidence is due to environmental agents. Physicians were surprised when this conclusion was first voiced a few years ago by cancer epidemiologists. Most of them have now become convinced, as increasing numbers of substances that are widespread in the environment have been shown to cause cancer in laboratory animals and are therefore suspected of causing cancer in people as well. These include the insecticides DDT, aldrin, and dieldrin, which have been banned (for most uses) for that reason. Workers exposed to asbestos, or vinyl chloride, have recently been shown to suffer an unusually high cancer incidence; both substances have been found in the environment. A recent National Cancer Institute survey of cancer deaths in all the counties of the United States showed that death rates from lung, liver, and bladder cancer are highest in areas that have a heavy concentration of chemical plants and refineries.

The scientific study of environmental cancer has its origins in Percivall Pott's classic account, in 1775, of the occurrence of cancer of the scrotum among chimney sweeps. About 100 years later it was discovered that such cancers are due to certain chemical substances found in soot and coal tar. They belong to a class of complex organic compounds, the polycyclic hydrocarbons—thus named because their basic structure is made up of a series of two or more joined hydrocarbon rings.

Coal conversion involves the chemical addition of hydrogen to the nearly pure carbon of coal. The process is likely to form a certain amount of polycyclic hydrocarbons. (In the original coal structure the carbon atoms are themselves often arranged in joined rings, which upon addition to hydrogen atoms become polycyclic hydrocarbons.) Since coal is not a homogeneous chemical substance, and the hydrogenation process is itself difficult to control precisely, a wide variety of chemical compounds are produced by coal hydrogenation. About 200 different compounds have been identified in the output of one coal-hydrogenation plant, including many polycyclic hydrocarbons.

The workers' health record at this plant, which operated in West Virginia from 1952 to 1959, stands as a somber reminder that the chemistry of coal conversion may produce powerful carcinogens. The plant, designed as a large-scale pilot plant with a capacity of 300 tons of coal per day, began operation only after seventeen years of extensive research. However, it was not until late in 1952, after the plant was already in operation, that the company toxicologist reported that some of its products caused cancer when rubbed on the skin of laboratory mice. As noted by the plant medical director, "This stimulated the introduction of protective measures for workmen who would be exposed." The plant's medical department set up an elaborate program of education, hygiene, and frequent medical examinations in order to prevent exposure and to detect skin cancers

as early as possible. Examination of 342 workers in the
plant with nine or more months' exposure between
1954 and 1959 detected 5 cases of verified skin cancer,
11 cases of probable skin cancer, and 42 pre-cancerous
skin lesions. The incidence of verified and probable
skin cancer in this group was between sixteen and
thirty-seven times higher than the incidence in similar
populations outside the plant. On these grounds the
plant medical officer's report concluded that, despite
the intensive hygienic precautions, "Heavy exposures to
coal hydrogenation materials, even those of relatively
short duration (less than ten years), are capable of
producing cutaneous tumors—both precursors and neo-
plasms [actual cancers]."

The chemical processes that occur during the production of oil from shale are similar to the coal-hydrogenation reactions. And it has been known since 1876
—when an English physician described cancer of the
scrotum in a Scottish shale-oil worker—that shale oil is
carcinogenic. Scottish shale oil was used chiefly as a
lubricant in certain cotton-spinning operations in England. Between 1920 and 1943 over 1000 cases of skin
cancer were reported among the English cotton spinners
who were exposed to shale oil—an incidence considerably in excess of the rate elsewhere in England. A
laboratory study in 1922 showed that when crude shale
oil was applied to the skin of mice, tumors occurred in
40 percent of the animals.

Coal conversion and shale-oil production are not
commercially feasible at this time; the production costs
are so high that the synthetic fuels cannot compete with
oil at even its present high price. Government agencies,
in particular the FEA, have paid a good deal of attention to these costs, including in their estimates the expenditures needed to prevent undue environmental im-
pacts. These have been evaluated down to rather fine
details, such as the effects of dust raised by the cars to
be used by the workers living in the area of projected
shale-oil operations. However, the carcinogenicity of
shale oil and the problem of controlling it are nowhere
mentioned in the FEA's 495-page report on that fuel. If
and when the problem of carcinogenicity is taken into

account in the design of coal-conversion and shale-oil plants—so that the plant work force, the people who live nearby, and everyone who uses these products are not exposed to this hazard—the plants' already high costs are likely to increase appreciably.

Coal, coal conversion, and shale oil are generally considered as alternatives to oil and natural gas. It is appropriate, therefore, to compare the environmental and health effects of these fuels. Apart from the aesthetic effects of huge oil derricks, the environmental impact of land-based oil and gas operations is less than those of underground coal mines, and very much less than strip mining and shale-oil production—which involve the displacement of huge amounts of material. The main environmental effects of oil production (excluding the refining and use of fuels, which will be taken up later on) are in the ocean. The growing tanker traffic in crude oil and the resultant dangers of collisions that spill huge amounts of oil into the seas have been effectively described in Noël Mostert's *Supership*. Belatedly, the industry has begun to develop methods for cleaning up oil spills, but these still occur frequently and place an ecological burden on the marine food cycles that is, thus far, poorly assessed. If oil pollution were to seriously affect the photosynthetic activity of marine algae, it might turn out to be a global catastrophe.

Another major environmental question about oil production is the impact of offshore operations. These are just now in the process of being assessed. The oil industry claims that, with newly developed precautions, the sort of disastrous blow-out that fouled miles of beaches around Santa Barbara, California, in 1969 can now be avoided. However, it is too soon to tell whether the precautions will work, and the problem must be regarded as still potentially serious.

Air pollution is probably the most serious environmental problem associated with the use of coal. Certain types of coal contain sulfur, which is oxidized to sulfur dioxide when the coal is burned. This is an especially pernicious pollutant, for it tends to interfere with the self-protective mechanisms in the lungs that help to reduce the effects of dust and other pollutants. As a result, the health effects of all other air pollutants are intensified in the presence of sulfur dioxide. Certain fuel oils are also high in sulfur content and contribute significantly to the sulfur-dioxide problem.

When coal is burned, it also tends to produce fine ash particles, some polycyclic hydrocarbons (including at least one which is carcinogenic), mercury, and other toxic metals. Precipitators that significantly reduce the emissions of ash are widely used. The Environmental Protection Agency (EPA) and the utility industry have been battling over the feasibility of stack devices that remove sulfur dioxide. Recent developments tend to support the EPA's contention that they are technically and economically feasible, but they are not widely used as yet.

On balance, the air-pollution problems created by burning coal are more serious (and therefore more costly to control) than those resulting from oil. Of the three fossil fuels, natural gas is clearly the most environmentally benign, and coal the worst.

In general, the main advantage of coal production over oil and natural-gas production in a future energy program would appear to be that, unlike the production of petroleum, coal production can be expanded without a reduction in capital productivity. However, this advantage promptly disappears if coal is to be converted into liquid or gaseous fuel. These are technically complex processes in which large amounts of coal go through a series of chemical treatments. For example, in a typical coal liquefaction plant the coal is made into a paste with oil, and then treated with hydrogen gas in a reactor at high pressure and temperature. The crude hydrogenation product is then separated into a series of different liquid products, some of which are further purified before being shipped. Such units are comparable to an oil refinery in technical complexity. As a result, the capital costs are very high compared to the cost of producing coal itself. For example, in 1970 a typical strip mine produced, per year, per dollar of capital invested, coal representing about 2 million BTU of heat energy. In contrast, if that coal were then liquefied, the amount of fuel produced per dollar of invested capital would represent only about 254,000 BTU of heat energy—a reduction of more than 87 percent in capital productivity. Similarly, coal gasification involves a 92-percent reduction in capital productivity, as compared to direct production of strip-mined coal. Shale-oil production yields about 420,000 BTU of fuel per dollar of capital invested.

Thus, if coal or shale is used to replace oil and natural gas, it would be impossible to escape the same problem—escalating capital costs—that makes the expansion of crude-oil production so difficult. This is reflected in the estimated price of synthetic fuels—which may be as high as $26 per barrel, well above the highest expected price of natural crude oil.

Despite these difficulties, the Ford administration is actively pressing for the development of coal conversion and shale-oil production. These schemes are economically feasible only if the price of the product which they are supposed to compete with—natural crude oil —is very high. When, following the 1973 embargo, the price of crude oil began to rise, seemingly without any foreseeable limit, commercial interests actively developed several experimental and pilot-plant coal-conversion and shale-oil operations. However, when the price of crude oil failed to rise sufficiently, some of these projects were abandoned because it was evident that their products would be unable to compete unless the price of crude oil increased further.

At this point the U.S. government tried to come to the rescue. Despite their earlier efforts to persuade the Organization of Petroleum Exporting Countries (OPEC) to effect a *reduction* in oil prices, Mr. Ford and Mr. Kissinger now attempted (unsuccessfully thus far) to persuade OPEC countries to agree to a *floor* to crude-oil prices. Thus in a speech in February 1975, Mr. Kissinger proposed to ". . . ensure that the price for oil on the domestic market does not fall below a certain level" so that investors in alternative energy sources—such as coal conversion and shale oil—would not be discouraged. A *New York Times* dispatch from the Paris meeting at which the Kissinger plan was adopted by the conference of oil-consuming countries stated explicitly:

> Countries with large domestic energy reserves, such as Canada and the United States, need a price floor to safeguard capital investments in the development of new energy sources such as oil shale and coal gasification. . . . The United States might preserve the floor by imposing a tariff or quota system on the imported oil or setting a special tax.

It seems to me that not only these efforts but also Mr. Ford's persistent attempts to raise the price of domestic oil by imposing a tariff on imported oil, or by lifting price controls, may be motivated less by the hope of reduced consumption (as he claims) than by his interest in making the synthetic-fuel industry (and, as we shall see, nuclear power) a safe investment for private capital.

Against this background, the pessimism in regard to the future of coal conversion that was exhibited at a coal conference held in Chicago in mid-1975 is understandable. It was reported that the cost of coal-conversion plants is so high that their products would need to be sold at a price equivalent to $26 per barrel of oil. Since such plants could not possibly compete on their own, potential operators were looking to the Federal government for help. However, a government representative reported that plans for a demonstration coal-conversion program had been held up because the industry was unable to raise its half-share of the total capital of $2.8 billion. The account of the conference closes with the comment that ". . . more funds to encourage domestic gas exploration might do more for our energy budget than would the big and expensive coal-conversion plants."

Now Mr. Ford has discovered how to make up for the inability of private companies to assume these risks. He is offering them public funds. This, after all, is the real meaning of the proposed $100-billion corporation designed to provide government guarantees against the risks of investing in synthetic-fuel production. If it succeeds, this move would eliminate the one barrier that has thus far held back this unnecessary, hazardous, and enormously expensive enterprise—the unwillingness of private entrepreneurs to risk their own money. But the new scheme has a special kind of irony. It proposes to use public funds to guarantee an enterprise that would burden the people of the United States with higher fuel prices if it succeeds or with higher taxes if it fails.

5

NUCLEAR POWER

IF THE U.S. GOVERNMENT can be said to have *any* policy for the solution of the energy crisis, it is that we will be saved by nuclear power. At the present time, nearly twenty years after the completion of the first nuclear power plant in the United States, the existing fifty-eight nuclear power plants provide only 8 percent of our electricity and about one percent of the nation's energy demand. Nevertheless, according to the Federal Energy Administration, "Today, although nuclear energy accounts for only 1 percent of the total energy demand, the atom is expected to account for about 15 percent of demand by 1985 and about 30 to 40 percent by the year 2000." Presumably the government believes that the nuclear industry is sound enough to carry this greatly increased portion of the nation's energy burden. Yet at the same time (July 1975), the following statement appeared in one of the energy industry's leading journals: "The nuclear industry was described last week by one of its titans [Richard McCormack, vice-president of the General Atomic Company] as a sick institution teetering on collapse."

The sharp clash between the government's view of the nuclear-power industry and Mr. McCormack's is but the latest evidence of the conflict that has troubled this industry since its ambiguous conception and birth. The creation of the U.S. nuclear-power program was motivated less by the need for energy than by the hope of covering the frightening prospect of nuclear war with a peaceful façade. Until President Eisenhower launched the "Atoms for Peace" program in 1953, the Atomic Energy Commission paid little attention to the development of nuclear power, concentrating nearly all its effort on weapons. By 1953 tests of nuclear bombs had revealed what military secrecy had until then kept hidden—that nuclear weapons are a fearful threat to human survival. The birth of the government's active interest in commercial nuclear power is marked by Mr. Eisenhower's speech to the United Nations on December 8, 1953, where, as he put it, in order "to hasten the day when fear of the atom will begin to disappear from the minds of people," he proposed a program, based on military stocks of uranium, "to devise methods whereby this fissionable material would be allocated to serve the peaceful pursuits of mankind. . . . A special purpose would be to provide abundant electrical energy in the power-starved areas of the world."

In responding to this mandate, the AEC turned over increasing amounts of nuclear material, previously under the exclusive control of the AEC and the military, to civilian use by power companies. But now the prospect that the nuclear-power industry will use plutonium fuel—which is easily made into bombs—means that power plants will have to be protected by a "security force" to guard against this possibility. As a result, the nuclear-power industry is a potentially explosive mixture of the civilian and the military.

The AEC also had a statutory responsibility "to strengthen free competition in private enterprise." In recognition of this, the AEC transferred to private corporations as much of the government's nuclear-power program as they have been willing to accept. However, until the development of the nuclear-power industry, most of the activities required to support these complex operations were under integrated government control. In several important sectors of the program, private operations have faltered and failed. As a result, the nuclear-power program is now an uncertain mixture of public and private interests.

A NUCLEAR POWER station produces electricity from energy released by the splitting, or fission, of certain types of very heavy atoms—in typical U.S. reactors, chiefly Uranium-235. Like any other atom, Uranium-

235 consists of a heavy central core—the nucleus—surrounded by a cloud of much lighter electrons. In Uranium-235 there are 92 electrons in the cloud that surrounds the nucleus. They are held there by attractive forces between their own negative electric charges and the nucleus' 92 positive charges. The nucleus is made up of 92 positively charged protons and 143 neutrons (a neutron has the same mass as a proton, but carries no charge); the atomic weight, 235, is the sum of the protons' and neutrons' weights.

Most atomic nuclei contain neutrons, which can be ejected from them by the impact of sufficiently energetic radiation. The earth receives such radiation from space —cosmic rays, which, on striking an atom, produce secondary showers of neutrons; in turn, these can collide with the nuclei of other atoms. The response of Uranium-235 is rare among natural atoms: When a neutron—moving sufficiently slowly—collides with it, there is a good possibility that the Uranium-235 nucleus will split. The fission products are two atomic fragments, each roughly one-half of the original atom, plus some free but fast-moving neutrons. All of these fission products, in their sum, are slightly lighter than the Uranium-235 nucleus from which they were formed. This slight difference in mass is converted to energy, in accordance with the famous Einstein equation which states that the amount of energy (E) is equivalent to the mass (m) multiplied by the square of the speed of light (c). Since the speed of light is a very large number, its square is enormous, so that a truly tremendous amount of energy is given off when the very small mass "disappears" (that is, is converted into energy) as a uranium atom is split.

A neutron does not split a uranium nucleus with the sureness of William Tell's arrow cleaving an apple. Atomic nuclei are so far apart compared to the size of the neutron that a hit is very rare. As the physicist Hans Thirring has put it:

> The chance of hitting a nucleus with an uncharged particle traversing the space of an atom is less than that of hitting a single fly in a large theatre with a pistol-shot without

aiming. Many millions of atoms must therefore be traversed by a neutron before it happens to hit a nucleus and to cause a fission.

If some of the free, fast neutrons produced when the Uranium-235 atoms split are slowed down and then collide with and split fresh Uranium-235 atoms, a chain reaction is set off which can quickly spread through a lump of uranium, releasing huge amounts of energy in a very short time. (In a nuclear bomb, matters are arranged to maximize this effect and the intense, sudden release of energy causes a huge explosion.) Although Uranium-235 is present in many ores, and although showers of neutrons regularly occur on the earth, nevertheless such explosions do not happen naturally because the chain reaction is blocked by another uranium isotope, Uranium-238. The Uranium-238 nucleus contains three more neutrons than the Uranium-235 nucleus, but both exhibit the same chemical behavior because that is governed by the atoms' electron shells, which are identical. Uranium ore contains 0.7 percent Uranium-235, almost 99.3 percent Uranium-238, and a trace of Uranium-234. Unlike Uranium-235, the more common Uranium-238 atoms are not split by neutrons, but rather capture them and, as a result, after some intervening steps, are transformed into Plutonium-239 (about which more later). Thus, in the natural situation, because Uranium-238 is the more prevalent isotope, it preferentially absorbs the neutrons and a Uranium-235 fission reaction cannot start.

In order to establish a chain reaction—without which no nuclear energy could be released—two features are built into the design of a nuclear reactor. The fuel is made from material in which the Uranium-235 has been enriched, its concentration increased from 0.7 percent to about 3 percent. This cuts down the chance of a chain-stopping neutron/Uranium-238 collision. (Enrichment is carried out in one of three huge government plants, where a gaseous uranium compound diffuses through numerous delicately designed porous membranes which gradually hold back the slightly heavier gas molecules that contain Uranium-238.) In addition,

in the reactor the uranium fuel is embedded in material
—the moderator—which slows down the high-velocity
neutrons that are emitted from the split uranium atoms.
One of the peculiarities of the Uranium-235/neutron
collision is that, unlike the collision with Uranium-238,
it is favored if the neutrons are slow. In a typical
reactor the uranium is formed into long, thin rods that
are submerged in water (the moderator), the entire
assemblage making up the reactor core. When Ura-
nium-235 atoms split, the fast neutrons they emit pass
quickly through the thin rods into the water, where,
following a series of collisions with the water molecules, the neutrons slow down to about a thousandth of
their original speed. These slow neutrons find their way
back into a fuel rod, where they are likely to collide
with a Uranium-235 atom and split it.

Once suitably enriched, the uranium is made into
fuel rods. When these are installed in the reactor moderator bath, a self-sustaining fission chain reaction
becomes possible. Like every self-propagating chain
reaction, such as an ordinary fire, the process must be
controlled or it will get out of hand. In a nuclear reactor, control is a rather delicate problem. One reason
is that the nuclear reactions are so fast that the chain
reaction can propagate itself very quickly; to avoid a
runaway reaction, an excessive rate must be corrected
within a tenth of a second. In the reactor the chain
reaction is controlled by inserting rods of a metal such
as boron into the core. Boron is a good neutron ab-
sorber and can therefore cut down the number of free
neutrons in the core, and reduce the overall rate of
the chain reaction. The speed of the chain reaction and
the reactor's rate of energy production are regulated by
varying the length of control rod that is inserted into
the core.

As the fragments of the split uranium atoms fly
apart, their kinetic energy is converted to heat. In
present U.S. reactors, water is used both to slow down
(moderate) the neutrons and to absorb the heat generated by the fission process. In one type of reactor the
fuel rods are bathed in water which is under presure, so
that it becomes quite hot (600° F.) without boiling.

The hot water is circulated through pipes which go through a secondary boiler, where they produce steam that is used to drive a conventional turbine electric generator. In another type of reactor (the "boiling water" reactor) the water that bathes the fuel rods itself boils and produces steam which is fed into the turbines. The steam is then condensed to water and returned to the reactor vessel. In both cases the water that bathes the fuel rods becomes highly radioactive and must be kept away from people and the environment.

After the reactor has operated for a time, the fuel becomes "spent": The accumulated fission products take up enough neutrons to block the fission chain reaction, which gradually slows down. At this point the fuel rods must be replaced, a task which is extraordinarily difficult because they have now become highly radioactive. (The various nuclear reactions that occur in the fuel rods produce a mixture of radioactive elements of different kinds.) In practice the spent rods are stored temporarily in a well-shielded container, usually under a deep layer of water. Sooner or later the spent fuel must be "reprocessed"—a step in which, by various chemical means, different atomic species are separated from the radioactive mélange. One product of the reprocessing is leftover Uranium-235 itself, which can then be re-used in new fuel rods. Another valuable product is Plutonium-239 (formed when a Uranium-238 atom captures a neutron), which is also a fissionable fuel. The rest of the material is useless waste that must be scrupulously contained for many thousands of years as its intense radioactivity slowly decays.

The various operations which constitute the nuclear-power system in the United States are scattered across the entire country. The uranium mines and refinery operations are in various Western states. From there the uranium is shipped to one of two plants in Illinois and Oklahoma, where it is converted into the gaseous form, uranium hexafluoride, that is used in the enrichment process. The enrichment plants are in Oak Ridge, Tennessee, Paducah, Kentucky, and Portsmouth, Ohio. Once enriched, the uranium is shipped to about a dozen fuel-rod fabrication plants that are spread across the country, as are the fifty-odd reactors themselves. The only plant for reprocessing reactor waste that has operated thus far is in upstate New York. The plant is now closed; if and when it reopens, the uranium and plutonium recovered at the plant will be shipped back to the fuel-rod fabrication plants and so re-enter the cycle. Permanent waste-storage facilities do not exist as yet. Thus, the materials involved in the nuclear-power system—uranium in its natural and enriched states and highly radioactive spent fuel and waste—are moved about a great deal, in trucks, railroad cars, and aircraft (until the latter practice was recently forbidden).

The economic structure of the nuclear-power system is equally complex. Most of the ore lies on Federal lands and is publicly owned until the mining rights are leased to private firms. Mining, milling, and conversion of the ore to uranium hexafluoride are now in private hands; but the next step, enrichment, is carried out at government-owned plants. Fabrication of fuel rods is done by private firms, although until recently, by law, the uranium remained the property of the government. Most of the reactors are owned and operated by private power companies. Reprocessing facilities for spent reactor fuel are privately owned, but all of the proposed schemes for permanent waste disposal, if and when they operate, are to be publicly owned. It should be added that the large and expensive research program that lies behind the entire nuclear-power system has been operated almost entirely at public expense, as is the regulatory part of the system.

Although most nuclear power plants are privately owned, government decisions strongly influence their economic feasibility. The cost of the electricity that the system produces depends on the cost of reactor fuel, which in turn is determined largely by the government's charge for enrichment. Since most of the cost of enrichment is the huge capital investment of government funds in the enrichment plants—several billion dollars—the price of this service can be quite arbitrarily determined by choosing a particular rate of capital amortization. The price of nuclear fuel, and therefore the cost of electricity produced from it, has been kept down by such government decisions. In addition, the government has made large amounts of technical information —the results of its vast research program—freely available to industry. This saves industry major development costs.

As it exists today, the U.S. nuclear-power system is a one-way process: Uranium ore goes in and electricity, highly radioactive waste, and the waste heat inevitably emitted by any power plant come out. Nuclear power plants produce more waste heat than most conventional plants of equal size and therefore cause more serious thermal-pollution problems.

The problem of permanently "disposing" of the radioactive waste—somehow keeping the damaging radiation away from people and environmental situations —has been studied for a number of years, but the problem has not yet been solved. The difficulties involved in finding some final resting place for this hideously dangerous material can be judged from the following: The waste produced by a billion-watt nuclear power plant (the typical size of recent ones) is equivalent in radioactivity to about 2500 tons of radium. In contrast, the total amount of radium used thus far in the world for medical and scientific purposes—all of it handled in very small amounts and elaborately contained and shielded—probably amounts to a few pounds. Another sobering comparison is that the radiation from the wastes produced by a city's nuclear power plant—if it were released into the environment —would be sufficient to kill 100 times the city's population.

In bulk, this radioactive waste does not amount to much—a fact that can readily lead to a highly deceiving conclusion. Thus, the head of the Federal Energy Administraion, Frank G. Zarb, in a recent speech in support of his conviction, relative to the nuclear-waste problem, that "the facts are reassuring," offered the following evidence:

A single aspirin tablet has the same volume as the waste produced in generating 7,000 kilowatt-hours, which is about one person's share of the country's electric output for an

entire year. Compared to large quantities of other harmful
materials, the volume of nuclear waste is minuscule. . . .

What Mr. Zarb fails to mention is that, unlike a real
aspirin tablet, his radioactive one is sufficiently toxic to
kill 100 people.

Nuclear wastes are persistent. Their radioactivity
will remain at a very harmful level, and will need to be
meticulously isolated from people and the environment
for about 200,000 years. This fact provokes a melan-
choly question: Who is to stand watch over this radioactive legacy? What social institution can promise to
last that long? One reply, from perhaps the most
thoughtful proponent of nuclear power, A. M. Weinberg, is that the task must be assumed by a kind of
nuclear priesthood:

> We nuclear people have made a Faustian bargain with
> society. On the one hand we offer—in the catalytic nuclear
> burner [the breeder]—an inexhaustible source of energy.
> . . . But the price that we demand of society for this
> magical energy source is both a vigilance and longevity of
> our social institutions that we are quite unaccustomed to.
> . . . In a sense we have established a military priesthood
> which guards against inadvertent use of nuclear weapons
> . . . peaceful nuclear energy probably will make demands
> of the same sort on our society.

This concept—which cloaks the devil in a laboratory
coat and the soldier in a cassock—is almost as forbid-
ding as the fact to which it seeks to respond.

The current status of the waste-disposal problem is
described in the latest government report on the nuclear-power industry. A diagram in the report depicts
the movement of uranium from the mines through the
successive phases of the nuclear-power system. A final
arrow marked "high-level solid waste" points to an impressive building labeled "Federal Repository." The
possible contents of such a repository are described in
three accompanying diagrams, but their effect is rather
spoiled by the notation that they are an "artist's concept." In fact there is no Federal repository for the
permanent storage of highly radioactive waste. The final

disposition of this enormously dangerous material remains, indeed, an "artist's concept."

Proposals abound, none of them satisfactory. One idea is to improve the present reprocessing method. This now leaves in the waste 0.5 percent of the long-lived radioactive isotopes originally present in the spent fuel; the proposed new method would reduce this residue to .0001 percent of the original material. That would shorten the time during which the waste is too dangerous for human contact from about 200,000 years to perhaps 1000 years. Depending on one's outlook, this might perhaps bring the storage problem within what one nuclear expert has called the "time horizon of present rational planning." Since the present reprocessing system is already so difficult that none of the three plants that are supposed to handle commercial-reactor wastes is now in operation, this approach does not seem to be a very practical one.

Another idea—to store the radioactive waste in the Antarctic ice—would violate a specific prohibition in the Antarctic Treaty of 1959. At one time the AEC proposed to store the waste in deep salt mines in Kansas. The people of Kansas rejected the idea, since no one was able to assure them that the radioactivity would not eventually leak into underground water supplies. The most elaborate and redundantly fearsome idea has been proposed by experts at the Lawrence Livermore Laboratory, one of the nation's leading nuclear-research institutions. They would set off an underground nuclear bomb beneath the waste-reprocessing plant, creating a large hole, into which the radioactive waste would be poured, to be contained—it is hoped—within the glassy walls created by the intense heat of the nuclear explosion.

The entire waste-disposal situation has been summed up by two experts who, as it happens, are optimistic about solving it, with the comment that AEC efforts ". . . have yet to produce, after a decade and a half, one operational long-term storage facility—a sign of both commendable caution and inadequate work."

With no acceptable outlet for its radioactive waste, the nuclear-power system's temporary storage facilities

have become heavily overloaded. Temporary storage is
provided next to each reactor, so that the spent fuel
can be safely stored while its initially intense radioactivity decays somewhat. Without an operational
waste-disposal system, these temporary facilities have
been used routinely to hold spent fuel. There are
enough such storage facilities for about 930 metric tons
of spent fuel. A recent survey shows that storage space
for all but 50 metric tons of fuel is now occupied;
many reactors have been deprived of their temporary
spent-fuel storage site. Our nuclear cup runneth over.

It is instructive to imagine how a nuclear reactor
would be designed if its fuel were as innocuous as, let us
say, coal—and the wastes as harmless as Mr. Zarb's
aspirin—and to compare it with the actual design that
is required by the radioactive realities. Such an imagined non-radioactive reactor could consist of the core of
fuel rods, immersed in a tank of water, contained in a
metal boiler. Steam produced in the boiler would be
conducted to a turbine; the spent steam would be condensed by cooling in the usual way and the resulting
water conducted back to the boiler. Control rods would
govern the rate of heat output from the core. Every
few years, fresh fuel rods would replace the spent ones,
which would be readily disposed of (they weigh only
a few thousand pounds), perhaps by burying them. The
only danger would be the possibility of accidental over-
heating in the core or a failure in the water-circulation
system, for either event could result in excessive boiler
pressure and a steam explosion. Such an accident could
be reliably prevented by existing boiler safety devices.
(Boiler explosions plagued steam-engine operations
100 years ago—for example, on Mississippi River
steamboats—but since then the technology has been
thoroughly mastered and, although high-pressure steam
is widely used today, boiler explosions are rare.)

When the intense radioactivity of the actual nuclear-
fuel system is added to this benign imaginary device, it
becomes enormously more complex—and dangerous.
The core is surrounded by a heavy shield to protect
workers from emitted radiation. The entire reactor is
sealed into a massive containment vessel—a concrete

hemisphere 150 feet across. In the vessel there are spray systems to drain off radioactive materials if the core should rupture into it. A complex system is provided for cooling down the core if the normal water-circulating system should fail. There are elaborate control and warning systems, often in multiples to reduce the risk of failure. Safety and environmental-control measures account for a large part of the cost of a nuclear reactor. All this is to avoid the consequences of a failure that might cause the core to overheat. If it became hot enough to melt, after a day the molten core could burn a hole through the bottom of the container and then release massive amounts of radioactive material into the environment.

Such possible reactor accidents, and their effects, have been very much on the minds of nuclear engineers, and the AEC has devoted a good deal of effort to studying them. In 1957 a report on reactor accidents was prepared for the AEC by its Brookhaven National Laboratory. This showed that a "credible" large-scale nuclear-reactor accident might kill 3400 people immediately, severely injure 43,000 others, and cause $7 billion of damage. A revised report was prepared by the same laboratory in 1964, taking into account the five-fold increase in the average size of reactors. It concluded that 45,000 people would be killed, with injuries and damage increased proportionally. This report was suppressed by the AEC and became available only recently through the intervention of the Union of Concerned Scientists, under the Freedom of Information Act. Understandably, the report had a chilling effect on the AEC's public stance on the issue. A memorandum on the report, also suppressed until recently, remarked: "The results of the study must be revealed to the Commission and the JCAE [Joint Congressional Atomic Energy Committee] without subterfuge although the method of presentation to the public has not been resolved at this time."

The AEC then asked for a new study, this time choosing a group at MIT to assess the probability of a reactor accident and the expected damage. After two years of work and an expenditure of $3 million, the thirteen-volume Rasmussen report was issued in draft form in August 1974. This report was much more optimistic than the earlier ones. It estimated that a reactor accident that had a one-in-a-million chance of taking place, per year, per reactor, would cause 70 deaths, 170 injuries, and $2.7 billion in damage. An accident that might cause 2300 deaths and 5600 injuries had a one-in-a-billion chance of occurring.

The Rasmussen report has been severely criticized by individual scientists and by two groups of specialists. One group—organized by the Union of Concerned Scientists—concluded from a detailed critique of the report's methodology that an accident killing about 50,000 people had a 1-in-100,000 chance of happening. Another group, organized by the American Physical Society, reached a similar conclusion from a separate critique of the report.

The AEC had asked that the Rasmussen study not only estimate the risks to the public from possible reactor accidents but also compare them with the risks from other hazards to which people are ordinarily exposed. In response, the report includes a table showing the chances of fatalities from various kinds of accidents. The risks encountered, per person per year, range from one in 4000 for automobile accidents, through one in 100,000 for aircraft accidents, to one in 2,500,000 for tornadoes. The computed risk of a fatality from a nuclear-reactor accident is one in 300,000,000. The former head of the former Atomic Energy Commission, Dr. Dixy Lee Ray, has compared this risk with the chance of being bitten by a poisonous snake while crossing a street in Washington.

Apart from deciding which of the risk estimates to believe, the basic problem is *how* to judge, from any estimate, whether the risk should be taken. This is, of course, a relative matter, since nothing in life is without risk. The question is: What comparisons should be made?

To begin with, it makes sense to compare reactor risks with the risks of other voluntary, man-made activities—excluding tornadoes, lightning, and so forth. Next it seems appropriate to note that building a reactor, unlike deciding to take an auto trip, is not an individual decision, but a social one. And the consequences of a reactor accident—let us say 5000–50,000 possible deaths in a single event—also represent a social rather than an individual issue. It should be noted as well that the extremely small probability relates only to whether or not the accident will occur, and not to its consequences. However improbable, when an accident does happen, it may be highly destructive.

Taking all this into account, it seems to me that the reactor accident question can best be stated as follows: Shall we build nuclear reactors which, with a very low probability, may suffer an accident resulting in, let us say, 5000 to 50,000 deaths and many more injuries and billions of dollars of damage? Stated this way, the uniqueness of the issue becomes clear: There is probably only one other existing man-made device which has the physical capability of causing such a catastrophe in a single event—a nuclear bomb.

One can perhaps get some sense of the moral background of the necessary decision in the following way. In the Rasmussen report's list of comparative risks of fatalities, the three highest are: auto accidents (55,791 deaths per year, individual risk one in 4000); falls (17,827 deaths per year, individual risk one in 10,000); fires (7451 deaths per year, individual risk one in 25,000). If these individual risks were to be converted to a single event (in the sense that the one-in-100,000 risk of dying in an air crash relates to single events in which several hundred people may be killed at once), we could perhaps begin to get a useful comparison with a reactor accident. Suppose, for example, that by some fictional device or Faustian bargain we were to arrange to eliminate all the random auto deaths and instead have the 55,000 deaths occur all at once, at some random moment. Or suppose that by a similar arrangement the 7500 annual fire fatalities were to occur, with some random probability, in a single fire at one time. However low the probability, would we build such a device or make such a Faustian bargain? My own answer is "No," but that is hardly relevant. What *is* relevant is that the answer must be given by society.

And this is hardly possible so long as the government persists in making misleading comparisons. In human, moral terms, it seems to me there is no valid comparison between the risks of personally tragic individual events like auto accidents and the risk of operating a device which has the acknowledged, designed capability —however improbable—of killing tens of thousands of people at once. It will be argued that this is precisely the kind of device that the United States has already built and dropped on Hiroshima and Nagasaki, and that we have ready in hand for use in another war. In my view, neither the nuclear bomb nor the nuclear reactor can be excused by postulating the acceptability of the other.

Despite the AEC's protestations that nuclear reactors are more innocent of risk than most of life's hazards, the government and the AEC have in fact acted as though the opposite were true. The Congress has acknowledged that the risk of huge losses from a reactor accident is so great as to require insurance backed by the wealth of the U.S. Treasury. When the first reactors were built, no private insurance company—or combination of them—was willing to provide the amount of insurance that the power companies wanted. As a result, Congress passed the Price-Anderson Act, which enables the government to insure against the costs of a reactor accident up to the sum of $560,000,000.

For its part, the AEC—or rather the Nuclear Regulatory Commission (NRC), which has taken over its regulatory functions—has established guidelines that prohibit the building of reactors close to urban areas. These guidelines, intended to limit the casualties and property damage from a reactor accident, cost the country a very appreciable potential benefit in energy savings.

As pointed out in the preceding chapter, a power plant necessarily rejects a good deal of the energy that enters it, as waste low-temperature heat. Nuclear reactors have a particularly low Carnot efficiency, so that they reject relatively more heat than do fossil-fueled plants of the same capacity. As indicated earlier, to maximize the thermodynamic efficiency with which energy is used, this waste heat should be distributed, as hot water or low-pressure steam, to heat or cool buildings. But this can be done only if the power plant is located in or near a city. Because nuclear power plants risk a catastrophic accident and have therefore been exiled from the cities, this kind of energy-conserving arrangement is impossible.

Apart from these disabilities, nuclear power is a kind of thermodynamic overkill. Various forms of radiation make up a spectrum of energetic effects. These range from the mild to the intensely destructive; from the molecular agitation stimulated by infrared radiation, through the chemical changes induced by visible and ultraviolet radiation, to the random breakage of molecules brought about by the powerful radiation emitted by radioactive materials. In a power plant, the basic task to which the energy source is applied is to boil water to produce the steam that drives the generator. If this task is to be accomplished with thermodynamic efficiency, it requires temperatures in the range of 1000–2000° F. At such temperatures, fuels produce chemicals (such as sulfur dioxide and nitrogen oxides) that cause pollution problems. The pollutants—and the cost of controlling them—are the unavoidable price that is paid to achieve the necessary thermodynamic linkage between the energy source and the energy-requiring task.

In a nuclear reactor the price is much higher, for the extreme energy of the ionizing radiation of the nuclear radiation is well beyond the range appropriate to the task of generating steam. Expressed in terms that are equivalent to the temperature scale, the energy associated with the nuclear fission process is in the range of a million degrees. All the difficulties and dangers due to the radiation associated with a nuclear reactor are, in this thermodynamic sense, unnecessary since the task of generating steam can be achieved by the much lower energies of ordinary fuels.

The use of nuclear radiation for the relatively mild task of boiling water violates the familiar caution against attacking a fly with a cannon. The fly is likely to be killed, but at the cost of considerable unnecessary damage. Thermodynamics tells us that a fly-swatter and a fuel-burning power plant would be more suitable to their respective tasks.

The nuclear-power program is completely dependent on the availability of fissionable fuel. The present one-way fuel system uses uranium ore, which, like fossil fuels, is a non-renewable resource. The amount of ore in different deposits, and their quality, varies a great deal. The richest ores, which are now being mined, are the least plentiful, but while they last they are the cheapest source of uranium for nuclear fuel.

A number of surveys of the future availability of U.S. uranium resources have been made. Since the cost of recovering uranium from ores of progressively lower quality rises steeply, the amount of uranium that can be produced depends on its sale price. At a selling price of $15 per pound, the total amount of uranium that can be recovered from U.S. mines is estimated at about 1.5 million tons of uranium oxide ("yellow cake"). At a price of $30 per pound, about 2.5 million tons are recoverable. (Until the 1973 oil crisis, uranium sold at about $8 per pound. In 1975 it reached a price level of $20–$24, but this may be temporary.) If present plans for building nuclear reactors are actually carried out, the amount of uranium that will be needed to operate them would be about 2.5 million tons by the year 2000.

THE NUCLEAR-POWER SYSTEM just described, based on "light-water" reactors (so named because they use ordinary rather than heavy water as a moderator), was developed by the AEC and gradually turned over to private industry between 1953 and 1965. At that time the AEC decided to cut back its development work on light-water reactors and to concentrate on a new, considerably more complex type. The new reactor was designed to produce more fissionable fuel than it used —a "breeder" reactor. Development of the breeder has since then taken up most of the AEC's research funds; it is expected to cost about $11 billion by the time the first experimental plant is built.

The reason for this costly move was economic. To the power companies the most persuasive fact about nuclear reactors was that they could produce electricity at less cost than fossil-fueled plants. This advantage depended a great deal on the cost of uranium fuel, which at the time (1962) was expected to account for about 34 percent of the total cost of nuclear-power production. However, the AEC expected the resources of easily mined—and therefore relatively inexpensive—uranium to be exhausted before the turn of the century. It was reasoned, therefore, that if the nuclear-power industry was to remain economically viable, fissionable fuel must remain plentiful and cheap.

The breeder promised to do just that. By turning uranium into a renewable, recycled source of nuclear fuel, the breeder could greatly expand the amount of fissionable fuel that can be produced from uranium ore. On that basis the AEC calculated that a breeder-based power system could sell electricity at competitive prices even if uranium cost up to $100 per pound. And at that price enough domestic uranium could be mined profitably (about 25 million tons) to support breeder-based power production at a rate sufficient to meet the country's power needs for hundreds of years. The breeder program promised a nearly unlimited supply of power—if it worked.

The breeder produces fissionable fuel by converting the common Uranium-238 isotope into Plutonium-239. As indicated earlier, this happens when a fast neutron collides with Uranium-238. Like Uranium-235, Plutonium-239 is fissionable; colliding with a neutron, it splits, releasing energy and two to three fast neutrons. Some of these neutrons can collide with another Plutonium-239 atom and split it, thus continuing the energy-producing chain reaction. The other neutrons are available to produce more Plutonium-239 by combining with Uranium-238. The breeder reactor under development in the United States is supposed to produce about three new Plutonium-239 atoms for every two atoms that are split and burned as fuel. It would literally produce more fuel than it used.

Thus, the breeder promised to solve the rapid de-

pletion of uranium fuel which would otherwise bring
the nuclear-power program to an early end. Having
persuaded the nation—over increasing opposition—to
develop nuclear power as a long-term solution to the
nation's energy problems, the AEC and the Joint Congressional Atomic Energy Committee were understand-
ably eager to see the breeder succeed. But it faced a
mounting series of obstacles.

The most serious difficulty relates to the breeder's
special product—Plutonium-239, the new fissionable
fuel that accumulates in the fuel rods as the breeder
operates. When the spent fuel rods are reprocessed, the
plutonium is separated from the other highly radioactive waste materials. It can then be made into fuel rods
and used in reactors to produce power. In effect, this
would establish a fuel-recycling system in which plutonium rather than uranium circulates. Such a "plutonium economy," in which fissionable fuel is recycled
between reactor and reprocessing plant, is essential to
the operation of the breeder; without it the breeder
cannot save the nuclear-power industry from the impending shortage of fuel. However, the plutonium
economy creates new problems that threaten to halt
the breeder program itself.

Plutonium-239 is much more toxic than uranium; it
is widely regarded as the most dangerous radioactive
material among the many that the Nuclear Age has
bestowed on us. Plutonium emits a particular form of
radiation, alpha particles, which consist of helium nuclei. An alpha particle is so massive that it is stopped
by living tissue after penetrating only a very short distance into it. Because the particle's energy is released in
a short distance, its effect is intensely localized and is
very damaging to the cellular material. If very small
particles of Plutonium-239 should become embedded
anywhere in the body, their radiation effects would be
particularly destructive. Unfortunately, plutonium released into the environment tends to form into very
small particles that readily become permanently trapped
in the tiny air spaces of the lungs.

The greatest danger to health from Plutonium-239
radioactivity is cancer, and an extraordinarily small

deposit of plutonium in the lungs carries with it a significant risk of that disease. One set of computations, based on the expected number of cases of cancer due to plutonium in fallout from nuclear tests, indicates that each pound of plutonium reactor fuel, similarly scattered into the environment, might cause some 600 cases of cancer over a fifty-year period. If the nuclear-power program is based on the breeder, according to current projection of power production it will eventually involve about 130 million pounds of plutonium. If only one millionth of this material were to escape into the environment as it circulated through the intricate steps of the "plutonium economy," some 78,000 cases of cancer would result, or about 1600 per year. If four/ten-thousandths of the material were lost to the environment, 600,000 cancers per year might result. The present annual incidence of cancer in the United States is also about 600,000 cases. If we are to avoid the risk of doubling the present cancer rate, as plutonium is carried through the far-flung network of the nuclear-power system we would need to avoid losing even .04 percent of it.

The foregoing figures are based on a particularly high estimate of the toxicity of Plutonium-239. But there is a great deal of controversy about this value. Experts differ by factors as much as 10,000 to 100,000 in their estimates of the cancer-inducing effect of a given dose of plutonium—a degree of uncertainty which is itself chastening. Nevertheless, in practice it would appear that when confronted with a personal choice, most experts make about the same judgment of the Plutonium-239 hazard. A staff member at the Lawrence Radiation Laboratory at the University of California, one of the government's leading nuclear-research institutions, performed an instructive and relevant experiment. A brief questionnaire was submitted to thirty-eight staff members regarding their attitude toward soil contaminated by plutonium to the level of about 6.5 millionths of a gram per square meter. To the question "Would you allow your child to play in this soil?" 86 percent said "No." Now this level of plutonium contamination, on the entire surface of the United States, would total about 60 million grams. This is about one-thousandth of the amount of plutonium that would be involved in the projected nuclear-fuel recycling system. In other words, if one-thousandth of that material were to escape and become distributed evenly over the soil of the United States, most knowledgeable experts would not want their children to play outdoors. Since the Plutonium-239 radioactivity would persist for tens of thousands of years once the plutonium cycle was in operation, this risk—and its consequences—would be confronted by the U.S. population for many centuries.

Another serious difficulty with the breeder is that the plutonium economy would tie power production directly into the dangerous issues of nuclear weaponry. Largely through the efforts of Dr. Theodore Taylor, a former designer of nuclear weapons, we now know that, unlike uranium, plutonium can be made into a devastating bomb by one or a few people working with material available from a hardware store and an ordinary laboratory-supply house. If the plutonium economy is established, the amount of plutonium in circulation would be enough for some 10 million bombs, each capable of destroying a medium-sized city. Someone successfully stealing one/ten-millionth of the circulating plutonium could threaten the destruction of a city.

In response, the government has acknowledged that the plutonium economy would need to include an absolutely theft-proof guard over the fuel plants, the power plants, the reprocessing plants, and the transport vehicles. Recent reports to the AEC call for elaborate military protection of plutonium-powered plants, including a mobile military "recovery force" and domestic espionage. There is a danger that the threat of terrorist attempts to steal plutonium—whether real or not—could be used to justify a system of miliary control over the entire nuclear-power system.

Another special problem is the breeder's heat-transfer system. Unlike conventional reactors, the breeder operates on *fast* neutrons, so that a neutron-slowing medium such as water cannot be used. Instead, in order to transfer the heat that they produce, the fuel rods are bathed in molten sodium which is pumped through a heat-transfer system that eventually generates the steam that drives the turbines.

Unlike the other elements that are encountered in the glossary of nuclear power—uranium, plutonium, radium—sodium has a familiar, comforting ring to it. After all, sodium chloride is on the dining table, and is the salt of the sea. Uncombined sodium metal, however, is not so benign. Unlike most metals, sodium is never found as such in natural ores. The reason is instructive. Even at ordinary temperatures, sodium metal reacts so strongly with two very common environmental constituents—water and oxygen—that in nature it is always found in a combined chemical form. The reaction of sodium metal with water is violent; a thimble-sized fragment accidentally dropped into a chemistry-laboratory drain causes a destructive explosion. In the breeder reactor the sodium metal is molten, circulating at a temperature of 1150° F. The slightest leak that brought it into contact with the air, or with the water of the steam circuit, might result in a serious explosion. A breeder in the U.S.S.R. has been reported to have suffered such an explosion in 1974.

Thanks to the National Environmental Policy Act, the AEC was required to prepare an environmental impact statement to define the effect of the breeder on the environment, in comparison with alternatives that might yield a better benefit/cost ratio. The AEC prepared such a statement, which covered only the two demonstration breeder reactors that the government plans to build. Since the demonstration reactors are pointless except as the basis for the large-scale development of a breeder program to extend the life of the fissionable-fuel supply, this action failed to satisfy environmentalists. The Scientists' Institute for Public Information (SIPI) went into Federal Court, represented by the Natural Resources Defense Council, in order to force the AEC to prepare an impact statement on the entire breeder program. As one of the editors of *Science* magazine reported at the time,

The SIPI suit asks, in effect, that the Federal Government put its national energy policy on a rational and explicit basis so that Congress and interested citizens can have a say in its formulation. It is a modest but nonetheless revolutionary request, and if successful it may provide the information necessary for a proper assessment of the breeder program.

This "modest but revolutionary" request succeeded. In 1973 the U.S. Court of Appeals in Washington, D.C., ruled in favor of SIPI, and the AEC was required by the court to prepare an environmental impact statement on the entire breeder program. While the resulting document did not lay out a rational energy policy, it did open the breeder program to criticism. SIPI found the draft statement so faulty that in hearings before the AEC it urged that the statement be withdrawn and rewritten. An evaluation of the impact statement made by the Environmental Protection Agency reached a similar conclusion, and EPA later suggested that the breeder program should be delayed.

By then serious technical difficulties were plaguing the breeder program. This is evident from the rapid escalation of the projected costs of the two demonstration plants, originally budgeted at $2 billion a few years ago. The present estimate is $10.7 billion. This increase greatly exceeds the effects of inflation and can only mean that appreciable, and expensive, modifications have been made in the original design.

This is not surprising, for breeder technology is considerably more complex than the technology of conventional reactors. The use of plutonium makes radiation protection more difficult, and the reactor control problem is more critical than it is in conventional reactors. The breeder program has run into unprecedented delays due to safety and environmental considerations.

The most serious technological failure in the proposed breeder program is described in a report recently issued by the AEC's successor, the Energy Research and Development Administration (ERDA). This report summarizes the status of the fuel-recycling process, which, as we have seen, is essential to the operation of the breeder reactor.

The report takes note of the government's stated goal for the development of nuclear power plants—a thirty-fold increase from the present capacity of 30 billion watts to about 1100 billion watts in the year 2000. However, according to the report, two as yet unsolved problems—how to find financial support to increase capacity for uranium enrichment, and how to activate the presently paralyzed program for reprocessing fuel and disposing of the resultant waste—"will limit the total nuclear electric capacity to the approximately 220 GW [billion watts] already on order." Even if these problems were solved, according to the report there are "insufficient known or projected supplies of uranium to support projected growth of the LWR [light-water reactor] industry beyond 1990–1995." This would freeze overall capacity at about 400 billion watts and would mean that the price of fuel would rise rapidly as readily accessible supplies diminished.

As we have seen, the government has planned to overcome this restraint by developing a system for recycling plutonium fuel and a commercially operable breeder-reactor program which would produce fuel as it generated power—the so-called back end of the fuel cycle. But once more, according to the ERDA report,

> . . . it is improbable that industry on its own will be able to carry through with commercialization of the "back end" of the fuel cycle. Some aspects of reprocessing have not been demonstrated commercially, fabrication of plutonium-bearing fuels has not been demonstrated on a full-scale production basis, the economic attractiveness of the plutonium recycle has not been proven, acceptable safeguard systems for the separated plutonium are yet to be established, and permanent disposal of the radioactive waste has not been demonstrated.

It is illuminating to document the facts behind ERDA's circumspect statement that "some aspects of reprocessing have not been demonstrated commercial-

ly." The relevant fact is that after commercial firms
had spent many millions of dollars to build several
reprocessing plants, none of them is now in operation.
Although one plant did operate from 1966 to 1972 at
West Valley, New York, after a series of violations of
radiation safety standards, the plant was shut down
"for modification." A new license must be issued, but
since this must be based on acceptable methods of recycling plutonium, and no such acceptable methods
are available, no one knows when the plant will actually
reopen. The brand-new $64-million reprocessing plant
built by General Electric at Morris, Illinois, is a total
failure. After several years of trying, the company has
concluded that the plant simply will not work. The
remaining reprocessing plant has been nearly completed by Allied-General Nuclear Services at Barnwell,
South Carolina. It was designed to produce and ship
reprocessed plutonium as a solution of plutonium nitrate. However, a recent ruling requires that all commercial shipments of plutonium must be in the solid
form. Meanwhile, the Nuclear Regulatory Commission
has been unwilling to issue a permit for the construction
of the plant addition needed to convert the nitrate solutions to a solid form. Thus, the entire commercial
reprocessing operation is in a state of paralysis.

In sum, there is no way at present to close the loop
in the one-way nuclear-fuel cycle, for the breeder reactor can only operate with plutonium. This failure
means that the nuclear-power industry must continue
to operate at the expense of a dwindling (and therefore
increasingly expensive) supply of uranium ore, accumulating spent fuel which, for lack of reprocessing
facilities, must be stored in temporary sites.

The impending failure of the "back end" of the new
fuel cycle that is needed to extend the life of the nuclear-power program has now been certified by two
important, if inconspicuous, government actions. In
June 1975, Secretary of Commerce Morton announced
that the breeder program had been demoted from a
demonstration of commercial feasibility to the status of
"research." This effectively reverses the government's
commitment, implicit in the establishment of the breed-

er demonstration program, for subsequent commercial development. The second action has been the decision of the Nuclear Regulatory Commission to delay by at least 18 months the preparation of an environmental impact statement on plutonium recycling. This action acknowledges that many of the basic issues are still too poorly understood to support an estimate of the environmental effects of this complex and enormously dangerous operation. Until this statement is prepared and adequately defended against public criticism, no reprocessing plant can operate, and the waste-disposal problem remains unsolved. In the absence of an acceptable method for handling plutonium, the breeder approach to fuel recyling is inoperable.

In effect, these government actions acknowledge that the breeder, although still in an extended and expensive period of gestation, has already outlived its usefulness. The purpose of the breeder was to stretch out the supply of uranium that could be mined at a price that would enable nuclear generators to sell their power in competition with coal-fired plants. It was reasoned that because, in the economy of conventional reactors, the cost of nuclear fuel represented a large part of the cost of producing nuclear power (about 34 percent in 1966), it would be impossible for the industry to remain competitive as the easily mined, cheap uranium ore became exhausted. Only the breeder, it was believed, could save the nuclear-power industry from stagnation and probable collapse by 1990–2000.

This reasoning seemed sound in 1957, when the decision to base future nuclear technology on the breeder was made, and even in 1962, when the decision was confirmed. However, since 1966 the situation has changed drastically: The cost of uranium fuel has become a progressively smaller part of the cost of producing electricity. In 1966, of the total cost of producing electricity from nuclear power, 34.2 percent was fuel costs, 49.9 percent capital costs, and the remainder operation and maintenance costs. By 1975 capital costs represented 77.1 percent of the total, and fuel costs had decreased to only 18.2 percent. This did not occur because the price of nuclear fuel declined, for in fact it

rose about 19 percent. Rather, there was a sharp rise
in the cost of constructing nuclear reactors—about 244
percent in that period. The trend continues. Orders
placed in 1965 for a nuclear-reactor system to be operational about ten years later resulted in average plant
capital costs of $300 per kilowatt of electric capacity;
for orders placed in 1968 the cost had increased to
$430 per kilowatt (these costs are given in 1973 dol-
lars, to eliminate the effect of inflation). There has been
a steady increase in the capital costs of nuclear reactors
which has now considerably reduced the significance
of fuel costs.

Thus, the original argument for developing the
breeder has lost its validity. The breeder is no longer
needed to keep the cost of fuel down because that factor has lost a good deal of its earlier influence on the
cost of nuclear power. The breeder has been rendered
obsolete by the escalating capital cost of conventional
nuclear power plants.

The reasons for this dramatic and (at least by the
AEC and the nuclear industry) unexpected increase
in the cost of constructing conventional nuclear power
plants have been analyzed by a group at the MIT Center for Policy Alternatives, headed by I. C. Bupp of
the Harvard School of Business. They have made a detailed study of the rapid-rise in the capital cost of
nuclear plants by evaluating, mathematically, the influence of a series of relevant factors. They report that
the factor which correlates most significantly with the
increase in capital costs is the length of the period in
which the AEC and state agencies consider whether to
license the construction of the plant. On its surface, this
would appear to validate a common complaint voiced
by the industry and government officials. They argue
that environmentalists have delayed the licensing procedure by raising questions about the safety and environmental effects of the plants, and that capital costs
increase because of interest charges and the costs of
inflation incurred during the added time. However,
Bupp's group reject this explanation, for they also find
that the lengthening of the period of *construction,*
which would also incur these economic penalties, does

not correlate well with increased capital costs. They explain the effect of licensing hearings on capital costs by pointing out that often, in response to environmental complaints voiced at these hearings, the power company is required by the AEC to make design changes that respond to these objections. It is these changes—and not so much the extended time of the hearings—that raise construction costs. Naturally, the longer the hearings, the more changes are likely to be called for, so that the length of the hearings is what statisticians call a "proxy" for the actual operational factor—which is that the plant's safety features need to be improved.

That environmentalists can in fact claim credit for most of the newly introduced changes in the design of nuclear plants is evident from a list of such changes required by the AEC since 1957. A series of design changes results from the adoption by the AEC of increasingly rigorous radiation-exposure standards—the results of long battles in the 1950s and 1960s between independent scientists and the AEC over the then less rigorous AEC standards. Several changes involve restrictions relative to the reactor site, especially with respect to the possible effects of earthquakes. This is a legacy of the successful effort by environmentalists to block the construction of a reactor at Bodega Bay, California, by introducing, for the first time, the need to take the earthquake hazard into account. A major impact on reactor design results from the enactment of the National Environmental Policy Act. A Federal court decision on the Calvert Cliffs reactor in Maryland required the AEC to adhere to the provisions of the act—again an outcome of environmental concerns.

All this demonstrates that the impact of environmental concerns has convinced the AEC of the need for major, and costly, changes in reactor design. The administration's response to this situation is something out of Alice in Wonderland—the AEC (and now the NRC) has been ordered to hasten the licensing procedure, in the apparent hope that the safety issues, and their costly consequences, will go away if no one mentions them.

Another argument advanced to explain the increasing cost of constructing nuclear plants is that the construction workers have become less efficient. Bupp's group, once more, supply us with the relevant data by comparing the rise in capital costs of nuclear power plants with other construction that involves similarly skilled workers—petroleum refineries and coal-fired power plants. For plants constructed to operate in 1976, as compared with those placed in operation in 1970, capital costs increased by 10 percent for refineries, by 60 percent for coal-fired power plants, and by 150 percent for nuclear power plants. Clearly the problem is not the declining efficiency of construction workers, but something unique to the nuclear plants.

Thus, the need for the breeder reactor—a far more complex machine than the conventional one—has been removed by a kind of technological irony: The conventional reactors have themselves become so much more complex, and therefore expensive, that the reduced cost of fuel which the breeder was supposed to achieve is much less economically significant. The cost of electricity now depends much more on capital costs than on fuel costs. The breeder is hardly the kind of power plant that can serve in this situation; compared with a conventional reactor, the breeder would reduce fuel costs, but greatly increase capital costs. Thus, the breeder has been rendered obsolete by the very instrument that it was destined to replace. One's intellectual pleasure in this novel turn of events is quickly dampened by the realization of the huge cost of the breeder program, not only in money but also in the confusion of public policy.

We come now to the denouement of this costly and chaotic technological extravaganza. Recall that the stated purpose of the nuclear-power program has been to produce electricity at economic and social costs that are less than those of coal-fired plants. Now as a result of the rapid escalation in their capital costs the conventional reactors appear to have successfully resisted displacement by the breeders. How has this affected the competitive position of the conventional reactors relative to coal-fired plants?

With respect to social costs, proponents of nuclear

power plants point to several advantages over coal-fired ones. One claim is that nuclear power plants are "clean"—that they have a lesser impact on the environment than coal-fired plants. Coal-burning plants that use high-sulfur coal are largely responsible for the often unacceptable levels of sulfur dioxide in urban air. In contrast, nuclear plants produce no *chemical* pollutants. They do produce some radioactive emissions, and certain of the recent design changes are intended to reduce these. In coal plants, sulfur dioxide and most of the other combustion wastes can be kept out of the air by suitable smokestack devices. Such anti-pollution devices add to the cost of the power plant and to the price charged for the electricity it produces. Nuclear plants also avoid the noise and dust often associated with the heavy movement of coal at coal-fired power plants, but these too might be reduced—at a price. In general, in both nuclear and coal-fired plants, the social cost represented by environmental degradation can be minimized by increasing the cost of the plant and its product.

The main justification for building nuclear power plants, and certainly the one that motivates power companies, is economic: They can produce electricity more cheaply than coal. Since power companies are public utilities, they receive a rate of return on investment that is fixed by state regulatory agencies. As a result, the reduced cost of producing power results in a lower price of electricity to consumers. At the present time, in certain parts of the United States (for example, in the New England area) electricity is produced more cheaply by nuclear power plants than by coal-fired ones. However, the costs change rapidly and the more relevant question is whether the competitive economic position of nuclear power can be maintained in the future.

It is possible to estimate, approximately, the future costs of producing electricity from the expected changes in the cost of the several relevant factors: capital, fuel, labor, and interest charges. Trend lines can then be computed, showing the expected cost of electricity produced by nuclear power plants and by coal-fired plants some years into the future. If the costs of the two types of plants rise, year by year, at about the same rate, the present cost advantage of nuclear power will be maintained into the future. On the other hand, if the cost of producing electricity in coal-fired plants is expected, with time, to increase more slowly than the cost of nuclear power, then at some "break-even point" the costs will become equal. Thereafter, if the trend continues, the competitive advantage will pass over to coal. Despite the difficulties of making such extrapolations, they cannot be avoided. Since it may take ten years before the decision to build a power plant is converted into reality, estimates of future costs are always necessary, however uncertain.

Such computations have been made by the group headed by I. C. Bupp, and have been brought up to date with respect to various relevant options by Robert Scott of the Center for the Biology of Natural Systems. Bupp's group have made a detailed analysis of the comparative rates of increase in capital costs of nuclear power plants and coal-fired plants. From a statistical analysis of the costs of 87 nuclear power plants ordered between 1965 and 1970 they report that the capital costs have been increasing at the rate of $31 per year per kilowatt of electric capacity. In contrast, an analysis of 102 coal-fired plants built during the same period showed that their capital costs increased at the rate of only $13 per year per kilowatt of electric capacity (in real, uninflated 1973 dollars).

If the capital costs per kilowatt of power-plant capacity of nuclear and coal-fired plants continue to rise at the rates of increase that they have exhibited since 1965, and coal continues to cost about $26 per ton and uranium about $25 per pound (these prices are in real, uninflated dollars), then the break-even point will be reached between 1979 and 1980. At that time the cost of electricity produced by the two methods will both be about 23.2 mills per kilowatt-hour (kwh). Thereafter the cost of uranium-based power will exceed that of coal-based power. For example, by 1984 electricity from nuclear power plants would cost an average of 26.5 mills per kwh, while the cost of electricity sold by coal-fired plants would be 24.6 mills per kwh.

If, in order to eliminate the disadvantage of coal-fired plants with respect to air pollution, about $100/kw is added to the capital cost of these plants to pay for sulfur-control devices (this would increase the plant's capital cost by about 25 percent), the break-even point is delayed to 1983. Again, thereafter the economic advantage lies progressively with coal. By 1986 nuclear power plants would sell electricity at 29.2 mills per kwh, and coal-fired plants at 27.4 mills per kwh.

In these computations it was assumed that the uninflated costs of the fuels would remain constant—that is, their prices would rise along with the general course of inflation. However, since 1973 the price of oil has begun to rise faster than general inflation, carrying with it the price of all fuels, including coal and uranium. It is useful to consider, then, what the trends will be if the uninflated prices of uranium and coal continue to increase in the future. If it is assumed, based on present trends, that the uninflated price of uranium will increase 5 percent per year and that of coal at an average of 4 percent per year, then the break-even point is in 1982, and once more coal has the economic advantage, progressively, thereafter.

Another relevant item in such computations is the *capacity factor*—the fraction of time at which a power plant is actually working and yielding the amount of power that it was designed to produce. According to the AEC, coal-fired plants and nuclear plants are expected to operate at an average capacity factor of .75. However, while coal-fired plants generally meet this expectation, nuclear plants do not, in recent years operating at an average capacity factor of .6. (They are shut down 40 percent of the time, often because unexpected faults turn up in their complex structures. The problems are often common to a number of reactors, so that when a particular faulty pipe is found in one reactor, the AEC usually requires that the others shut down for inspection.)

If the capacity factor of nuclear power plants were to increase from the present figure of .6 to .8, the switch in the present economic advantage enjoyed by nuclear power relative to coal could be delayed to about 1994, but not prevented. Although the AEC has promised that this improvement will be made, there is no evidence at this time that it will actually occur. The AEC's optimism is based on the notion of the "learning curve"—that as experience with the new technology is gained, the plants can be made to operate more efficiently. Actually, the nuclear power plants seem to follow a different learning curve: The capacity factor seems to increase in the first two or three years of operation and then it declines.

Taking into account the necessarily low precision of these estimates, we can nevertheless conclude that sometime before 1985 the average price of electricity produced by nuclear power plants will probably catch up with and thereafter exceed the price charged by coal-fired plants.

According to Scott's analysis, there are only two ways to escape the eventuality that the economy of coal plants will overtake nuclear plants sometime in the next ten to fifteen years. One way would be a striking improvement in the nuclear-power industry's capital-cost figures relative to coal-fired plants, so that these costs would no longer increase at three times the rate of coal plants. The other way would be an abrupt 50-percent increase in the price of coal.

This alternative—that nuclear power can be made economically viable by arbitrarily imposing a sharp increase in the price of coal—should not be lightly dismissed just because it seems absurd. As indicated earlier, the administration has taken the position that the price of oil must be kept high enough to make investments in coal conversion and shale-oil production attractive to investors. Toward this end, Mr. Ford has already used his tariff-regulating authority, has proposed levying other taxes on crude oil and gasoline, and has vetoed a Congressional bill to continue the regulation of oil prices. Once it becomes plain that the nuclear-power industry will collapse in the next decade or so unless the price of its chief competitor, coal, is arbitrarily increased, Mr. Ford's philosophy would mandate the imposition of a "coal tax." Given recent experience with the spreading effects of increased energy prices, such a move might save the nuclear industry, but it might well destroy the economy.

U.S. difficulties with nuclear power have their parallel in most of the other countries that have undertaken nuclear programs. In June of 1975 six of Japan's twelve nuclear reactors were shut down for repairs or for unscheduled safety inspection; this is only the latest manifestation of a series of problems there, ranging from radiation leakage to clogging of cooling pipes by jellyfish. In January 1974 the Soviets' prototype breeder apparently suffered an accident when molten sodium came in contact with steam. In England the magazine *The Economist,* commenting on the start-up of a small prototype breeder reactor in Scotland, commented:

> Despite the confidence of the nuclear establishment in Britain, France, Russia, America and other countries that the breeder will develop into the most important commercial reactor of the 1980's and 1990's, there is now growing up around the world a counterbalancing body of opinion that holds that the breeder's merits have been exaggerated. . . .

What emerges from these considerations is the likelihood that the entire nuclear program is headed for extinction. It will leave us with a monument which people will need to care for with vigilance if not affection for thousands of years—stores of intensely radioactive wastes and the powerless, radioactive hulks of the reactors that produced them.

How can we account for the inability—here in the most advanced technological society the world has known—to create the energy system that was supposed to usher us into a new Nuclear Age? The chief difficulties appear to arise at the troublesome interface between energy technology and the economy.

At every phase in the chaotic development of the nuclear-power industry, technological difficulties have led to unexpected economic problems. When private corporations took over the manufacture and sale of conventional reactors, they followed customary business practice and offered prospective customers very favorable terms. According to Bupp's group, "The reactor manufacturers, Westinghouse and G.E., more or less consciously risked substantial financial losses to secure market shares in what they viewed as the power generating technology of the future."

In selling their reactors, the manufacturers made construction-cost estimates which later proved to be far too low. For example, for reactors to be placed in operation in 1971, the average expected cost was $123 per kilowatt of electric capacity, but the actual cost was $261 per kilowatt, a 112-percent increase (these prices are quoted in fixed 1973 dollars, so that inflation is not involved). Six years later, for reactors supposed to be in operation in 1977, the expected cost was $183 per kilowatt and the actual cost $490 per kilowatt, an increase of 167 percent. Thus, the costs were not only seriously underestimated but became increasingly so, because—as we have seen—the original designs did not deal adequately with problems of safety and environmental protection.

Power companies were also persuaded to purchase nuclear rather than fossil-fueled plants by offers from reactor manufacturers of guaranteed supplies of fuel at contractually fixed prices. However, in recent months the price of uranium has risen so sharply that these obligations cannot be met except at a great financial loss to the reactor manufacturers. As a result, the Westinghouse Corporation has recently proposed, unilaterally, to abrogate its contracts to supply fuel to the companies that ordered its reactors. It would appear that in the chaotic milieu of nuclear power, at least this one corporation has difficulty in meeting the customary obligation of private enterprise to accept the consequences of its own financial risks.

Another striking example of this same failure on the part of private enterprise is Mr. Ford's recent proposal to have private corporations build the new enrichment plants that are needed if the nuclear-power program is to expand as planned. It should be recalled that the so-called front end of the nuclear-fuel cycle—uranium mining and enrichment, and the design of reactors— was accomplished at considerable public expense by intense government development. When government effort had brought each of these processes to the point of successful operation, it was turned over to private industry, with the exception—until now—of the enrichment process. However, unlike the "front end" processes, the activities involved in the "back end" of the fuel cycle were given over to private companies for *both* development and commercial operation. As indicated earlier, the resultant failures have been spectacular. They will be rewarded, if Mr. Ford has his way, by assigning to private industry the one remaining publicly owned part of the nuclear-power system —enrichment.

In making this proposal Mr. Ford presumably expressed his confidence in the private sector's ability to meet the huge financial responsibility—risking an investment of about $30 billion in the next ten to fifteen years on the proposition that the nuclear-power industry will remain in business, and that the new enrichment plants will work. But private finance is unwilling to take this risk. At the White House conference that led to Mr. Ford's decision, the consortium that proposes to build the next enrichment plant asked for and received guarantees that "If the enrichment operation owned by private business fails, the government would buy the plant and meet all commitments for shipments. . . ." A participant in that conference has revealed why the guarantee was asked for. He reported that the conference discussed the question: ". . . why doesn't UEA [the private consortium] just go ahead and do it?" The reply was in the form of another question asked by the bankers who were interested in possibly financing the operation: "Well, the private sector has never built a plant. What if it doesn't work?"

Thus, in proposing to turn over uranium enrichment to private enterprise, both parties have acknowledged that the step is possible only if the risk of failure of this costly enterprise is borne by the government.

This is a fitting summation of the nuclear-power program as a whole. It is a lopsided partnership between the private and public sectors, in which the rewards have been private and the huge risks—the hazards to life, the waste of billions of dollars, the rising cost of power, the impending collapse of the nuclear-power program, and the ensuing economic chaos—have been assigned to the public.

6

THE SUN

By now the reader is aware that we cannot depend indefinitely on our present energy sources—fossil fuels and uranium. The supplies of oil, natural gas, and uranium are limited and rapidly becoming more demanding of capital and higher in price as the readily exploited deposits are depleted. While coal is more plentiful, converting it to liquid and gaseous fuels that can substitute for oil and natural gas demands large capital investments, and the products are very costly. Expanded use of these fuels would worsen environmental deterioration and, in the case of nuclear power, create new and unmanageable hazards. It is now accepted as inevitable that future energy supplies, unlike present ones, must be renewable and less harmful to the environment.

The only renewable source of energy is the sun—which, after all, comes up every day and will continue to do so, its radiant energy essentially undiminished, for billions of years into the future. As the energy crisis has developed and people have become more acutely aware of the importance of renewable energy sources, some attention has been paid to this basic fact, but until very recently not much. For years the only research on solar energy in the United States was done by a handful of poorly supported scientists and engineers. Progress was made, but given little notice. Not many people were aware that more than ten years ago Farrington Daniels, until his recent death perhaps the leading solar scientist in the United States, summarized what was then known about solar energy in these words: "There is no gamble in solar energy use; it is sure to work. It has been demonstrated that solar energy will heat, cool, convert salt water into fresh water, and generate power and electricity."

Since the 1973 oil crisis, interest in solar energy has increased sharply, first among the public, and then— apparently in response—among government agencies and commercial firms. But just as the sun itself has generated a powerful mythology, solar energy has become clouded by a set of firmly held but poorly founded beliefs: Solar energy is too diffuse to achieve the power needed by a modern energy-intensive society; it is impractical because it is unavailable at night or on cloudy days; the equipment is too expensive. Such objections provided a plausible excuse for the nearly total lack of government support for research on solar energy. As late as 1973, Federal expenditures for the development of practical uses of solar energy amounted to less than one percent of the total energy-research budget.

Solar energy has been largely ignored in the current debate over national energy policy—usually dismissed as only a faint, distant hope, irrelevant to current concerns over the price and availability of fuel. When the facts are known, however, it turns out that solar energy can not only replace a good deal, and eventually all, of the present consumption of conventional fuels —and eliminate that much environmental pollution— but can also reverse the trend toward escalating energy costs that is so seriously affecting the economic system.

THE SUN BATHES the earth in a huge amount of energy, which reaches the planet by an enormously rapid passage through essentially empty space, traversing the 93 million miles that separate the earth from the sun in about eight minutes. All the other forms of energy that we have considered thus far—mechanical motion, chemical energy, and nuclear energy—are transferred in close association with matter. The sun's energy is of a different sort; it does not travel in company with matter, but as "pure" energy—_radiation_. (Unfortunately, the realities of the modern world have encumbered this word with the misleading idea that radiation is invariably dangerous and destructive. In the technical sense, the term includes not only dangerous X-rays and nuclear radioactivity, but also the warmth radiated by a hot stove. Light is the most commonly experienced form of radiation.)

Solar radiant energy has its origin in electrons—the fundamental units of matter which carry the negative electrical charges that balance the positive ones of atomic nuclei. The electrons' energetic behavior explains the special properties and effects of such radiant energy, and how it can be used.

The first successful, if partial, explanation of the relation between the energy of an atom and the behavior of its electrons was made by Niels Bohr in 1913. He deduced that electrons, moving about the nucleus, could occupy only certain discrete orbits, which differ in their distance from the nucleus. In this "Bohr atom," the energy is constant as long as the electron remains in a particular orbit. It can only change abruptly. If the electron leaps to an outer orbit, the atom's energy state shifts to a correspondingly higher level; if the electron drops into a lower orbit, the energy state shifts to a lower level. In the 1920s Bohr's view of the atom was replaced by a more accurate representation based on wave mechanics—a theory that regarded the electron as a wavelike thing rather than as a particle. Bohr's orbits were reduced to statements about the probability of finding an electron in a particular region about the nucleus, but the notion of discrete energy states was confirmed.

From the law of conservation of energy we know that when an atom falls from a high energy state to a lower one, the extra energy cannot simply disappear; it must go somewhere. The extra energy leaves the atom, emitted into the surrounding world as radiation. Just as the atom's energy can change only in discrete steps, so the energy of the emitted radiation is also given off in separate packets—photons—which correspond in their energy content to the difference between the atom's original energy state and the lower one to which it has fallen. Conversely, when the atom goes into a higher energy state, it must absorb radiant energy from some external source. And because there is a discrete gap between two successive energy states, the atom must absorb a photon that is sufficiently energetic to at least match that gap.

When atoms are joined to form a molecule, many of the electrons originally associated with the individual atoms collectively form new energy states. These molecular energy states also occur at discrete levels, giving rise to characteristic energy gaps that enable the molecule to absorb photons of corresponding or larger size.

The characteristics of radiation can also be expressed in terms of wave-length, which is based on the (older) view that radiation is a wavelike disturbance rather than a stream of energy packets. It is helpful to keep both aspects of radiant energy in mind, taking note of the basic relationship between them: the shorter the wave-length of the radiation (or the higher its frequency), the greater the energy content of the photon.

It is useful, then, to think of atoms and molecules—and of the materials which they comprise—as containing energy traps that will specifically absorb radiation characterized by a particular wave-length (or by a photon of a particular energy content). The absorbed energy alters the arrangement of the electrons of the molecule or atom. Since this arrangement determines how the substance will react chemically, the absorbed energy may induce a chemical change. Otherwise, the absorbed energy is soon converted into generalized molecular agitation and contributes to the temperature of the substance.

The sun's energy is produced by a nuclear fusion reaction deep in its vast interior. This reaction is a complex cycle in which nuclei of hydrogen, carbon, nitrogen, and oxygen interact, with the net result that two hydrogen nuclei fuse to yield a helium nucleus plus some high-energy particles. (Experimental fusion reactors are being built in an as yet unsuccessful attempt to reduce this process to a new energy-producing technology, which will be discussed later on.) The products of the sun's natural fusion process have a slightly smaller mass than the starting material, and in keeping with the Einstein equation, the minute amount of lost mass (about 0.75 percent of the original) is converted to an extremely large amount of energy. As a result, the sun loses weight constantly—at the rate of some four million tons per second. However, the sun is so large that it will not change perceptibly for some billions of years. In effect, the sun is a huge, essentially eternal nuclear reactor, assembled by the play of cosmic forces rather than by the hand of man.

The energy of the sun's fusion reaction is released mainly in the form of very energetic gamma radiation. As the gamma radiation streams outward from the sun's core, it collides with the nuclei and electrons in the surrounding 300,000-mile-thick blanket that makes up the rest of the sun. These collisions absorb some of the energy of the gamma photons, and the radiation gradually diminishes in energy until most of it is in the form of X-rays. Near the sun's outer layer are numerous hydrogen atoms; striking them, the X-rays tend to push their electrons out of close-in orbits to more outlying ones. As these energized electrons fall back to lower energy states, the atoms lose energy by radiating photons, chiefly of visible light and lesser intensities of ultraviolet and infrared. These stream outward from the sun, spreading radially into space. By the time the solar radiation reaches the earth, it has been spread over a spherical surface of about 100,000 trillion square miles, and has become quite diffuse.

Less than one billionth of the energy radiated by the sun falls on the earth. There it interacts, first with the constituents of the atmosphere that surrounds the planet, and then with the material on its surface: water, land, and vegetation. Most of the solar ultraviolet radiation is absorbed at the outer edge of the atmosphere by a layer of ozone—a molecule which happens to have an energy gap that corresponds to the energy content of ultraviolet photons. The ozone layer thereby shields the living things that inhabit the earth's surface from the damaging effects of ultraviolet radiation, such as skin cancer. (In the past few years it has been discovered that this protective layer of ozone is being threatened by pollutants from supersonic aircraft and by chemicals used to pressurize aerosol cans.)

Infrared photons match certain energy gaps in water and carbon-dioxide molecules, which occur in the lower atmospheric layers. These molecules therefore absorb most of the infrared radiation, which increases their general molecular agitation and heats up the atmosphere. Some of the solar radiation that approaches the earth is scattered in different directions by dust and other particles in the atmosphere. Clouds reflect solar radiation; over a cloud-covered part of the earth 80 percent of the solar radiation may be reflected back into space.

These processes prevent most of the sun's ultraviolet and infrared radiation from reaching the earth's surface, so that the radiant energy that does get through is mainly in the visible part of the spectrum. What happens to the light energy that reaches the earth's surface depends on the color of the material that it strikes. A substance's color is an indication of which wave-lengths of light radiation, if any, it absorbs. White materials, such as snow, absorb almost none of the light that falls on them, reflecting it instead. A green leaf absorbs red and blue light, reflecting green wave-lengths. A red rock is likely to absorb blue and green wave-lengths, reflecting the red ones. Black soil (or the asphalt street) absorbs all the visible wave-lengths, so that almost no light of any kind is reflected from it.

On the earth the only chemical reaction that is driven by energy absorbed from the sun is photosynthesis, which converts some of the radiant energy absorbed by the green leaf into the potential energy of the organic substances that the leaf produces. The potential energy in foodstuffs, cotton, and wood is therefore derived from solar energy; agriculture and lumbering are the main ways in which solar energy is captured and put to use at present.

Except for photosynthesis, the radiant energy striking the earth's surface simply raises the temperature of whatever absorbs it. This has a considerable effect on the earth's temperature. Thus, black soil or the asphalt street efficiently converts the light that strikes it into heat. In contrast, snow reflects back into space a good deal of the energy that would otherside warm the soil, and a snow cover tends to reduce winter temperatures further.

As a result of such absorption processes, most solar energy simply heats up the earth's surface and the atmosphere. At night this heat is re-radiated, as infrared photons, back toward space. However, not all of it gets out, for the carbon dioxide in the atmospheric layer around the earth acts as a valve: During the day it lets the sun's visible radiation through, but when that energy is transformed to heat on the earth's surface and re-radiated as infrared energy, the carbon-dioxide layer absorbs a good deal of it. This resembles the way in which glass helps to warm a greenhouse on a cold winter day, for glass, like carbon dioxide, is transparent to visible light energy but absorbs infrared. The global "greenhouse effect" tends to keep the earth a little warmer than it would be otherwise.

The earth is not heated uniformly by the sun. Wherever clouds are overhead, a good deal of the incoming solar energy is reflected back into space. The amount of solar energy that is scattered and reflected also depends on the thickness of the atmospheric layer that the sun's rays must traverse. That thickness varies with the latitude, the season, and the time of day. For example, near sunrise or sunset the sun's rays come slanting through the layer of air around the earth and must go through more of it than they do when the sun is directly overhead. The same effect governs the intensity of solar radiation at different latitudes.

Because of these variations and the random drift of clouds, the atmosphere is warmer in some places than in others. These differences drive the movement of air. Where the air is hot it will tend to rise and cooler air will move in to replace it—this is the origin of winds. Wind is therefore a form of solar energy, and a windmill is a device for capturing it.

As surface waters absorb solar energy, they become warmer and some of the water molecules evaporate. Water vapor, carried upward by heated air to the cooler upper layers of air, may condense there into the droplets that make up clouds. Eventually rain forms and falls to the earth, where it may collect for a time, let us say, in some mountain lake. The kinetic energy of the water in the streams that rush down the mountain is therefore also a form of solar energy, which can be captured by a water wheel or a hydroelectric plant.

Solar energy is the richest resource on earth, and the least used. If the solar energy reaching the earth were converted into electricity and sold at current prices, it would be worth more than $500 billion a day. Yet we use only a few hundredths of one percent of that energy, chiefly to raise crops for food, fiber, and lumber. What can be done to make more use of this huge resource? Can it reasonably be expected to replace the dwindling, expensive, and environmentally hazardous non-renewable fuels on which we now depend?

As late as 1973 the conventional answers to these questions—for example, those usually provided by government agencies—have been uniformly negative. The following summary of the potential value of solar energy in a 1973 report of a task force of the National Petroleum Council's massive study on the "U.S. Energy Outlook" is typical:

> Because it is so diffuse and intermittent when it reaches the earth, solar energy can be put to no foreseeable large-scale use over the next 15 years, even with appreciable improvements in technology. The large area over which solar energy must be collected and the cost of collection and conversion equipment prevent the widespread use of such devices as solar evaporators, solar desalinators, solar heaters, solar cookers, solar furnaces, solar cells, solar houses, etc.

For a long time this view has dominated the government's attitude toward the development of solar energy and has contributed to the general public impression that solar energy is some sort of visionary, faintly ridiculous idea that might—or might not—turn out to be helpful sometime in the next century.

What is most unfortunate about such evaluations of solar energy is not so much that they are pessimistic putdowns and perhaps motivated by the self-interest of the purveyors of oil, coal, and uranium. (The chairman of the NPC task force quoted above was an officer of the Gulf Research and Development Company, the research subsidiary of a firm engaged in producing all three non-renewable fuels.) Much more distressing is the fact that the supposed disadvantages of solar energy —its diffuse nature and the economics of constructing solar devices—turn out, when properly understood, to be precisely the reverse: Just because it is diffuse, solar energy has certain major thermodynamic advantages over conventional sources of energy. And the economics of solar installations are uniquely capable of overcoming the devastating effects of conventional energy production on the economy—in particular, rising capital costs and inflation.

To understand these remarkable and unexpected advantages of solar energy, we need to recall a basic consequence of the principles of thermodynamics. From the Second Law of Thermodynamics we learn that the value of energy lies in its capability, upon being transferred, to do work; that this capability is always reduced when work is done; and that the efficiency with which work can be obtained from the flow of energy depends on how well the thermodynamic properties of the energy source are matched to the properties of the energy-requiring task.

The thermodynamic properties of a task can be conveniently characterized by the temperature at which the required energy needs to be applied to it. Some common examples of such tasks, and the required temperatures (in degrees Fahrenheit) are: space heating, 70–80°; hot-water heating, 140–160°; air-conditioning (heat-driven), 180–200°; cooking, 250°; efficient steam generation of electricity, 1000°; internal-combustion engine, 3000°; metallurgical furnace, 1000–2500°. We can also characterize the thermodynamic "quality" of an energy source by its temperature. Energy delivered at high temperature has a high capability of doing work (it is low in entropy) and vice versa. As we have seen, the chief reason for the very low Second Law efficiencies that characterize many of the ways in which energy is now used is that high-quality energy (such as electricity) is used for low-quality tasks (such as producing hot water). Similarly, when oil is burned in a furnace at 500° F. to warm a room to 70°, we are using high-quality energy to accomplish a task that could be done just as well by a low-quality energy source, such as the waste heat rejected by a power plant. Thus, in many of its present conventional uses, energy is produced at an unnecessarily high source temperature and then applied, inefficiently, to processes that require a lower quality of energy. Conventional energy sources usually operate, so to speak, downward in quality and therefore, in thermodynamic terms, are often inefficiently coupled to the tasks to which they are applied.

Perhaps the most remarkable feature of solar energy is that it can operate just the other way around. We know from personal experience that solar radiation is delivered to the earth at a rather low temperature, compared to conventional energy sources. It is generally recognized that solar energy is therefore quite suitable for tasks that require low-quality energy—such as producing hot water or space heat. What is much less appreciated is that, nevertheless, solar energy is intrinsically of very high quality and can readily be applied to a task that requires high-quality energy. Solar energy is therefore thermodynamically suited to *any* energy-requiring task, and can substitute for the present sources of energy in any of their present uses.

The reason for this surprising situation is that the thermodynamic quality of radiant energy is determined by the temperature of the source that emits it. In this case, the source is the luminescent surface of the sun, which has a temperature of about 10,000° F. Solar radiation is therefore inherently of very high thermodynamic quality. The low temperature that direct sunlight produces when it is absorbed at the earth's surface (about 100–120° F.) does not mean that the quality of the energy has been degraded en route. Rather, it signifies that the energy has spread out enormously in its long radial journey from the sun. To demonstrate that the intrinsic high quality of solar radiation is still retained when it reaches the earth, we need only perform a familiar experiment. If sunlight is sharply focused with a lens, it will set paper or wood aflame (at ignition temperatures of 400–450° F.). All that is required to deliver solar energy at any desired temperature, up to the 10,000° temperature of the solar source, is to concentrate it from a sufficiently large area. A three-inch lens will gather enough light to produce a temperature of a few hundred degrees, and the huge parabolic mirror of the French solar furnace in the Pyrenees will gather enough to melt tungsten, at a temperature of nearly 6000° F.

Thus, there is a sharp contrast between the thermodynamic consequences of using conventional fuels and using solar energy. Conventional fuels almost always generate energy at temperatures much above those needed for most energy-requiring tasks, so that the thermodynamic quality of the energy is wastefully downgraded in the process. In contrast, solar energy can readily be *brought up* to any desired temperature by concentrating it, and thus it can be precisely matched, thermodynamically, to any given task. And this can be achieved without chemical combustion and the inevitable release of noxious chemicals to the environment. Nor is destructive nuclear radiation involved —all that having been safely left behind, 93 million miles away, in the sun's interior.

It is precisely the fact that solar radiation is spread so diffusely across the surface of the earth that makes it uniquely capable of being thermodynamically matched to a wide range of tasks by concentrating it to the degree desired. The practical value of concentrating solar energy is nicely illustrated by the only solar power technology that is now in regular use—hydroelectric power. The energy that drives the huge turbines at hydroelectric power stations is, of course, generated by water falling from a height, to which it is raised by solar radiation.

Like sunlight, the energy of falling rain is widely diffused across the earth, and its gentle force would seem to hold no promise of delivering power sufficient to run the energy-hungry tasks of modern society. As pointed out by Nicholas Georgescu-Roegen, who has written extensively on the economic implications of entropy, it is precisely this seemingly ineffectual force that generates the considerable amounts of high-quality electric energy produced by hydroelectric plants. What transforms the diffuse "impractical" energy of the rain into the eminently useful power of the hydroelectric plant is the process of concentration: The great flow of water that drives the hydroelectric turbines is the collective result of widely diffused rain falling over the large watershed, which, like a huge funnel, collects the water in the impoundment that feeds the power plant. For example, the hydroelectric plant at Hoover Dam, which has a capacity of 1345 million watts, achieves this output with a flow of 4.2 trillion gallons of water per year. This is the amount of rainfall collected by about 168,000 square miles of watershed.

What emerges from these considerations is an exceedingly simple—and, as we shall see, quite practical—principle for delivering solar radiation to an energy-requiring task at whatever temperature is most appropriate to it, thermodynamically: Light is gathered and concentrated from an area that is enlarged as the required temperature increases.

The temperature that can be achieved when solar radiation is absorbed by a collector (the term usually given to the absorbing device) depends on how intensely the collector concentrates the energy. The simplest ones do not concentrate the radiation at all. Such a collector is simply a flat plate, painted black and encased in an insulated, glass-covered box. As the black plate absorbs light and heats up, it tends to lose some of its heat as infrared radiation. The glass cover prevents this loss (through the "greenhouse effect") without impeding the entry of light energy. Such a collector can reach temperatures up to about 200° F. Equipped with a suitable way of transferring the heat (by circulating water through a pipe attached to the black plate, or by passing air over it), it can readily provide space heat and hot water.

For somewhat higher temperatures—let us say, to drive a heat-operated air-conditioner—the light is concentrated by means of a curved mirror, and the device is rotated (for example, by means of a clockwork motor) to track the daily movement of the sun. Such devices can reach temperatures up to about 1000° F.

To generate high-pressure steam, and from it electricity, light can be further concentrated—for example, by focusing an array of mirrors on a central tower containing the boiler. Temperatures in the range of 4000° F. can be achieved in this way. A steam turbine can operate quite efficiently at 1000–2000° F.

The _amount_ of energy absorbed from solar radiation (as distinct from the temperature achieved) is determined only by the overall area of the collecting surface and by the angle between the plane of the surface and the direction of the sun's rays. Maximum energy is absorbed when the surface is at right angles to the direction of the sun, so that the collector squarely intercepts a beam of light of a cross-section equal to the collector's area. If the collector is tilted off the perpendicular, it will intercept less than its own area and receive that much less solar energy. This means that for maximum absorption a collector should track the daily and seasonal movement of the sun so that it constantly faces directly toward it.

The amount of solar energy received by a given area of collector varies, of course, with the time of day, the season, and the weather. In the United States, about 11.8 watts of power (expressed in terms of electricity) are received per square foot, year round. The relation of this amount of power to the amounts that are needed for household tasks can be judged from the following: An average U.S. household uses about 6400 watts of power—about 57 percent (or 3600 watts) of the total for space heat, about 15 percent (or 960 watts) for heating water, and the rest for other household tasks. A flat solar collector will readily provide energy of the quality (temperature) suitable for space heat and hot water. To provide enough power for the household's space heat under the most demanding conditions (December in the central part of the United States) W. E. Morrow of MIT estimates that about 1300 square feet of collector would be needed, or a square about 36 feet on edge. This is slightly more than the roof area of a typical suburban two-story home.

Of course the situation is complicated by the shape and arrangements of the building relative to other buildings, trees, and nearby obstructions. Nevertheless, these numbers tell us, in general terms, that for most current one- or two-story residential and commercial buildings there would be sufficient space available on the roof, southern walls, and surrounding areas to install solar collectors capable of supplying low-quality energy needed for space heat and hot water. Suitably designed, tall buildings can be provided with a good deal of their low-quality energy needs by installing collectors on the southern wall. This is true *on the average*, and ignores the problem of storing heat for nighttime use or when the sky is cloudy (which will be discussed later on).

The remaining household needs for energy are largely for tasks involving mechanical motion (washing machines and so forth) and therefore require energy of a high thermodynamic quality. This is supplied most effectively as electric power. It is of interest, therefore, to determine the collector area that would be required to meet the nation's need for electric power. According to Morrow, if the entire present U.S. output of electric power were to be produced by solar-powered steam-electric generators of the central-tower design, operating at 30-percent efficiency (an attainable figure), about 780 square miles of collectors would be needed. This represents about .03 percent of the land area used for farming, or about 2 percent of the land area used for roads. There is room enough.

It is sometimes objected that these large areas of collectors would use massive amounts of material, such as glass and metal—which themselves demand considerable energy in their production. Several points are relevant here. First, it should be noted that light can be effectively reflected by a mirror made by depositing a film of metal no more than a few molecules thick. Such a film, supported on a plastic base and protected from the weather by a glass or plastic covering, would make an extremely light-weight reflector that could be used, in numbers, to concentrate considerable solar energy—for example, on a steam boiler. Flat-plate collectors that are suitable for space heat and hot water are readily made from aluminum and glass. So are the huge numbers of throwaway containers produced in the U.S. If these were banned and replaced by returnable glass bottles, each year enough glass would be made available to equip 8 percent of the nation's homes with solar collectors, and enough aluminum would be made available for about 1.5 percent of the homes. With additional metal obtained by, let us say, reducing the size and number of cars in use, material for solar collectors for all U.S. homes could readily be available over a fifteen-year period, even without increasing the total aluminum and glass output.

I have refrained from describing in even slight detail the design and construction of actual solar devices for space heat, hot water, or steam-generated electric power because there is nothing very novel about them. In these applications, all that is done is to link up a suitable solar collector with an already well-known device: a hot-water plumbing system; a forced-air home-heating system; a heat-operated air-conditioner; a steam-driven electric generator. The engineering problems are quite straightforward and involve no insuperable technical barriers. In one experimental installation, in which an array of mirrors is used to focus light on a steam boiler for electric-power generation, the most difficult technical problem was how to keep the mirrors clean. It was solved by designing a tank truck that traveled around the array and intermittently sprayed the mirrors with a cleaning solution. In general, the most difficult task in developing such devices is to keep the cost of manufacturing the mirrors low enough so that the price of the system is within competitive reach of present power plants. As Morrow has understated it: "It is fair to say that the engineering problems to be solved in making solar energy practical are considerably simpler than those of the breeder reactor. . . ."

It would appear, then, that rather uncomplicated devices could take care of the national energy requirements for space heat, hot water, and, if built on a sufficiently large scale, electric power—a total of perhaps 38 percent of the total national energy budget. But the remaining energy-requiring tasks could not be readily accommodated by such devices, for these largely involve transportation, which, except for electrified railroads, requires a transportable, preferably liquid fuel. Yet with a greater engineering effort this need, too, can be met by solar energy.

Hydrogen is the key to converting solar energy into a widely useful, transportable energy source. Solar-generated electricity can be used to produce hydrogen, by passing it through a slightly salty solution. The water molecules are split, and hydrogen gas and oxygen gas are produced.

Hydrogen has a number of advantages as a fuel. It can be made from water, which is everywhere available; compared with other fuels, it has a high energy content; when burned in air, the only waste product is water; it can be used to drive various types of engines (in the National Urban Vehicle Design Competition of 1973, two of the winning entries were designed for hydrogen fuel). On the other hand, the *Hindenburg* disaster is a reminder of the serious hazards that are involved in handling hydrogen. However, one recent engineering analysis states that, with suitable precautions, hydrogen used as a fuel ". . . should not be more hazardous than conventionally-applied fossil fuels."

Hydrogen is conventionally stored as a gas or a liquid; in either case, storage facilities may be very expensive. However, experimental methods of storage based on the reversible formation of an easily stored hydrogen compound are being developed.

The conversion of solar power into a liquid fuel also helps solve the problem of storing solar radiant energy to provide for energy needs during times when the sun does not shine. Hydrogen stores can be built up when the sun shines, and then used to maintain power production when light is not available. This can be done with the aid of a remarkably simple and efficient device, the *fuel cell,* which, if supplied with streams of hydrogen gas and oxygen gas, produces electricity (water is the only by-product). The fuel cell has no moving parts and is very simply constructed. It is also the most efficient means of converting fuel energy into electricity.

Conventional systems (using diesel engines or turbines) can convert fuel energy to electricity with a maximum First Law efficiency of about 38 percent. The maximum efficiency practically attainable with a fuel cell is about 60 percent. Conventional power plants can achieve their optimal efficiency only when they have a high power output. For that reason, there is a tendency to build very large power stations, which places a serious limitation on their location. While the efficiency of fuel cells also falls at lower output, the effect is less marked than in conventional systems. Fuel cells are therefore promising ways for the efficient operation of small-scale power stations, thereby enhancing the organizational flexibility of a power system.

Other ways of storing solar energy, once it has been converted into electricity, are known and some are in use: Water may be pumped to an elevation during daylight hours and allowed to run downhill to produce power when it is needed (several such "pumped-storage" plants are now used to store conventionally produced electric power for use in periods of peak demand). Other suggested power-storage devices include compression of air in underground cavities, and large fly-wheels. For storage of solar energy as low-temperature heat, insulated tanks of water or piles of gravel or rock are usually used.

In the common methods of converting heat into electricity, the power is derived from the difference between a high input temperature and a lower output temperature, which is achieved by cooling the generator with ambient air or water. As Carnot first pointed out, what is crucial in determining the amount of work that can be gotten out of such a system is the *difference* between the two temperatures. Thus, if a temperature reservoir that is colder than ambient temperature can be found, it is possible to construct a heat engine to convert that difference into work.

The impact of solar radiation on the ocean creates such an opportunity by heating the surface water to a temperature well above that of deep water. In the Caribbean Sea, for example, water at 2000 feet is about 40° F. colder than the surface water—a difference sufficient to power a heat engine, provided a suitable working fluid is used. Designs of such devices have been proposed; they would float in the sea and generate electricity that could be used to produce hydrogen (and oxygen) for shipment to shore. A survey by the physicist Clarence Zener points out that the temperature differences in the Gulf Stream are enough to generate 180 million billion watts of power per year, or about six times the total amount of energy that the United States is expected to use in 1980.

All this gives substance to Farrington Daniels' claim that the technical means for converting sunlight into useful work exist. Examples of most of the different kinds of solar devices have been built and successfully operated, some of them a long time ago. A solar still for producing fresh water from salt, covering 50,000 square feet, was built and operated in Chile in 1872; a solar steam engine ran a printing press at a Paris exhibition in 1878; a 4.5-horsepower solar steam engine operated in Pasadena, California, in 1901, a 20-horsepower engine in St. Louis in 1908, and a 50-horsepower engine pumped irrigation water from the Nile in 1913. Solar collectors for home heating have been common in many countries (including Florida and California in the United States) for a number of years, and research to improve them was active at MIT and the University of Colorado in the 1940s. Windmills are of course ancient, as are hydraulic energy sources.

Such accounts are often regarded as quaint sidelights on the history of industrial technology—a kind of museum of devices that have been left behind in the march of energy technology because they were not commercially feasible. However, as the economics of energy production rapidly changes, these devices, or their technological descendants, do become practical. That working examples already exist is an important step toward that goal, for they give the engineer something to work on, to modify and improve.

It is useful at this point to contrast solar energy with the only other source that might be regarded as equally long-lasting: nuclear fusion. Since the development of the hydrogen bomb, we have had evidence—indeed, more than most of us want—that huge amounts of energy can be derived from the fusion of atomic nuclei. The technical problem is to "tame" this enormously energetic process so that it can produce energy usefully, in a device that is not likely to be vaporized in the process. The temperature involved in the fusion process is so high that no known substance can withstand it, and the reacting material must be contained by magnetic forces in a field derived from intense electric currents. Elaborate and enormously expensive research to develop such devices is under way, supported by $74.7 million in the 1973 Federal energy-research budget (compared to $4.2 million for solar energy). Apart from the "thermodynamic overkill" involved in attempting to boil water with a source that operates at some 100,000°, the effort to develop a fusion reactor appears to be grossly out of balance relative to the effort given solar energy, for no one can be certain that fusion will *ever* work, or that if it does, it can be reduced to economic practicality.

The reason usually advanced for the remarkable failure to make practical use of what we already know about solar energy is that the devices are so expensive as to be uncompetitive with conventional sources of energy. (It might be noted that this argument has never been advanced relative to nuclear fusion, although it is clear from theory alone that the capital costs of such devices—if they ever work—will be very much greater than the costs of solar devices of the same capacity.) However, unlike physical realities, the realities of economics, particularly as they apply to energy, are far from eternal. For example, the overall price of energy in the United States has increased by more than 125 percent since 1970. And we have already noted how rapidly economic changes have altered the competitive positions of nuclear and coal-fired power plants. Thus, it would seem worthwhile, given that solar power devices do exist and can perform very useful tasks, to find out what it would take in financial costs to bring them into commercial operation.

Such an assessment has been made by a panel of government experts that was assembled under the leadership of Dr. Alfred Eggers of the National Science Foundation in order to help conduct a study entitled "The Nation's Energy Future," under the direction of Dr. Dixy Lee Ray (head of the AEC at the time) in response to a presidential directive. The report, which was published in December 1973, recommended a five-year, $10-billion research program, of which $200 million, or 2 percent, was to be devoted to research on solar energy. Some $1.45 billion was assigned to research on fusion, and the breeder reactor received $2.844 billion, or 28 percent of the entire budget. Nuclear energy as a whole received about 40 percent of the total research budget.

The report was supposed to plan a research program to develop new sources that might alleviate the energy crisis. It is appropriate, therefore, to examine the research priorities assigned to the breeder, fusion, and solar energy (as indicated by the proposed expenditures) in comparison with the contribution that each of these three new sources of energy might make to the nation's future energy budget—if the research actually succeeded.

To begin with, we can dismiss fusion from this evaluation. Since no one knows whether it will work at all, no one has had the temerity to assign any part of a future energy budget to this source. On the other hand, the AEC has made such an estimate of the expected contribution of the breeder program in the environmental impact statement referred to earlier in Chapter 4. The AEC estimated that in the year 2000 the breeder program would produce 434 million kilowatts of electric power, or 23 percent of the projected demand for electricity in that year.

According to the Ray report, the investment of $10 billion in the proposed research might be expected to increase the total amount of energy available from domestic sources from the equivalent of about 34 million barrels of oil per day to 57 million barrels per day. The investment of 40 percent of the research funds in nuclear power (largely for the breeder) was expected to account for 32 percent of this increase. Solar energy (together with geothermal and hydroelectric power)

was expected to contribute 1.7 percent of the anticipated increase in domestic energy. Since solar energy
was assigned 2 percent of the research budget, there
seemed to be a reasonable match between the report's
research priorities and the expected results.

When the report appeared, I was surprised and troubled by the smallness of both the proposed solar-
research budget and the expected results. Accordingly,
I attempted to obtain a copy of the report of the Solar
Subpanel (IX), which, I knew, comprised a distinguished group of experts in the field, assisted by an
equally distinguished list of fifty-six consultants. In response to my first inquiries I was told that there was
no such thing as a Subpanel IX report. Since such an
omission would have meant a revolution in bureaucratic procedure hardly credible in the Washington of
1973, I enlisted the aid of someone whose inquiries
might perhaps receive a more helpful response from
the AEC—Senator James Abourezk of South Dakota,
who is vitally interested in solar energy. His efforts also
failed. When the White House, at Senator Abourezk's
request, asked the AEC for the Subpanel IX report, all
that that supremely powerful institution (Mr. Nixon
was President at the time) received and sent on to Senator Abourezk (and eventually to me) was only
another copy of the "Futures" report to add to my own.
Finally, like a genie materialized by the appropriate
incantations, the report's existence was confirmed, and
the Senator was informed that a copy was available in
the AEC document room. This turned out to be a dim
photocopy of a hazy carbon; but it has brilliantly illu-
minated the obscurities of solar utilization.

The Subpanel IX report describes in meticulous detail what it would cost in research expenditures to bring
the various types of solar devices into practical operation and how much they could contribute to the national energy budget. If the various solar technologies
were developed according to the subpanel's recommen-
dation for "an accelerated orderly program having a
high probability of success" at a cost of $1 billion, they
would contribute a total of 21 percent of the nation's
electrical demand, or about 5.5 percent of the total

energy budget, in the year 2000. (Dr. Ray's report recommended an expenditure of $200 million, or half the amount the subpanel recommended for a "minimum viable" research program.)

The contrast between the AEC's attitude toward solar energy, as revealed in the "Futures" report, and Subpanel IX's conclusions is worth some further consideration. A particular solar device, the _solar cell,_ is an illuminating testing ground. This device (technically known as the photovoltaic cell) is remarkably simple in its operation, but thus far difficult and costly to produce. It consists of a thin slice of a crystal of treated silicon (the element which together with oxygen makes up the chief chemical constituent of sand, silicon dioxide) sandwiched between two electrical connections (electrodes), the upper one an open grid. When light strikes the upper layer, the photons raise certain electrons in the crystal to higher energy levels, which allows them to move through the crystal. As a result, an electric current flows from one electrode to the other. Large arrays of such solar cells are used to power space satellites; a panel a few inches square will drive a toy electric motor and whirl a small propeller.

Solar cells are now made by a series of rather delicate hand operations and are therefore so expensive that it would cost about $10,000 for one kilowatt of electric generating capacity, compared to current costs of $460 per kilowatt for nuclear reactors and $300 per kilowatt for coal-fired plants. Citing such disparities, the AEC assessment of solar energy as an alternative to the breeder (in the breeder environmental impact statement) claimed that useful solar electric power could not be achieved in the "foreseeable future."

The Subpanel IX approach to the potential of the photovoltaic cell was to work out what research effort would be needed to reduce the manufacturing costs—for example, by producing thin silicon crystals in a continuous ribbon rather than slicing up a thick one by hand. This approach was in keeping with earlier experience with the manufacture of transistors (which are quite similar to photovoltaic cells in structure and operation): Mass-production methods reduced the price of early transistors about a hundredfold.

On this basis Subpanel IX proposed an "orderly milestone schedule" for the development of solar power from photovoltaic cells: in 1977, cell-manufacturing technology developed to bring costs to $5,000 per kilowatt; 1979, costs reduced to $500 per kilowatt and a central power-station design completed; 1985, 10-million-watt photovoltaic systems installed in communities and large industrial plants; 1986, completion of a pilot plant to manufacture photovoltaic cells to provide power at $300 per kilowatt; 1990, construction of photovoltaic power systems of 100-megawatt capacity for use in towns and power networks. In sum, according to the Subpanel IX report:

> ... the achievement of the cost goals of this program will result in the production of economically competitive electrical power (cost of ten mills per kwhr) by the year 1990. The projected rate of implementation of this solar energy conversion technology will produce more than seven percent of the required U.S. electrical generating capacity by the year 2000.

To reach this goal, Subpanel IX proposed research expenditures of about $250 million; this was reduced to $35.8 million in Dr. Ray's final report. Thus, whereas the breeder was assigned $2.844 billion in research funds in the hope (now abandoned) that it would contribute 21 percent of electrical demand in the year 2000, the photovoltaic cell, which was capable of achieving one-third of that power output, was assigned about one percent of that amount. And the overall solar-energy program, which was expected (by Subpanel IX, but not by Dr. Ray) to contribute 21 percent of the national electrical budget in the year 2000, was assigned a total of $200 million in research funds. For approximately the same expected contribution to the energy budget, the breeder was assigned more than fourteen times the research support given to solar energy.

Such gross disparities in the effort being made to

develop nuclear and solar energy, which still persist despite recent efforts by Congress to redress the balance, help to explain why, despite its inherent practicality, solar energy remains a tenuous dream in the United States.

There is, to be sure, a considerable air of unreality about such reports, which predict that x millions of dollars will be transmuted by scientists and engineers into a device which—if and when it is manufactured and installed—will produce y millions of kilowatts of power. However accurate and perceptive, the reports about solar energy which emanate from government agencies and academic institutions tend to be remote from the realities of the energy crisis as they are experienced not by the people who study energy, but by the people who use it. In the real world, energy is perceived not in BTU, but in dollars—the cost of buying the energy required to do some needed work. In the real world, it is more informative to think about how best to perform a particular task than how best to produce a particular source of energy—even one so inherently beneficial as solar energy.

Let us consider how best to perform a task that figures prominently in every householder's budget—producing space heat and hot water. As we have seen, *all* of the present sources of energy are thermodynamically unsuited to such low-quality tasks: the Second Law efficiencies for existing space-heat and hot-water processes are extraordinarily poor. And although the waste heat of power plants can be efficiently used for space heat and hot water, this is very difficult to arrange except as new communities are built. There remains, therefore, the problem of providing a thermodynamically suitable form of energy for these uses in the homes that people live in now.

The simplest, most easily constructed solar collectors can quite reliably produce precisely the low-temperature heat needed for these tasks. The collectors are now available on the open market in the United States, although not yet manufactured on a mass scale, and they can readily be built by local craftsmen or even as a do-it-yourself project. But what can the householder expect to gain by using solar energy for space heat and hot water?

Bernard Yudow at Washington University has recently studied how solar energy might contribute to part of this task—providing a steady supply of hot water in amounts sufficient for household uses, at a suitable temperature (140° F.) and minimum cost. Electricity is one of the energy sources now commonly used to perform this task, especially in new homes, and Mr. Yudow worked out how a solar collector might serve as an alternative, and at what cost. A conventional hot-water heater of suitable size, operating on electricity supplied at $.03 per kwh (the current rate in St. Louis), would cost about $105. The solar collector would cost $12 per square foot (commercial units are available at that price), and would be purchased through a fifteen-year loan at an 8-percent interest rate. Data on variations, during the year, of the temperature of the tap water that enters the heater and of the daily amount of sunshine are available.

Taking these and other relevant data into account, Mr. Yudow computed the cost of hot water to the St. Louis householder, for a series of designs in which electricity and solar energy provide varying proportions of the total hot-water heat. The results are instructive. The cost of producing a unit of hot water (representing one million BTU of heat) by electricity alone is $9.90. If the householder were to invest in a thirty-square-foot solar collector and a six-cubic-foot storage tank (at a cost of about $660), the solar collector would provide about 46 percent of the hot-water supply, the remainder being supplied electrically. This mixed system would supply hot water at a cost of $8.90 per million BTU—a 10-percent saving over the cost of hot water produced only by electricity. If a sixty-square-foot solar collector and a twenty-four-cubic-foot storage tank were installed (at a cost of $1196), the solar collector would supply 75 percent and electricity 25 percent of the hot-water heat at a cost of $11.25 per million BTU. In order to provide *all* of the hot water, the solar collector would need to be expanded to 120 square feet; the system would then cost $1916 and produce hot water at $14.15 per million BTU. Thus, it pays the householder to install a solar system, but only one large enough to produce about half of the needed heat.

If the price of electricity were to increase to $.04 per kwh (given present trends, this is likely to occur in the next few years), the hot water produced by electricity alone would cost $13 per million BTU, and in the most favorable mixed system (46 percent solar, 54 percent electric) hot water would cost $10.34 per million BTU—a saving of 20 percent. However, even with electricity at this price, the mixed system would become uneconomical when the proportion of solar heat exceeded about 85 percent. An all-solar system becomes economical only when the price of electricity is about $.06 per kwh—about double the present rate.

These computations give us a valuable insight into the origin of some of the common beliefs about the supposed impracticality of solar energy. At first glance, the study seems to confirm the conventional wisdom that, except in unusual circumstances, solar energy is more expensive than conventional sources, for it would indeed cost more to operate a completely solar hot-water system than an electrical one, given the present price of electricity and of solar collectors. But taking a more flexible, *task-oriented* rather than source-oriented approach, it becomes apparent that by suitably combining the solar and electric sources, the householder can save 10 percent of his hot-water bill right now, and more later as the price of electricity continues to rise.

These computations also help to answer the conventional complaint that solar energy is unreliable because it is available only intermittently. On its surface, the objection has merit; after all, water should be hot (and rooms warm) at all times, whereas the supply of solar energy rises and falls with day and night and fluctuates with the weather. The daily variations can be accommodated by including a modest storage tank in the system. But if the sun is to be the sole source of heat, the collector and the storage tank must be large enough to maintain the needed energy supply during the relatively few days in the year when a stretch of bad weather prevents the collection of solar energy. Since this extra capacity is not needed during the rest of the year, it contributes very little energy relative to its cost. Therefore, the productivity of invested capital (that is, the amount of hot water produced per dollar invested in the system) will fall sharply as the capacity of an all-solar system approaches 100 percent. The answer to this fault is, then, obvious: Use solar radiation to produce not quite all of the needed heat, relying on the conventional energy source, as a standby, to take care of the short periods in which the solar source is insufficient.

This type of analysis also illuminates the interplay of private and social concerns. The private concern of the householder is to have a reliable supply of hot water at least cost. One social concern is for saving energy—making the most efficient use of the non-renewable fuels that are now burned to produce electricity. Mr. Yudow's computations show that the methods of producing hot water which best satisfy the private concern and the social one are not the same. Thus, a system 46 percent solar and 54 percent electric will be best for the householder's pocketbook, but a 100-percent solar system will save most fuel. An 85-percent solar system would maximize the social value of saving fuel at no cost to the householder.

Another social concern is to make better use of the increasing amount of capital that is needed to produce and use energy. At first glance, the solar method of heating water seems to require a larger capital expenditure than the conventional one. Even the smallest solar system costs considerably more than the electric heater: $660 as compared with $105. Although the investment is an economical one for the householder, one might question whether it serves society to tie up a seemingly large amount of wealth in solar equipment. In fact the difference is not as large as it seems, for the cost of the solar collector should be compared not only to the cost of the electric heater, but to the capital cost of producing the electricity as well. A typical hot-water heater operates at a power of 5000 watts; since the heater is ordinarily on about one-tenth of the time, it calls on

500 watts of the power plant's generating capacity. At the present time the capital cost of a coal-fired power plant is about $300 per 1000 watts (it is higher for a nuclear plant). When to the power-plant capital required to support the heater's demand for electricity are added the capital needed to produce the necessary coal and the cost of the heater itself, the *total* capital invested in producing the householder's hot water is about $320. Considering that mass production is certain to reduce the cost of the solar system, it would appear that the total amount of capital involved in it is not very different from the capital needed to produce hot water by electricity. What *is* different is that the capital cost of the solar system is borne by the householder, while the cost of the electric system is borne by the coal company and the power company. This illustrates the decentralizing effect of solar energy; the capital needed to provide domestic heat is broadly held by households, rather than concentrated in large power companies.

A comparable study of how combined solar/conventional systems can be used to supply space heat is being carried out by Ali Shams at the Center for the Biology of Natural Systems. Preliminary results show that the relationship between the cost of providing space heat and the percentage supplied by a solar collector is similar to that computed by Mr. Yudow for mixed solar/electric hot-water systems.

For example, in the city of Albuquerque, New Mexico, heating a typical home electrically now costs about $350 per year. If a solar heating system capable of producing one-half of the needed space heat is installed at its market price of $1600 and paid for with a 9-percent fifteen-year loan, the annual heating cost would be $325. If a householder bought the parts and installed such a solar system himself (thereby reducing the cost by one-third), the annual heating bill would fall to $250—a saving of $100 relative to the all-electric system. This saving can be gained from a combined system up to a ratio of 85 percent solar to 15 percent electric. A combined system that is 95 percent solar and 5 percent electric produces space heat at a cost about equal to a conventional all-electric system. This would enhance the social value of saving fuel at no added cost to the consumer. Clearly, solar space heat is a paying proposition in Albuquerque.

In St. Louis, which has about 40 percent less sunshine each year than Albuquerque and more severe winters, the situation is not so favorable at present. A small savings in heating bills can be achieved with a system 50 percent solar and 50 percent electric, if the solar installation (for a hot-air heater) is of the do-it-yourself variety. However, if the cost of electricity should increase to $.048 per kwh, even in St. Louis about 20-percent savings in fuel bills could be achieved with heating systems up to a ratio of about 75 percent solar to 25 percent electric.

While these results are still approximate, the general trends are clear: Solar installations to provide between 50 and 75 percent of the low-quality energy for space heat and hot water are *now* economically advantageous in certain places (such as Albuquerque) and in other places under limited circumstances (for example, in St. Louis if the solar equipment is installed by the householder). Given that the present costs of solar collectors are based on small-scale manufacture and should fall significantly as production is expanded, and given that conventional energy prices are increasing rapidly, such mixed solar/conventional installations could become the most economical alternative in most parts of the United States within the next few years.

There is a tendency in some quarters—perhaps in reaction to the sweeping denials of the usefulness of solar energy—to regard it as a panacea for the energy crisis. Enthusiasm for solar energy is understandable; in the long run, it does come close to being the perfect energy source. It is renewable; it is available everywhere; its environmental effects are negligible. (The only effect of any solar technology on the environment is that it changes the geographic pattern of the earth's absorption and re-radiation of energy. The natural pattern is represented by the weather; this is itself so variable that the effect of any solar device is likely to be unnoticed in the random fluctuations of the weather.) Most recent studies of long-range energy problems con-

clude that midway through the twenty-first century, or
even somewhat sooner, we could obtain all, or nearly
all, of our energy from the sun.

But solar energy by itself is not the solution to our
immediate problems. It is, rather, a valuable way to
make more rational use—economically as well as thermodynamically—of existing energy resources, gaining
time while the full development of solar energy gets
under way. The catalytic effect of solar energy is evident not only in the matter of producing hot water in
St. Louis, but also in the more weighty matters of national policy: the disastrous rate of inflation, largely
impelled by the rising price of energy, which is eroding
most families' earnings; unemployment in auto and
other major industries, much of it worsened by the high
cost and threatened shortage of energy; the growing
demand for capital, especially by energy industries,
which is outrunning the supply and threatens industrial
development; the still unmitigated curse of environmental degradation; the feelings of frustration and im-
potence of the citizen or the community confronted
with the concentrated wealth that is symbolized by
billion-dollar nuclear power plants.

None of these problems can be swept away in a
flood of sunlight; but solar energy can play its special
part in the effort to solve each of them. Solar energy
could at once begin to supply a large part of the energy
now used for space heat, hot water, and—with very little further development—air-conditioning. The householder would not only enjoy reduced bills, but would
also be relieved of the specter of constantly increasing
ones. In effect, by purchasing a solar heater now, the
householder can establish a hedge against inflation—
investment in goods that will retain their use value into
the inflated future. And if solar collectors were to be installed on a sufficiently large scale, the resultant decrease in the demand for fuels might, if the law of
supply and demand retains any of its force, reduce the
rapid rate of escalation of energy prices, and thereby
help to check the pace of inflation generally. Any
major effort to install solar collectors in the nation's 60
million homes would require the construction of up to

$200 billion or so of equipment. Unlike oil refineries or nuclear power plants, constructing these solar systems would be simple in technology and ample in its demand for diverse kinds of labor. The devices could be built by auto workers in idle auto plants or by plumbers, carpenters, and metal workers in small community-based shops. Such a program, based, for example, on government loans to support the manufacture and purchase of solar systems, could significantly reduce unemployment.

Nor is the manufacture of solar devices—not only simple collectors, but solar steam plants and photovoltaic power plants—likely to contribute to the growing shortage of capital. The chief reason for the increasingly intense demand for capital for the production of conventional sources of energy is that they are heavily affected by the law of diminishing returns. Every barrel of oil that is produced makes the production of the next barrel more difficult and more costly in invested capital; every new environmental and safety problem that is uncovered in a nuclear power plant makes the next one more complex, and more demanding of capital. In every conventional energy source, the productivity of capital—the energy produced per dollar of capital invested—has fallen sharply with increased production. In contrast, the capture of solar energy can be continuously expanded with no decrease in capital productivity because the production of one unit of solar energy in no way makes it more difficult or costly to produce the next. Sunlight falls continuously all over the earth, and its use in one place does not diminish its availability elsewhere—any more than corn growing in the Ukraine interferes with corn growing in Iowa. And so, unlike conventional energy sources, solar energy will not become progressively more demanding of capital as its use expands. What is more, as solar energy replaces conventional sources, the latter can be gradually phased out, thus reducing the most intense demand for capital in U.S. industry.

For all these reasons, solar energy is ideally suited to local or regional development. No giant monopoly can control its supply or dictate its uses. And since a large solar installation is not basically different from a smaller one (it is only a larger aggregate of collectors, mirrors, or photovoltaic cells), there are no significant economic advantages to be gained by size as there are in, let us say, nuclear power plants. Economically and thermo-dynamically, solar energy can be effectively applied—at first in judicious combination with conventional sources, and eventually alone—to the needs of a single home or a city. It offers a wide range of policy options; local, regional, and national development are equally feasible.

There is a broader lesson to be learned in what we know of the special properties of solar energy. Since it is *radiant* energy, it is an ephemeral thing; unless it is used, it is quickly transformed into heat and lost to space. Unlike oil or uranium, sunlight is not a com-modity to be bought and sold; it cannot be possessed; its value is not inherent, but derives from its use—the outcome of its relation to a process, to a task. Solar en-ergy enjoins us to attend to the task; to find the best way to link the task to resources; to cherish the re-sources that nature lends us; to find value in their social use, rather than profit in their private possession.

7

THE USES OF POWER

WE HAVE THUS FAR been concerned with the sources of energy. But the principles of thermodynamics tell us that the amount of work that can be obtained from an energy source—which is its only value—depends on how well the source is matched to a work-requiring task. This can be measured by its Second Law efficiency, and the recent APS study of such efficiencies reveals that in the United States most tasks are rather poorly coupled to their energy source:

About 28 percent of the national energy budget is used for low-temperature tasks such as space heat, water heating, cooking, air-conditioning, and refrigeration; on an overall national basis, their estimated Second Law efficiencies range between 3 and 6 percent.

About 25 percent of the energy budget is used for various forms of transportation, chiefly autos and trucks; their Second Law efficiencies are estimated at 10 percent.

About 37 percent of the energy budget is devoted to industrial uses, most of them requiring a high-quality source; the estimated Second Law efficiencies are 25–30 percent.

Several percent of the energy is consumed by the conversion of petroleum and natural gas into petrochemical products, such as synthetic fibers, plastics, pesticides, and fertilizers. There is some doubt as to how the Second Law efficiency of such uses of energy ought to be computed; for reasons to be discussed later on, my own estimate of their Second Law efficiencies is nearly zero.

From these statistics it would appear that the overall Second Law efficiency with which energy is now used

145

in the United States is probably no more than about 15 percent. There is a very large gap between the minimum amount of work needed to produce the goods and services that we now enjoy and the much larger amount that we actually use to accomplish these tasks. Or, put the other way around, by improving thermodynamic efficiency we could greatly reduce the amount of energy that we now use, without sacrificing any of its present value. In theory, we could save 85 percent of the amount of energy that we now use; practical limitations suggest that the possible savings are probably about 55–60 percent. In any case, it seems clear that there is room for a drastic reduction in energy consumption (more than enough to eliminate imports, if that seems desirable) without reducing the standard of living.

A low Second Law efficiency is not the result of a leaky fuel tank or some other loss of stored energy. Rather, it means that energy is being wasted *while* it is used; that its available work is poorly directed toward work-requiring tasks; that there is a faulty relationship between source and task. The imperatives of thermodynamics tell us that even at its best this relationship— in which energy flows from the source to the task— involves some loss of the available work. And even a small departure from this most efficient condition can considerably worsen that loss.

The relationship between the energy source and the energy-requiring task is in part built into the design of the instrument that mediates the flow of energy—the furnace, the diesel engine, the heat pump, or the cornfield. But it is also affected by how that instrument is used. A diesel engine is a relatively efficient way to convert the fuel's energy into electricity; but much of its efficiency is wasted if the electricity is then used to produce hot water. A field of corn is an effective way to trap solar energy, but (as we shall see) a good deal of that advantage is wasted if it is heavily fertilized with inorganic nitrogen.

If we wish to understand, as a prelude to doing something about it, why the U.S. production system makes such shockingly inefficient use of energy, we need to understand not only the design of the various energy devices and of the instruments of production that they drive, but also how each of these machines is used, and how it might better fit into the production system. Where in that system does it make sense to use a furnace, a diesel engine, or a heat pump; an electric motor or an electric heater? What energy relationships call for the design of a new instrument or a different pattern of production? What economic considerations —which, after all, govern how the instruments of production are designed and used—have so uniformly imposed on them features that drastically curtail their thermodynamic efficiency?

To answer these questions, we would need a kind of encyclopedia of production, a detailed catalogue of the processes of agriculture, industry, and transportation and of their various productivities—what we put into them in the form of labor, capital, and energy, and other resources relative to what they produce. Such a catalogue does not exist. Various useful fragments are available. Some of them (such as the input-output tables which give the dollar value of certain contributions of one production sector to another) have been created by economists in the last twenty to thirty years. More recently, physical scientists concerned with resource problems have made more detailed estimates, chiefly based only on the First Law of Thermodynamics, of the amounts of energy used in different industrial and agricultural processes relative to their output. But these are only the small beginnings of a monumental task.

It is chastening to discover that the huge, enormously complex U.S. production system has been built not only without a plan, but also without a guidebook that explains, or even merely describes, its existing intricacies. It is not difficult to provide convincing evidence of this lamentable fact. The first detailed account of the pattern of energy distribution in the U.S. production system, ordered by the White House and carried out by one of the country's leading research institutions, begins quite appropriately with the following statement:

The availability of energy, and the impact of the utilization of energy upon the environment, are urgent issues in the United States. However, much of the information required to deal effectively with these issues is not available. An obvious gap has been the absence of statistics on how energy is used in the United States, broken down into meaningful end uses and compiled on an overall energy basis.

The laudable ring of these words is spoiled by two unfortunate facts: The study was published in 1972, at least two decades after most of the present production patterns were firmly established; and the entire analysis takes no account of the Second Law of Thermodynamics, which in 1972 had been known for some 150 years. This explains the report's naïve optimism regarding the efficiency with which energy is used in the United States:

. . . efficiencies in the industrial sector vary from a low of 64 percent for process steam production using natural gas to a high of 90 percent for electric drive. In the residential and commercial sectors, the lowest efficiencies are in air-conditioning and refrigeration—30 percent for gas and 50 percent for electricity—and the highest efficiency is in electric space heating, at 95 percent.

This last statement, which stands thermodynamics on its head, perpetuates an idea that ranks high in the mythology of power companies.

So it is unfortunately true that even at this late date in the history of the U.S. production system we have no comprehensive picture of its design that might support an effort to describe, let alone correct, its serious thermodynamic faults. In its absence I shall fall back on the expedient of considering, as examples, several narrower segments of production in which the available data and my own knowledge happen to coincide. That is the purpose of this chapter; it considers the design and economic relations, relative to energy, of three areas of production: agriculture, transportation, and the petrochemical industry.

FOR ANYONE, such as myself, who approaches it from the outside, agriculture in the United States presents a picture of enormous and apparently successful change. The storybook farm, with its menagerie of animals personally attended by the farmer and his family amid checkered fields of corn, oats, hay, and clover and a garden of fruits and vegetables, is long gone. Nearly all the horses have disappeared, their place before the plow taken by tractors, which—in a kind of parody of their predecessor's evolution—each year grow in size and power, many now riding on seven-foot wheels and carrying an air-conditioned cab. Most of the cattle have been banished to feed-lots—enormous pens where thousands of animals are fattened on truckloads of grain, tended more by bulldozers than by people. The chickens are no longer in the barnyard, scrambling about for food and laying eggs in nests of their own making; now they are congregated in long buildings, confined in rows of cages, their food and water delivered and their eggs and waste removed by endless belts.

Now the once-variegated fields are uniformly covered with a single crop. The corn no longer dries in the sun, but is harvested as moist grain which is fed into gas-burning drying ovens and trucked to feed companies—that supply the penned cattle and the caged chickens. Where once the animals' manure made the fields fertile, now it has become feed-lot waste. Instead, the crops are nourished by purchased chemicals. Other chemicals are used to kill weeds and insect pests, no longer kept in check by shifting crops from field to field.

The farm land, once a place where in almost every season some green leaf shimmered in the sun, is now more often bare ground, green for only a few summer months, when the single crop that is mandated by the market is rapidly grown, harvested, and turned into cash. And most of the people have left, no longer needed to tend the animals or to manage the seasonal variety of planting and harvesting. Those who remain are no longer preoccupied with daily decisions about how to mediate between the complex needs of their livestock and crops and the harsh demands of nature. Their decisions are now less numerous but much more portentous—whether to plant all of one crop or all of another, to take advantage of an expected market price; or whether to buy an expensive new machine or chemical, in the hope that it will increase their income sufficiently to cover the cost of the loan needed to pay the high purchase price.

All of these changes—most of them in the last thirty years—have been accompanied by spectacular improvements in agricultural production. Compared to 1950, in 1970 an acre of land planted to corn yielded three times as much grain; a broiler chicken gained nearly 50 percent more weight from its feed; a hen laid fifty more eggs per year (a 25-percent increase). In that time, farm output as a whole increased by 40 percent. And, as the proponents of the new agriculture are fond of reminding us, in 1950 each farm worker produced enough food for about 15 people and today the figure is well over 47 people per farm worker. If people have left the farm, it is because they are no longer needed there.

But there is also a major economic mystery here. Since the productivity of farm labor has increased nearly threefold and most of it is still supplied by farm families, we might expect them to be that much better off, economically, than they were. But they are not. Despite the huge increase in agricultural labor productivity and in total output, the real income of U.S. farms *decreased* from about $18 billion in 1950 to $13 billion in 1971. (These and the following figures are given in 1967 dollars to eliminate the effect of inflation.) Because the number of farms also decreased by 50 percent, the income per farm rose by 46 percent (from an average of about $3200 in 1950 to slightly under $4600 in 1971). However, this is much less than the average increase in the family income of *all* U.S. families in that period, 76 percent. Meanwhile, the total mortgage debt of U.S. farms rose from about $8 billion in 1950 to $24 billion in 1971.

These statistics tell us that the farm families which

have accomplished the remarkable gains in agricultural production have not reaped most of the fruits of their labor. As a recent report of the National Academy of Sciences points out: "Agriculture as a major segment of the total economy has had to produce far more in order to earn as much; the terms of trade between agriculture and the rest of the economy have shifted against agriculture."

Who, then, *has* gained from increased agricultural production, if not the farmers?

My first clue to this puzzle came as I heard a lecture by Professor D. M. Woodruff, a distinguished and innovative agronomist at the University of Missouri. Professor Woodruff likes to begin his lectures by asking the question "What is the purpose of farming?" The usual answer, which is enshrined in every agronomy textbook, is: "To produce food and fiber"; but the answer that Professor Woodruff prefers is: "To capture solar energy."

This is a powerful insight. Once given this lead, it takes only a little reflection to realize that although only a minute fraction of the solar energy that reaches the earth is turned into useful work, nearly all of that energy is captured by agriculture and forestry. Agriculture is an energy-requiring process, and energy is the clue to the curious disappearance of the new wealth that farms have generated during the post-war gains in production.

A useful place to pick up the trail and begin the pursuit of the lost farm income—and to appreciate the force of Professor Woodruff's insight—is the great biological cycle that supports agricultural production —in particular, the movement of carbon and nitrogen. In nature, carbon and nitrogen move through a familiar ecological cycle: Grass growing in the field takes carbon dioxide out of the air and water and nitrate out of the soil (along with other essential nutrients) and synthesizes from these simple inorganic ingredients thousands of different kinds of organic (that is, carbon-containing) compounds. Thermodynamically, these synthetic reactions require energy (this is generally true of an inorganic-to-organic process), which the plant

derives from sunlight. (The needed energy is initially
trapped by chlorophyll molecules; it is then transferred
through a series of intricate biochemical reactions that
finally incorporate the energy, in a potential form, in
the carbohydrates, proteins, fats, and other organic
compounds that make up the substance of the plant.)
Cattle eat the grass, and use its organic matter partly to
obtain the metabolic energy that supports their activity
and partly to form their own organic matter. The cattle's waste, which is also largely organic, drops to the
ground and is acted upon by a series of bacteria and
molds in the soil, the nitrogen and some of the carbon
eventually accumulating in the form of humus. Humus
serves as a store of nitrogen in the soil, which is
gradually broken down by bacteria into inorganic forms
(that is, molecules in which the nitrogen is no longer
linked to carbon)—ultimately, as nitrate, which is tak-
en up by the roots of the grass, thus closing the circle.
Bacterial metabolism, along with the metabolism of
cows, people, and other animals, releases carbon dioxide, which the plants can use, and the carbon cycle is
thereby closed.

Thus, carbon and nitrogen move in a cycle from
plants to animals, to a series of soil bacteria, and back
again to plants. Thermodynamically, this cycle is an
energy-requiring process; it will not run unless energy
flows into it—unless it is driven. The active agents that
drive the cycle are the bacteria that carry out the
various chemical transformations in the soil, and the
green plants themselves. The bacteria obtain the
needed energy by metabolic combustion of soil organic
matter. The energy used by the plant itself—for example, to pull nitrate and other nutrients into the root
cells—is also obtained metabolically from the organic
products of photosynthesis.

Nitrogen also enters the cycle by way of nitrogen
fixation—the conversion of chemically inert nitrogen
molecules in the air into biologically useful forms. This
is accomplished by bacteria living freely in the soil or
in the roots of legumes such as clover or beans. Nitrogen fixation is also an energy-requiring process, and

again the bacteria obtain the needed energy, metabolically, from organic matter.

Organic matter is the fuel that drives the great cycles of the ecosystem which support not only agriculture, but all life. Solar energy, trapped by the living plants, produces that fuel; Professor Woodruff is right.

The basic fact that agriculture is absolutely dependent on the energy contained in photosynthetically produced organic matter, and ultimately derived from the sun, has, of course, long been recognized in traditional farming practice. For example, one long-established principle was to maintain green crops on the ground for as much of the year as possible. This maximizes the capture of solar energy and the production of the organic matter that drives the soil cycles. Crops were grown in a yearly sequence, beginning with ones that green up early in the spring, through a summer crop, ending with one that remains green late into the fall.

The traditional scheme of combining animal and plant production on the same farm also recognizes the importance of organic matter for the soil cycle, energetically as well as in other ways. If the cycle is broken by growing a crop in one place and feeding it to animals in another, then their organic waste is not returned to the soil, but accumulates at the feed-lot. This practice converts manure from a useful carrier of solar energy and plant nutrients into a pollutant. Obviously, to maintain the integrity of the soil cycle, manure should be returned to the soil, where its nutrients can re-enter the biological cycle and its organic matter can provide the energy needed to drive it.

Crop rotations that include legumes are another good way to trap solar energy. The legumes' photosynthetic activity captures the energy needed to drive nitrogen fixation (by way of the organic products of photosynthesis) and thereby enriches the soil. Grasses seem to encourage the activity of nitrogen-fixing bacteria in the soil, perhaps by the organic matter sloughed off from their roots.

Given what we know about the natural cycles that maintain the fertility of the soil, and particularly their dependence upon energy, a system of agriculture that used solar energy efficiently would be based on a sequence of crops that are green for the longest possible yearly period, that are in a rotation which includes legumes, and that are mixed with animal production. This is, of course, the pattern of traditional agriculture. But this pattern has been largely destroyed by the post-war changes in agricultural production. By tracing the resultant effects on the farm's energy relations, and their economic consequences, we can find out where the added wealth produced by the new agriculture has gone.

In the U.S. Corn Belt, the common crop "rotation" is now usually corn-on-corn (corn planted in the same field year after year) or corn-on-soybeans, with the two crops planted in alternate years. This means that the soil is covered with energy-catching green leaves for only a short time each year. Corn matures in about ninety days and the leaves are full-sized and able to catch much sunlight for only perhaps half that time. And so, if only corn is grown, solar energy is trapped effectively for less than three months. For the rest of the year, the energy that the sun sheds on the land adds nothing to the economy of the farm, or the nation. In the new agriculture, legume rotations have been drastically reduced; legume seed production declined 60 percent between 1959 and 1973. Even when soybeans are grown, they are usually on land that has been previously fertilized, so that nitrogen fixation (which is inhibited by nitrate in the soil) is rather inactive. And finally, with the animals raised in separate feed-lots, the only organic matter returned to the soil is the stalk residue of the crop.

Thus, in a typical modern agricultural system, such as the Corn Belt, the soil cycles have been disrupted and deprived of a good deal of the solar energy needed to drive them. For this reason, and because the natural store of nitrogen in the humus has been greatly depleted over the years, large amounts of inorganic nitrogen fertilizer must be added to the soil each year in order to grow a successful crop. But the laws of thermodynamics are inescapable; if plants must have nitrate and if the synthesis of nitrate from the earth's great store of nitrogen in the air demands energy, then no technological trick can avoid the expenditure of that energy. Ammonia, one of the common Corn Belt fertilizers (which in the soil is rapidly converted to nitrate), contains nitrogen fixed from the air; it is produced in factories that get the necessary energy by burning natural gas or some other petroleum fuel. Because of the shift from manure, legumes, and other organic fertilizers, the crop's nutrition is no longer provided by a biological cycle, driven by renewable, freely available solar energy; instead, by using inorganic fertilizer, it has become dependent on non-renewable, increasingly expensive fossil fuels.

Another example of this kind of shift in the energy dependence of the farm is the matter of drying grain. Corn, like most grains, is an enormously valuable food because it can be easily stored well past the harvest season. Grain resists decay because it is too dry to support the attack of bacteria and molds. In nature, corn readily dries on the stalk in the autumn sun, and in traditional agriculture the field-dried ears were harvested and stored, as such, in ventilated bins. But the familiar corn-crib is gone. In the late 1950s new harvesting machines appeared which stripped the still-moist grains from the ear, in the field. To be preserved, the grain had to be dried within a few days after harvest in large ovenlike machines fueled by propane. Once more an essential energy-requiring task was diverted from solar energy to fossil fuel.

Thus we must add to the conventional glowing picture of post-war agriculture a feature that is more subtle and less praiseworthy than the increased yields of corn and chickens: Particularly with respect to energy, the farm has become less self-reliant, more dependent on the outside economy. To maintain production, the farm must now rely on factories and refineries for more and more of the energy that is needed "to produce food and fiber." The farm's link to the sun has been weakened, replaced by a new and—as we shall see—dangerous liaison with industry.

The energy that the modern farm now imports from

the industrial sector is delivered in diverse forms: as gasoline and diesel fuel (to run tractors and other machinery); as propane (to fuel grain driers); as electricity (to power milking machines, grain driers, and other stationary equipment); as fertilizers, insecticides, and herbicides, all chemicals that are synthesized in energy-demanding processes.

The relatively few analyses of the productivity of energy in agriculture that have been made thus far are all First Law computations. The major expenditures of energy in corn production (using Illinois agriculture in 1974 as an example) are for nitrogen fertilizer (47 percent), fuel for field equipment (18 percent), fuel for drying (19 percent), and other fertilizers (9 percent), with the remaining 7 percent used for a variety of minor purposes. According to the APS estimates, we can expect that fuel for driving tractors and other field equipment is used with a Second Law efficiency of about 10 percent, and that used for drying at an efficiency of about 5 percent.

There remains the puzzling question of how to compute the Second Law efficiency of the use of nitrogen fertilizer—the largest use of energy in modern corn production. Recall the definition of the Second Law efficiency: the ratio between the minimum amount of work required for a given task to the amount of work represented by the energy actually used to accomplish the task. The denominator in this ratio is readily computed from the energy budget of a nitrogen-fixation factory at about 19,700 BTU per pound of fertilizer nitrogen. If we define the task as the incorporation of nitrogen into the soil in a form useful to the plant, then it can be accomplished biologically with much less energy. A fall planting of a legume, vetch, plowed under in the spring, adds 133 pounds of nitrogen per acre to a cornfield. The external (non-solar) energy required to grow the vetch is about 360,000 BTU per acre, or about 2700 BTU per pound of nitrogen incorporated. On these grounds, conventional nitrogen fertilizer involves an efficiency of about 14 percent. Thus, when a farmer uses commercial nitrogen fertilizer, the amount of thermodynamic work expended to produce it is seven times greater than the minimum amount of work that is needed to accomplish the same result by planting vetch. But the external energy required to grow vetch *could* after all be reduced to essentially zero (for example, by using a horse fed on farm-grown corn). On this albeit impractical standard, the fertilizer's thermodynamic efficiency is zero.

U.S. agriculture now consumes only about 4 percent of the total national energy budget. It would make little sense to cut down the agricultural uses of energy, however inefficient they are, in order to reduce the overall energy demand. Nor is there much logic in complaining that the farmer is "wasteful" because he makes less use of the sun than before. Solar energy is renewable, and, like the milk in the fable's miraculous self-filling pitcher, there is no way to waste it.

The real problem created by the shift to outside energy sources is economic (apart from the environmental problems due to fertilizer leaching into streams and lakes and the very serious toxic effects of insecticides and herbicides). This is evident in the farmer's balance sheets, as they are averaged out in standard U.S. Department of Agriculture (USDA) reports. And they tell us quite clearly where the increased wealth generated by the post-war development of "agribusiness" has gone.

In 1950 U.S. farms had a gross income of about $32.3 billion. Their expenses amounted to about $19.4 billion, yielding a net income of $12.9 billion. By 1970 gross income had increased to $57.9 billion (a 79-percent increase); but expenses had gone up even faster, to $41.1 billion (an increase of 112 percent), leaving a net income of $16.8 billion. With inflation taken into account, the net income of U.S. agriculture had actually *decreased* in that twenty-year period despite the introduction of the new technological marvels that have so greatly improved agricultural production. Or, rather, because of them. The largest item in the farmers' rising costs is interest on loans and depreciation of machinery. These costs largely reflect the carrying charges of purchased material. These are the inputs brought into agriculture from the industrial sector, most of them—machinery, fertilizers, and chemicals—based on the intensive use of energy.

Looked at from the farmer's point of view, what happened between 1950 and 1970 was that the financial level of his operation increased, but with no gain—and in real dollars even a loss—in net income. Agribusiness has forced the farmer to operate at a higher economic scale, taking greater financial risks, with no real gain in net income. As one farmer remarked recently, "We don't make any more money, but we do handle a lot more of it." This trend has forced out the smaller farmers, who are less able to muster the amount of credit needed to handle such large-scale operations. This helps to explain why the number of farms in the United States decreased by half between 1950 and 1970.

Part of the problem is not only that agriculture has been using more and more industrial goods, but that in some cases their use yields progressively less output. This is particularly true of nitrogen fertilizer. For example, in the United States the average amount of nitrogen fertilizer applied to corn annually has increased steadily. Between 1950 and 1959 the rate of nitrogen application increased by 26 pounds per acre and the average yield of corn increased by 16 bushels per acre (.62 bushels per pound of fertilizer). Between 1960 and 1970 the rate of nitrogen application further increased by 71 pounds per acre, but the yield by only 27 bushels per acre (.38 bushels per pound of fertilizer). In other words, the productivity of nitrogen fertilizer—the crop produced per pound of nitrogen applied—has been declining as the rate of application has increased. This reflects a basic biological fact: that there is a limit to the amount of growth that a plant can sustain, so that yields obtained for a given increment of nutrient element inevitably decline as more and more is supplied to the plant. There has been a similar decline in nitrogen productivity in U.S. agriculture as a whole: Between 1950 and 1970 the amount of nitrogen fertilizer used per unit of crop produced increased fivefold. In the same way, as insect pests become more resistant to the new pesticides, the amounts of these chemicals used have also risen faster than agricultural output. Such effects mean that the farmer gets progressively smaller returns in income from increased expenditures of this sort.

Thus, in economic terms, the great post-war change in agricultural production technology did a great deal more than simply increase output. It displaced farm labor with energy-dependent inputs: machines, power, and chemicals. As the amount of labor involved in farming went down, the amount of capital went up; the assets used in agriculture, per farm worker, rose from $9400 in 1950 to $53,500 in 1970. This figure measures the demand of agriculture for capital relative to its demand for labor. As we shall see later on, this capital/labor ratio has a good deal to do with two major economic problems—the shortage of capital and unemployment (the shortage of jobs.). Production processes with a high capital/labor ratio tend to worsen both problems.

Since 1950 agriculture has joined the ranks of those sectors of production with the highest capital/labor ratios. The 1970 figure for agricultural assets per worker places farming second only to the petroleum industry ($117,865 of capital per worker in 1971) in this list. Moreover, in becoming more dependent on industrial inputs, agriculture has contributed to the importance of precisely those industries that are themselves characterized by high capital/labor ratios —petroleum and chemicals. The term for the new system of agricultural production—*agribusiness*—is well deserved; agriculture seems to have joined industry in generating the serious economic problems that now trouble us.

Here we can begin to see an explanation for the puzzling disappearance of the economic gains that one might expect farmers to receive from their additional production: Most of that wealth has been drained off by the industries—such as petrochemicals—that provide the new inputs, which substitute fossil-fuel energy for the solar energy on which agriculture has long depended.

By shifting its energy dependence from the sun to

petrochemical companies, the U.S. farm has become linked to a multibillion-dollar industry which not only sells fuel to the farmer, but competes with him for it when it is in short supply. Propane is an illuminating example. The chief consumers of propane are farmers and the petrochemical industry, in which it is a major raw material for the production of plastics and synthetic fibers. In the 1973 energy crisis the industry cheerfully bid up the price of propane, so that farmers had trouble finding the propane they needed to dry their grain and then in some areas had to pay triple its former price. Unlike the farmer, many of the petrochemical companies that produced plastics were not worried about the high price of propane. Many petrochemical operations are part of a vertically integrated corporation which deals in everything from crude oil to the plastics that are made out of it. Because they manufactured it themselves, for such petrochemical companies the high cost of propane was a purely bookkeeping transaction.

Propane, ammonia, and other farm chemicals represent a kind of lever which connects the farm with the petrochemical industry. But the two ends of the lever carry very different economic weights. In 1974 the average U.S. farm had assets of $148,600, whereas the average petrochemical company is a multibillion-dollar corporation. Obviously, the economic power is largely held by the petrochemical industry; inevitably, the farmer suffers.

Until the 1973 oil crisis this sort of economic vulnerability remained hidden. In the 1950s and 1960s, as the farmer became increasingly dependent on fuels and energy-intensive chemicals, their prices remained relatively low, in part because (as we have seen in Chapter 3) the cost of the petroleum products from which they were manufactured remained constant, and even fell slightly (in uninflated dollars) between 1950 and 1973. As long as the price of fertilizer remained low, it did not really matter that its agricultural productivity was falling; it was still a worthwhile investment.

Then came the oil crisis of 1973, which, as we have

seen, was the signal for a sharp and escalating rise in the price of fuel. And with it the prices of energy-intensive products such as fertilizers and other agricultural chemicals increased drastically. Between 1970 and 1975 propane increased in price by 101 percent; nitrogen fertilizer by 253 percent; and pesticides by an average of 67 percent. In 1973 rising farm prices more than made up for the rising costs of fertilizer and other energy-intensive inputs, but these gains were lost by 1975. The process has left U.S. agriculture in a vulnerable economic position; if the selling price of farm commodities should fall, farmers will be hard pressed to meet the elevated prices of agricultural chemicals, and of fuel, that have been imposed on them by the energy and petrochemical corporations.

One can almost admire the enterprise and clever salesmanship of the petrochemical industry. Somehow it has managed to convince the farmer that he should give up the free solar energy that drives the natural cycles and, instead, buy the needed energy—in the form of fertilizer and fuel—from the petrochemical industry. Not content with that commercial coup, these industrial giants have completed their conquest of the farmer by going into competition with what the farm produces. They have introduced into the market a series of competing synthetics: synthetic fiber, which competes with cotton and wool; detergents, which compete with soap made of natural oils and fat; plastics, which compete with wood; and pesticides that compete with birds and ladybugs, which used to be free.

The giant corporations have made a colony out of rural America. Like Standard Oil forcing its product on old China, U.S. industry has molded the nation's farms into a convenient market and a weakened competitor. In both cases the economic weapon was energy.

All this suggests that if the modern farmer could find some way to reverse the direction of this technological "progress" and to reduce the use of energy-intensive inputs such as fertilizers and pesticides, he might suffer little or no loss in net income, the reduced gross income compensated by a comparable decrease in costs. Strangely enough, at least a few farmers in the Corn Belt have managed to do just that.

Farmers are, after all, independent folk, and despite the conventional wisdom as expounded by the USDA and most agricultural-research institutions, some farmers have remained skeptical of the value of the intensive use of chemicals. Some are concerned over the environmental effects of fertilizers and pesticides; some fear that exposure to pesticides is unhealthy; some have a moral commitment to maintaining the natural fertility of the soil. For one or more of these reasons, a few farmers (no one really knows how many) operating commercial farms on which they rely for their livelihood have given up the use of inorganic fertilizers and chemical pesticides, becoming, in effect, "organic" farmers. (The idea of "organic" farming or gardening, stripped of overzealous exaggerations and unsupported claims, has a firm scientific foundation. From what has already been said, it should be clear that the maintenance of organic matter in the soil cycle is a good indication of the system's natural fertility. There is also good reason to believe that organic substances which do not naturally occur in living things —such as synthetic pesticides—are likely to risk biological harm, so that excluding these substances from agriculture wherever possible also has a scientific justification.)

The existence of these farms creates the opportunity to test the validity of the conventional wisdom that the success of current agricultural practice—its level of production and economic returns to the farmer—would be impossible without the intensive use of inorganic fertilizers and synthetic pesticides. The position has been forcefully laid down by Secretary of Agriculture Earl Butz:

Without the modern input of chemicals, of pesticides, of antibiotics, of herbicides, we simply couldn't do the job. Before we go back to an organic agriculture in this country somebody must decide which 50 million Americans we are going to let starve or go hungry.

Having located a number of such "organic farms," the Center for the Biology of Natural Systems was able to set up a simple way to test the validity of Mr. Butz's dictum: It compared these farms with neighboring conventional ones.

A research group headed by Dr. William Lockeretz studied sixteen commercial-sized organic farms that use neither inorganic fertilizer (other than phosphate rock) nor chemical pesticides, and sixteen conventional farms similar in size, location, and soil properties that used these inputs. Both categories of farms were combined crop-livestock operations; they raised about the same types of crops—corn, soybeans, wheat, and oats —except that the conventional farms raised relatively more corn. Both used about the same amounts and types of machinery (including grain driers).

The group analyzed the production of these farms for the 1974 season. The market value of the crops produced by the conventional farms was an average of $179 per acre, while the average value for the organic farm was $165 per acre. However, the operating costs of the conventional farms averaged $47 per acre, and those of the organic farms $31 per acre (the difference is largely due to the cost of the nitrogen fertilizer and pesticides used by the conventional farmers). As a result, the net income per acre of crop for the two types of farms is essentially the same: $134 per acre for organic farms and $132 per acre for conventional ones (this is not a statistically significant difference). The yields of different crops obtained by the two groups of farms are about equal, except for a small excess (12 percent) of corn yields on conventional farms as compared with organic farms.

The organic farms used only 6800 BTU of energy to produce a dollar of output, while the conventional farms used 18,400 BTU. Thus, organic farms appear to yield about the same economic returns as the conventional ones, but do so by using about one-third as much energy. In the terms of the farmer quoted earlier, they have managed to make as much money, without handling so much of it.

These observations, being based on only one year's results, must be regarded as tentative. As the study continues and we learn more about how the conventional and organic farms compare in their production, costs, and income, it will be possible to evaluate measures that might restore farming to a more thrifty use of energy, without undue loss in production. We hope to learn how to help the farmers find their way back to the sun.

TRANSPORTATION DOMINATES the energy picture. It is the largest single end use of energy, consuming 25 percent of the total U.S. energy budget. The fuel on which transportation depends—petroleum—has become the nation's major energy source. Together, the transportation and petroleum industries and the industries that depend on them (in particular, chemicals) are dominated by a group of only twenty major corporations that are worth a total of $181 billion and produce about $248 billion in sales, or 18 percent of the gross national product. (However, these corporations employ only 2.7 percent of the labor force.) The success with which this huge industrial complex has been concentrated in so few hands suggests that transportation has been firmly established as a vital, effective, and profitable sector of the U.S. production system.

Yet, by any objective standards, the U.S. transportation system is, in many ways, a failing industry: Nearly all the major railroads that serve the most heavily industralized area of the country, the Northeast, are bankrupt. For months one of them, the Penn Central (the nation's largest railroad), was so close to actually ending operations that the major industries in the area found it necessary to issue public warnings about the economic catastrophe that would follow. As the Congress struggles futilely with the problems of the Northeast lines, railroad bankruptcies threaten to spread, like some rail-borne disease, into the Midwest and beyond. Their economic failure only symbolizes the physical decay of the railroads; trackbeds are deteriorating (as one unhappy indicator of their condition, the number of railroad accidents increased by 42 percent between 1964 and 1972) and equipment is obsolete; passenger service has all but disappeared. (Relative to their total revenue, U.S. railroads provide less than a tenth of the passenger service common among European railroads.)

The major transportation industry, auto manufacturing, is itself in trouble. In the last two years the industry has been running at about 60 to 80 percent of its 1973 production rate, with as many as 300,000 workers laid off. And it faces a grim economic future. Under the impact of the energy crisis, the auto industry has begun a massive turn toward the production of small cars, despite the evidence that the rate of profit on such cars is much lower than the profit on the larger ones that have been produced up to now. (As Henry Ford has put it: "Minicars make miniprofits.")

The airline industry is in constant trouble. In the last five years, several major airlines have posted significant losses, and the major overseas line (Pan Am) has come close to collapse, hoping—thus far in vain—for financial help from the Iranian government. Mass-transit efforts have turned out to be far more costly and less effective than expected. At the same time, massive highway systems have been built at huge public expense, becoming the major carrier of commuter traffic. Yet, in almost every city, rush-hour traffic has become a nearly unbearable frustration.

Finally, the vehicles that power the U.S. transportation system themselves represent a huge, inefficient drain on the fuel supply. The worst offender is the standard U.S. passenger car (which accounts for 29 percent of national petroleum consumption). Between 1945 and 1972 its average gasoline mileage fell by 10 percent as, year by year, its engine increased in power and compression ratio. These same changes converted the automobile from a relatively benign environmental intruder into, literally, a smog generator. (Pre-war engines, operating at low compression ratios, and therefore at relatively low temperatures, did not produce enough nitrogen oxide in their exhaust to trigger the

photochemical process that is responsible for the smog
that now envelops nearly every city.)

How can we account for the sharp disparity between
the dominant position that the transportation industry
has won in what is presumably the world's most powerful production system and the extraordinary faults
that it now exhibits? Why is the U.S. economy unable to
sustain a rational development of transportation facilities? How did the present situation develop and what
is its portent for the future?

Like every sector of the production system, transportation is a means of using resources, available from
the ecosystem, to produce goods and services that
society values. The resultant wealth enters the economic
system, which in turn re-invests part of it, as capital,
in further production which, it is hoped, will maximize
the return of the investment. Clearly, in the case of
transportation these relationships are not working very
well: There are faulty interconnections among the
ecosystem, the production system, and the economic
system. If we wish to understand these faults—and learn
how to correct them—we need to analyze the performance of the various parts of the interlocking set of
systems.

How can we measure performance? Both physics and
economics are concerned with such measures. We have
already seen how thermodynamics is used to measure
the performance of a process such as heating a house:
First the task is defined, then the minimum amount of
work required to achieve that result is determined, and
is finally compared with the actual amount of work that
is used, as represented by the amount of fuel consumed. This is the Second Law efficiency of the process;
it describes the efficiency of the link between the energy resource (more generally, the ecosystem) and the
physical output of the heating system (more generally, the production system).

By quite similar means, economics can be used to
measure the performance of processes that link the
production system to the economic system. In this
same example, the economist might wish to measure a
heat pump's economic performance by determining

how much capital has to be invested in it, relative to a furnace, in order to obtain the same physical result. This would measure the productivity of the capital invested in the task of home heating.

Both thermodynamic efficiency and economic productivity measure the relationship between what is used to operate a process (technically, *input*) and what is gotten out of it (technically, *output*). Efficiency is the ratio: output divided by input, usually expressed as percent. Productivity is the same ratio: output divided by input, but usually expressed as a unit of output per unit of input because the two types of unit are not the same. For any given production process, such as transportation, one can compute the efficiencies with which physical resources, such as energy, are used and the productivities that characterize the use of economic inputs such as capital and labor.

Fortunately, such a productivity analysis is relatively easy to carry out in transportation, as compared with other sectors of the production system, largely because the output of transportation is so simple. The task, or use value, of transportation is to carry people and goods over distance. The output is, then, readily measured by the amount of material (or people) carried, the distance moved, the speed of transport, and some lesser factors such as the ease of access to the vehicle. (This is in sharp contrast to other sectors of production, in which the outputs are so varied as to forestall comparisons of their relative productivities except in monetary terms. Information about the input and output of different sectors of production is generally available from the astonishing mass of statistics about production activities that is published regularly by several departments of the U.S. government. The data are based on detailed, ongoing surveys of the thousands of corporations that do the actual business of production. One difficulty with such data for the computation of productivities is that the standard groupings combine information that usually needs to be looked at separately. A standard statistical category, such as "electrical equipment," reports collectively on the production of thousands of items, many of them with very different use values. For that reason, their separate productivities cannot be computed without going back to reports of individual companies—a laborious and often impossible procedure. Because the output of the transportation industry is so simple, it is a good place to begin the otherwise intimidating, but urgent, task of developing a productivity analysis of the production system as a whole.)

The basic production inputs are labor, capital, energy, and other resources. Given these data, and measures of output, one can compute, for various modes of transportation, the amount of a given output obtained from an amount of a *specified* input. The outputs for freight are ton-miles, and for passenger traffic, passenger-miles. (Ton-miles is the number of tons carried times the distance in miles carried. Passenger-miles is the number of passengers carried times the number of miles traveled.) The performance of the different modes of transportation can be judged by comparing the various productivities: labor productivity (ton-miles, or passenger-miles, carried per man-hour of labor used); capital productivity (ton-miles, or passenger-miles, per dollar of invested capital); energy productivity (ton-miles, or passenger-miles, per BTU of fuel).

From such a set of numbers one can determine what it will cost, in fuel, labor, and invested capital, to achieve a particular output from a given mode of transportation. At the same time, the economic performance can be described in terms of the cost of transportation to the users of transportation, the amount of capital required, and the profit to the investors. (This information can then be compared with relevant social goals. Depending on what social decisions are made, such goals might be that reliable and inexpensive home-to-work-place transportation should be available; that fuel should be conserved; that employment opportunities should be maximized; that acceptable profits should be made on invested capital; that entrepreneurs should be free to invest the profits from a transportation enterprise wherever they see fit; that, on the contrary, such profits should be re-invested only in transportation.) With this kind of information in hand, it may be possible to discover where, in the relationship of transportation to the ecosystem on the one hand and to the economic system on the other, the faults which are now so evident arise.

In the last few years, energy productivities have been computed for all the major modes of inter-city transportation. Railroads and buses have the highest energy productivities for passenger traffic: 630 and 340 passenger-miles per million BTU of fuel, respectively, as compared with 110 for auto travel and 120 for airlines. Railroads also have the highest energy productivity for general freight: 1300 ton-miles per million BTU as compared with 360 for inter-city trucks and 20 for airlines. Waterways and pipelines have higher energy productivities (1470 and 5260 ton-miles per million BTU, respectively), but they are quite restricted in the type of freight they carry and in their geographic distribution.

Computations of the productivities of capital invested in various modes of transportation are rather more complex. Since the highways are used in common by autos, buses, and trucks, the capital cost of construction and maintenance must be suitably apportioned among these users. About 80 percent of highway usage (measured in vehicle-miles) is due to autos and about 19 percent to trucks, with buses accounting for less than one percent. However, because of their size and weight, trucks do a disproportionate amount of highway damage. When all this is taken into account and the capital costs of the vehicles themselves and of terminal facilities are added, a total capital requirement for each mode of transportation can be computed.

In 1970, total capital invested in inter-city auto travel amounted to about $236 billion; in commercial inter-city trucks, $30 billion; in inter-city buses, $825 million. In comparison, the total amount of capital invested in *non*-highway modes of transportation in 1970 was only about $70 billion (railroads, $41 billion; airlines, $18 billion; pipelines and waterways, $11 billion). Even taking into account that some capital invested in autos relates to urban rather than inter-city travel, the capital invested in inter-city highway transportation is considerably greater than the capital invested in all the other modes combined.

The comparison between trucks and railroads is particularly striking. It is often assumed that a chief drawback of railroad transportation is its heavy demand for capital. Yet, the existing capital stock invested in railroads in 1970 was less than half the total capital stock invested in truck freight. Moreover, capital stock in railroads is essentially at a standstill, while capital invested in truck freight more than doubled between 1960 and 1970.

From this information and the available data regarding the two relevant outputs (passenger-miles of passenger travel and ton-miles of freight) we can compute the several capital productivities. The productivities of capital invested in auto, railroad, and air passenger travel are approximately the same—6.43 to 8.10 passenger-miles per year per dollar. Bus passenger traffic stands out as yielding the largest output per dollar of invested capital—23.31 passenger-miles per year per dollar. (However, the value for railroad passenger traffic is very inaccurate; only 3.0 percent of U.S. railroad revenue is derived from passenger traffic, and it is difficult to apportion the railroads' capital accurately to such a minor activity.) With respect to freight traffic, railroads clearly yield the highest capital productivity: about 20 ton-miles per year per dollar invested, compared with about 7 ton-miles per year per dollar for trucks. Again, the two limited modes of transportation—water transport and pipelines—yield higher returns, 41 and 99 ton-miles per year per dollar, respectively.

With respect to labor productivity, in passenger traffic, buses produce 294 passenger-miles per man-hour, railroads about 230, and airlines about 188. In freight traffic, pipelines, which use relatively little labor, have the highest labor productivity (12,000 ton-miles per man-hour), followed by water transportation (1200 ton-miles per man-hour); railroads (about 700 ton-miles per man-hour); trucks (94 ton-miles per man-hour); and airlines (19 ton-miles per man-hour).

The labor productivity of railroad freight appears to be about seven times higher than that of truck freight.

Analysis of the productivity of the land used by different modes of transportation shows one surprising result: The land productivity of airlines for passenger traffic is not very different from that of autos and railroads: 69,000, 85,000, and 93,000 passenger-miles per year per acre of land used, respectively. For freight traffic, land productivity of railroads is four times higher than the comparable value for trucks.

One of the social costs of transportation is accidents. The high risk involved in auto traffic is well known (33 million passenger-miles per fatality) along with the surprisingly high figure for railroads (25–100 million passenger-miles per fatality), which is probably the result of the recent deterioration in the upkeep of these operations. The comparable figures for air and bus travel are 100 million and 3125 million passenger-miles per fatality, respectively.

Other factors that influence the performance of different modes of transportation do not readily yield such quantitative data, but some general statements can be made. As far as environmental impact is concerned (noise and air pollution), railroads are definitely superior to both the private auto and to airlines. Air pollution from transportation can be judged by the amount of fuel burned; because of its superior energy productivity, the effect of railroads on air pollution is least, relative to productive output, among the three modes of transportation. Noise effects are more difficult to compare, but common experience would indicate that railroads are the least noisy mode of transportation.

Now consider speed and convenience. While airplanes travel through the air quite rapidly (averaging about 400 mph), there is generally at least a one-hour delay at each end of the journey, due in part to the distance between airports and areas of dense population. Traffic and weather delays in landing may add considerably to this figure. Ordinary railroads travel at an average speed of 41 mph, but delays at the terminals are relatively brief, because the stations can be centrally located within urban areas. High-speed trains such as those now common in Europe and Japan, that can travel at over 100 mph, can readily compete with air travel's speed and convenience for distances up to about 500 miles. Such trains could be equally competitive with auto travel (average inter-city speed, 50 mph) in respect to these same criteria.

In this information we have at least the rudiments of the catalogue of data that we need in order to understand what value can be gotten out of different modes of transportation relative to the resources that are put into them. A few generalizations stand out. One is that with respect to the investment of capital, labor, land, and energy, railroads yield by far the highest overall returns in both passenger and freight traffic. However, it is worth remembering that their relatively high labor productivity means that much less opportunity for employment.

The inter-city bus performs well with respect to energy and labor; its capital productivity is higher than that of the railroad (for passenger traffic), but here it must be kept in mind that more than half the capital is represented by the publicly supported highways.

Private automobiles, in their aggregate, represent the largest investment of capital in transportation—$236 billion, of which $73 billion represents their share of the investment in highways. In return for this huge investment, the owner has the free use (traffic permitting) of a vehicle which is the least efficient means of converting fuel energy into the movement of passengers (even less so than the much faster airlines).

To what extent can the present features of the various modes of transportation be improved? Since all of the thermodynamic efficiencies are low—10 percent or less—there is obviously a good deal of room for improvement in energetic efficiency. The APS study referred to earlier considered various ways of improving the thermodynamic efficiency of the passenger car: reduced weight; the use of more efficient engines (such as the diesel); improved transmission designs (automatic transmissions may be quite wasteful); improving the efficiency of tires (which, in flexing continuously, waste part of the car's kinetic energy as heat).

The study offered two proposals that make use of these potential improvements. Their "modest proposal" achieves a 33-percent reduction of present gasoline consumption, or a saving of about 4 percent of the total U.S. energy budget. A "less modest proposal" achieves up to 60-percent gasoline savings, or 8 percent of the national energy budget. Similar improvements could probably be applied to buses and trucks, but reduced somewhat because their present engines, most of them diesels, are already closer to maximum efficiency than are present auto engines.

The railroad, already the most thermodynamically efficient vehicle, can be further improved. Nearly all U.S. locomotives have diesel engines which operate fairly close to the Carnot limit of efficiency; that is, not much improvement can be expected in the fraction of the fuel's available work which is transformed into the train's motion. Thus, the main way to improve the thermodynamic efficiency of the locomotive is to make use of its waste low-temperature heat—an expedient which would be extraordinarily difficult in a device that moves about. However, as pointed out in Chapter 4, if the railroad is electrified, then the mechanical power of the generator can be converted to electricity, and the latter to the train's motion, with nearly 100-percent efficiency. In this case, the waste low-temperature heat is produced at the power plant, where—if the plant is suitably located—it can be used for space heating and other low-temperature tasks. Based on APS computations on total electric systems, this approach could considerably improve the efficiency with which a fuel is used—probably doubling it. Accordingly, if the railroads were electrified, they too could save about as much fuel as the APS-modified cars, buses, and trucks, and the present thermodynamic advantage of railroads over these vehicles would be maintained. In fact, it could even be increased by using the train's electric motors, reversed to serve as generators, to slow down the train.

We can now make a kind of inventory of the available and possible vehicles, in decreasing order of energy productivity, or thermodynamic efficiency. (Pipelines and waterways have been omitted because of their specialized uses.)

1. The electrified inter-city railroad: This is clearly the most thermodynamically efficient means of moving people and freight at average speeds, on ordinary track up to about 50 mph, and on improved track (based on Japanese experience) up to about 120 mph. Capital productivity would be equal to any other mode of transportation, even taking into account that present railroad capital would need to be doubled to make the necessary improvements in trackage and for new equipment. Labor productivity is high only if passenger traffic is minimal. With suitable passenger traffic (e.g., representing, as in European railroads, 25–50 percent of revenues), labor productivity would be reduced considerably—that is, more jobs would be available. Air pollution would occur only at the power plant and could be controlled with suitable stack devices.

2. The electrified urban railroad: Recognizing the considerable advantages of the electrified railroad, it has recently been proposed that a "light electrified railroad" could be very useful for urban passenger transport, as a replacement for diesel buses. The vehicle would have approximately the size and passenger capacity of the present bus and, like many present bus systems, operate in designated lanes in city streets, on tracks (but not necessarily), drawing electric power from overhead wires. This is, of course, the new name for an old vehicle—the trolley.

3. The (present) diesel-operated railroad: This is less thermodynamically efficient than the electrified railroad; its diesel engines produce considerable air pollution for which there are, thus far, no adequate controls; capital and labor productivity are about the same as electrified railroads.

4. The (present) diesel-operated bus: This is an energy-efficient passenger vehicle, but less so than a railroad operating at good capacity. Access on less-used routes would be better than railroads, in that a smaller

investment would be involved in establishing such new routes.

5. The (present) diesel-operated truck: This is, energetically, the least efficient way to move freight (except for air, which of course has a considerable advantage in speed). Capital productivity, relative to railroads, is inferior. Labor productivity is low (employment opportunities are good). Relative to railroads, it has the advantage of smaller, more frequent shipments; it is a considerable source of air pollution.

6. The private car: Inherently very inefficient, thermodynamically, for inter-city travel, but more efficient for urban travel if properly designed and used to capacity. Its main advantages are enormous flexibility and freedom of access. It is the major source of urban air pollution.

7. Airlines: For passenger traffic their energy productivity is very low, approximately equal to the autos'. For freight, energy productivity is less than a tenth of that of trucks. Their main advantage is speed, but that holds good—relative to efficient high-speed trains—only for distances greater than about 500 miles.

How does this catalogue compare with the use that we are now making of the alternative modes of transportation? Less than one percent of U.S. railroad locomotives are electrified; a few lines were electrified about twenty-five years ago, but many have now been replaced by diesel locomotives; the railroads are overwhelmingly diesel-driven. Railroad usage as a whole is declining; passenger services are minimal, having declined to about 15 percent of their former (1951) size; the fraction of freight traffic carried on railroads has fallen from 69 percent of all ton-miles (1945) to 40 percent (1970), being displaced by truck freight. The "light electrified railroad" (trolley), once a dominant form of transportation in the United States, has all but disappeared; it has been displaced by diesel buses. Passenger cars have grown in use at about 5 percent annually; together with airlines and buses, they have almost entirely displaced railroad passenger traffic.

Thus, with remarkable precision the U.S. transportation system has favored those modes of transportation that are thermodynamically inefficient and low in capital productivity. As a result, the U.S. transportation system now consumes much more fuel and capital than it needs to, relative to the use value that it yields.

How can we explain this seemingly inverted state of affairs? In the U.S. economic system, most productive enterprises are privately owned and attract investment generally in accordance with the expected rate of return—the profit. In transportation, the situation is complicated by the participation of public funds, which supply all of the capital needed to build and maintain highways and airports and which—many years ago—contributed land to the railways. Nevertheless, the expected rate of profit is likely to govern the flow of investment funds into different modes of transportation, and therefore their relative rates of development.

In the three years preceding the impact of the energy crisis (i.e, 1971, 1972, and 1973) the industries associated with the various modes of transportation showed characteristic, and strikingly different, rates of profit. Trucking firms reported average profits (returns, after taxes, on stockholders' equity) of 21 percent; automotive manufacturing, 14–16 percent; in airplane manufacturing (largely military), profits increased from 5.4 percent to 11.4 percent; airline profits fluctuated, reporting 2.1 percent, 6.7 percent, and 5.2 percent in the three successive years; railroad profits were 6.3 percent to 6.2 percent. The profits for 1974 were similar except that the automotive industry's profits fell from 16 percent in 1973 to 7 percent in 1974, as a direct result of the 1973 oil embargo.

It seems clear, then, that the profitability of the different modes of transportation—which governs the extent to which they are developed—tends to be associated with a low productivity of energy and capital.

This analysis suggests, at least as a hypothesis, that the reason for the failure of the present U.S. transportation system to perform effectively—that is, to move people and freight at the least cost in physical and economic resources—is that its operational design has been governed by profitability rather than performance, as measured by the relevant productivities.

Obviously, to test this hypothesis we would need the information that specifically describes how and why decisions to establish the present faulty designs were made, or evidence that, given the choice between maximizing performance and maximizing profitability, the latter option is taken. As it happens, there are such records available relative to the transportation system's failure to develop the two modes of highest performance: trolleys and railroads (especially electrified ones).

The electrified trolley was not only the main form of urban transportation; it also covered the areas surrounding the cities so well that it was possible, by making sufficient transfers, to travel by trolley over long distances. In E. L. Doctorow's *Ragtime,* Tateh and his daughter, fleeing New York, board the No. 12 Streetcar on the East Side, ride up Broadway to the Bronx, through a series of Connecticut towns, and three days later are in Springfield, Massachusetts, on their way to Boston. The fare for each ride is 5 cents for Tateh and 2 cents for his daughter—a total of $3.40 for both from New York to Boston. Both enjoy the trip, as the electrified cars rocket through the countryside, the sights and smells unobscured by pollution. In the period of *Ragtime*—the turn of the century—every U.S. city had an effective trolley system. For example, Los Angeles was served by 3000 vehicles, on lines that radiated seventy-five miles from the city's center, the routes winding their way through the valleys between the numerous hills that divide that urban area. As late as 1936, 40,000 streetcars operated in the United States. By 1955 only 5000 remained.

The process that dismembered this extensive, high-performance transportation system has now been documented in a remarkable report prepared by Bradford C. Snell for the Subcommittee on Antitrust and Monopoly of the Senate Committee on the Judiciary. In great detail, Snell describes how urban trolley lines were dismantled by corporations established by the General Motors Corporation as it set out to create a market for its new line of buses. According to General Motors' general counsel (as quoted by Snell), the corporation "decided that the only way this new market for [city]

buses could be created was for it to finance the conversion from streetcars to buses in some small cities."
General Motors organized a company that bought up trolley lines, to begin with, in Kalamazoo and Saginaw, Michigan, and Springfield, Ohio. Once in control of the company, General Motors dismantled the trolley line and replaced it with GM buses. According to the general counsel, in each case the company "successfully motorized the city, turned the management over to other interests and liquidated its investment." Thus, General Motors' interest was not to provide the cities with transportation but to sell buses. Censured by the American Transit Association for these actions, General Motors dissolved its transit corporation, only to form a new one a few years later in collaboration with Standard Oil of California and the Firestone Tire Company, which went about the same business of buying up and then destroying trolley lines. According to Snell, "By 1949, General Motors had been involved in the replacement of more than 100 electric transit systems with GM buses in 45 cities including New York, Philadelphia, Baltimore, St. Louis, Oakland, Salt Lake City, and Los Angeles."

In Los Angeles the buses replaced a trolley system which, according to one transportation specialist, "could have comprised the nucleus of a highly efficient rapid transit system, which would have contributed greatly to lessening the tremendous traffic and smog problems that developed from population growth."

In March 1949, General Motors, Standard Oil of California, and Firestone Tire Company, among others, were convicted in Chicago Federal Court of having criminally conspired to replace electric trolleys with gasoline- or diesel-powered buses. General Motors was fined $5000, and its treasurer, who had participated in the dismantling of the $100-million Los Angeles trolley system, was fined $1.

Los Angeles is perhaps the best-known victim of the bus and the automobile; photochemical smog, the distinctive pollutant of these vehicles, made its first recorded appearance in Los Angeles in 1943 and has since then enveloped most major cities in its noxious fumes. In Snell's work we have evidence of how this came about: by the deliberate decision on the part of major transportation companies to replace the high-performance electric trolley with the much inferior petroleum-driven bus and automobile. This case history does appear to confirm the hypothesis that the tendency of the U.S. transportation system to favor inefficient modes of transportation derives from the effort of transportation companies to maximize their profits in preference to improving the performance of the transportation system.

An equally informative case history explains the reduced use of the railroads, first for passenger traffic and later for freight. Railroads once carried essentially all of the inter-city passenger traffic, but now carry almost none. It is widely believed that the disappearance of nearly all passenger traffic from the railroads is the result of a natural preference for private autos and airlines. However, if this explanation is correct, it is a phenomenon that is somehow peculiar to the United States. In every European country, railroad passenger traffic remains at a very high level, despite competition from airlines and private cars. It would appear that there must be some other, specifically American explanation for this effect.

There is. It has been clearly described in the discussions, during the last few years, of what to do about the bankruptcy of the Northeast railroads. When the Penn Central railroad went bankrupt, the Department of Transportation prepared a bill designed to reorganize the Northeast railroads in a viable form. In the last few years the proposal has gone through a series of legislative transformations, but the fundamental plan remains the same. By then the railroads were already largely out of the passenger business, so that the plan related only to freight traffic. However, as we shall see, in the course of the argument for the reorganization plan it became clear why, in the previous twenty-five years, the U.S. railroads had abandoned most of their passenger traffic.

The reorganization plan is based on a rather simple, straightforward approach: the Northeast railroads went

bankrupt because their operational costs exceeded their
profits. The profitability of different parts of the railroads varied, in general being poorest on branch lines
that carried relatively little freight. The proposed solution was to abandon the unprofitable trackage so that
the reduced rail system could carry freight at a profit.
It would then be a suitable investment for private capital and would be taken over by some new owners who
found the investment attractive.

The plan faces some huge economic obstacles. Since
the railroads are heavily in debt, are operating with
frequent periods of loss, and are desperately in need
of new capital to restore crumbling roadbeds and to
replace obsolete equipment, no private investor is
now willing to take over the railroads from the re-
ceivers. Since the Penn Central bankruptcy, several
hundred million dollars have been granted by the U.S.
government to the railroads merely to keep them going.
What is now proposed is that after being stripped of
their unprofitable trackage, the railroads would be operated by a supposedly "private" company founded on
the basis of at least $3 billion in government funds.
After a period of at least twenty years the corporation
would presumably begin to pay off its debt to the
government and revert to fully private ownership. In
other words, what is proposed is to re-establish the
viability of the railroads—as a profitable private enterprise—by investing a very large amount of public funds,
and by actively reducing their scale of operations.

In times past, such a proposal would have been described in purely financial terms and argued in Congress largely on the basis of the merit or hazard (depending on one's point of view) of spending public
funds on such a venture. But since 1970, with the passage of the National Environmental Policy Act, a new
element must be at least considered before the government undertakes any major action. NEPA requires the
preparation and public dissemination of an "environmental impact statement" which is supposed to describe the impact of the proposed action on environmental quality, project its long-term effects on natural
resources, and consider "alternatives to the proposed

action." In effect, the statement must consider how well the proposed action makes use of natural resources (such as fuel) in comparison with alternative actions.

A Department of Transportation (DOT) environmental impact statement that accompanied the original bill to reorganize the Northeast railroads gives a rather good insight into the motivation not only for the new plan to handle freight traffic, but also into the earlier, successful moves to abandon passenger traffic. To begin with, we should note that the reorganization plan would shift about 20 percent of the freight presently carried by the Northeast railroads to inter-city trucks. This would increase total national fuel consumption for freight transportation by about 2 percent and, of course, worsen air pollution in the area. In other words, a reorganization plan designed to restore profitability would inevitably worsen environmental impact and the drain on fuel resources—contradicting the stated purposes of NEPA.

This difficulty was recognized in the DOT impact statement. However, the statement concluded that the only alternative to its plan, nationalization, would be unsound under the NEPA criteria (to "encourage productive and enjoyable harmony between man and his environment") because "experiences elsewhere have made it abundantly clear that nationalization only means increasing subsidies and declining resource efficiency." The evidence offered to support this claim is that the railroads of European countries and Japan, all of which are nationalized, lose money, while the U.S. railroads and the privately owned Canadian one are run at a profit—not including, of course, the bankrupt railroads that are the subject of the plan. To prove its point, the impact statement reproduced a table taken from an earlier analysis by the Union Pacific Railroad.

The Union Pacific study is worth reading, for here at last is an explanation of why the U.S. railroads have been decaying. What the study's statistics show is that the nationalized railroads do indeed run at a loss, and that, in particular, they gain much less revenue per worker than U.S. railroads—between $4000 and $9500 of revenue per worker as compared with the U.S. average of $23,200 per worker. But the report also shows that the workers on U.S. and European (and Japanese) railroads do very different things to bring in the railroad's revenue. Whereas the privately owned U.S. railroads gain almost none (about 3.0 percent) of their revenue from passenger traffic, the nationalized railroads gain between 25 percent and 75 percent of their revenue from passenger traffic. In other words, the main reason why the nationalized railroads are not profitable is that they are heavily—*and by policy*—engaged in a service which, as we have been frequently told by the managers of U.S. railroads, is unprofitable: carrying passengers. (One reason for this is that passenger service requires much more labor than freight: A passenger train has a much larger crew than a freight train, relative to the income it generates; more personnel are required at passenger terminals than at freight terminals, relative to the value of their respective services.)

The evidence seems, then, to be quite clear. Railroads are an eminently efficient means of moving people and freight, but relative to the required physical and economic resources, they yield less profit—compared with alternative investments—especially if they carry passengers and provide freight services to relatively small branch lines. There does appear to be a conflict between using the railroads as a means of providing maximum social benefits or as a means of maximizing private profit. In Europe and Japan the choice has been made in favor of the railroads' use value, and their revenues have been employed, together with some subsidies, to further improve their high level of performance (among the nationalized railroads of Europe and Japan, 36 percent of the locomotives are electrified, while in the United States the figure is less than one percent). The nationalized railroads of France and Japan have pioneered in developing high-speed operations which, as we have seen, can successfully compete with airlines for speed for distances up to 500 miles.

The U.S. government's position on the railroads exemplifies the grim travesty that has been made of transportation policy. The railroads are the form of land transport that is best suited to an age in which liquid fossil fuels will be increasingly expensive and progressively more scarce. Their value to society is now being judged on a kind of free-enterprise Procrustean bed: What will not fit the frame of private profitability is to be lopped off. This may serve the ideology of private enterprise, but it will help destroy the production system that yields its wealth.

THE ENERGY CRISIS is a relatively recent affliction, due chiefly to sweeping changes in the production system that began about twenty-five or thirty years ago. Many of these changes have occurred within a given sector of production, such as agriculture or transportation. But in one case the process has created a wholly new industry—petrochemicals.

Petrochemistry has a cunning talent for producing an enormous variety of substances from very few starting materials, chiefly petroleum and natural gas. Thus, unlike other industries, the petrochemical industry not only burns fuel, it also converts it into finished products. In 1971 the energy used by the chemical industry (most of it now producing petrochemicals) corresponded to about 605 million barrels of crude oil used as fuel and an additional 480 million barrels used as raw materials. Taking both types of uses into account, the chemical industry is the largest industrial consumer of fuels; it uses 28 percent of the energy used by industry, or about 9 percent of the total national energy budget.

Petroleum and natural gas are a mixture of hydrocarbons. These are organic chemicals, and the petrochemical industry is the practical application of the science of organic chemistry. In its first stages the science was largely concerned with identifying and characterizing the numerous carbon-bearing compounds that are found in living things—hence the term *organic* chemistry. Later on, organic chemists learned how to synthesize such compounds in the laboratory, starting from simpler, inorganic raw materials. Increasingly elaborate molecules were made. The record is probably the synthesis of insulin, a molecule containing 867 atoms of carbon, hydrogen, oxygen, nitrogen, and sulfur. Now organic chemists can almost at will put together organic molecules according to specifications; this is the scientific base of the petrochemical industry.

If progress consists of producing something new, then the petrochemical industry is certainly the cutting edge of progress in production technology. Almost everything it makes is new—materials that did not exist until they were invented by chemists. Synthetic fibers, plastics, detergents, pesticides are the most evident petrochemical products. Their novelty is a natural outcome of the special properties of organic compounds. These can be produced in an enormous variety because their carbon skeletons form chains and rings that combine with other atoms in an almost infinitely interchangeable way. As a result, only a few different types of atoms can form a large number of different molecular arrangements. For example, compounds made of 6 carbon atoms, 6 oxygen atoms, and 12 hydrogen atoms can be put together in over 70 different molecular forms. The known organic compounds now number over 125,000, but in fact chemists have stopped counting.

The inherent variety of petrochemical products is at once the source of their social value and their social cost. Because they are almost infinitely variable in their design, the molecules of petrochemical products can be tailor-made. For example, if a drug has certain valuable properties but also produces undesirable side effects, then by determining which parts of the molecule's structure are responsible for each effect, a new molecule can be synthesized that retains the pharmaceutical value with reduced side effects. In the same way, chemists can make plastics that vary in their flexibility, transparency, and resistance to heat, yielding a product that is well suited to a particular task.

But this same variability means that petrochemicals can go beyond the range of molecular designs that occur in living things. Life depends on the elaborate interactions of thousands of different natural organic compounds. This network of reactions has evolved over a three-billion-year period of trial and error and often does not tolerate the intrusion of new man-made substances that have not participated in the harmonizing process of evolution. This may explain why synthetic organic compounds are so often harmful to living things. For example, in a survey of 835 organic chemicals that represent about two-thirds of the major products of the petrochemical industry, nearly half of the ones that have thus far been tested for toxicity toward people were listed as having a "high" level of toxicity (the highest of a three-point score). In fact, only a small percentage of the petrochemical products that have already been thrust into the environment (and to which the workers who produce them may be heavily exposed) have been adequately tested for their toxic effects, especially for delayed harm such as cancer. The hazards of many long-used substances are just now coming to light. The latest example is vinyl chloride, a substance used to produce massive amounts of "vinyl" plastics—and now revealed as a cancer-producing agent.

Since the ecosphere operates in closed cycles, every natural substance produced by living things can also be broken down by them; every natural substance is biodegradable. (If living things produced a substance that they could not degrade, the ecological cycle would be converted into a one-way route ending in the accumulation of that substance.) However, many synthetic petrochemical products are so different from natural materials that the enzymes which in living things break down organic substances are unable to attack them. They are therefore non-degradable and accumulate as trash. Every pound of synthetic fiber, for example, that has ever been produced, if it has not been burned, is still with us.

The petrochemical industry is aptly named, for it was created by joining two pre-existing industries: petroleum refining and the chemical industry. In a refinery, crude petroleum, delivered by pipeline or ship from a well, is passed through a heated column of metal plates enclosed in a tall cylindrical tank and distilled, so that the different volatile constituents are separated according to their boiling temperatures. The most readily vaporized constituents are drawn off the top of the still—chiefly gases such as ethane, propane, and butane. A little lower down, gasoline is drawn off, and then, in descending order, jet fuel (kerosene), diesel and fuel oils, and heavier oils. The residue yields asphalt and wax. Originally these were the final products of refining, most of them used as fuels.

Then organic chemistry took a hand. Its main practical lesson was that organic chemicals can be made to combine in particular ways if they are brought in contact, under specified conditions of temperature, pressure, acidity, and so forth, with various kinds of catalysts. (These are often fine screens made of various metals, on which the reacting molecules can come in contact in a way that enhances their likelihood of forming joint chemical bonds.) By choosing the right sorts of catalysts a chemical engineer can set up a network of pipes that carries the starting chemicals through a sequence of reactions, emitting at the other end a steady output of some final product. A relatively simple example is the separation of the gas ethane from the refining operation, then "cracking" it in a high-temperature reactor to produce ethylene, which is reacted with chlorine to form ethylene dichloride; this is in turn converted to vinyl chloride, which, piped or trucked to a new plant, is made into the plastic polyvinyl chloride, which is, finally, turned into upholstery, floor tiles, "vinyl" garments and shoes, and other plastic objects. The production of these objects is also a flow process: The plastic is formed by being extruded from a die, or automatically molded, in a continuous process. In effect, petrochemical production is an unending flow of materials, stretching from the oil well to the final fabrication. Most petrochemical sequences are even longer and more complex than the production of polyvinyl chloride. In the largest petrochemical complex in the United States, around the Houston Ship Channel, dozens of different plants are linked together by thousands of pipes into a kind of gargantuan, odoriferous spaghetti bowl.

Since World War II the petrochemical industry's

pipes have disgorged a truly astonishing mass of materials: in one year, 1972, 7 billion pounds of synthetic fibers; 8.5 billion pounds of synthetic detergents; 22.4 billion pounds of plastics; and 1.2 billion pounds of synthetic pesticides. Total production of synthetic organic chemicals rose from about 300 million pounds in 1946 to 39 billion pounds in 1974. These statistics only confirm the common experience that the visible products of petrochemistry—plastics, synthetic fibers, detergents, and pesticides—have rapidly penetrated everyday life, flooding upon us in wave after wave of new materials and objects.

Civilizations are often identified—as the Stone Age, or the Iron Age—by the material that dominates their production technology. The petrochemical industry has already made a semi-official bid to designate our own as the Synthetics Age. In an article appearing in the trade journal *Modern Plastics* it was argued recently that the use of synthetic petrochemicals is growing so fast that they will soon overtake iron as the most common material, at least when computed by volume rather than weight. On these grounds, the article proposes: "Considering that . . . sometime between 1980 and 1990 the volume consumption of iron, which still marks our age, will have been surpassed by that of synthetics, it seems justified to mark that time [1984?] as the beginning of the synthetics age."

This trend, if not the plastic industry's cultural interpretation of it, is confirmed by the relevant statistics regarding the annual rates of increase in the production of various materials (over the period 1948–70) in the United States: lumber 0.4 percent; leather 1.2 percent; petroleum 3.5 percent; steel 4.3 percent; paper 4.8 percent; plastics 15.9 percent. (The compound-interest law is at work here: After twenty-three years a 15.9-percent annual increase in rate represents an overall rise of more than 2800 percent.)

To make all this clear, the *Modern Plastics* article translates such statistics into robot-like figures representing the amounts of various material consumed. In 1966 the robot's torso and one arm are made of iron, and only one leg is plastic: an Iron Age person. By the year 2000 the torso, one arm, and one leg have been engulfed by plastics. The other leg is iron and the second arm is aluminum; about half the head is composed of synthetic rubber. This is the Plastics Person.

By any ordinary measure, the petrochemical industry would appear to be a huge success; its products have taken over major markets such as textiles, furniture, home furnishings, paints, and building materials. The chemical industries' total assets are now second only to those of the primary-metals industry. But, as we have already seen from the post-war changes within agriculture and transportation, the productive activities that grow most rapidly are not necessarily the best performers in respect to the efficiency with which energy and capital are used or employment is generated.

In this case, we need to compare the performance of the petrochemical industry with that of other industries, particularly those which produce alternative goods (such as leather, which in many of its uses competes with plastics). Here we face the problem of comparing outputs which are physically different. The only available measure that is common to different goods is their value or sale price. However, such a measure is not an accurate picture of the actual value resulting from the production operation itself. For example, the production effort involved in manufacturing a steel watch and a gold, diamond-encrusted one may be approximately the same, but their sale prices will differ enormously. To avoid this kind of bias, economists have introduced the concept of *value added:* the value of the product less the cost of materials and energy used in making the product. This is the customary output that is used to compare the productivities of different manufacturing processes.

In 1971 (the date of the latest available statistics) the average *energy* productivity for all manufacturing was $14.42 of value added per million BTU of fuel. Among the twenty-one major sectors of manufacturing, five (paper; chemical; petroleum; primary metals; and stone, clay, and glass products) had the lowest energy productivities, ranging from $1.90 per million BTU (petroleum refining) to $7.64 per million BTU (paper products). The value for the chemical industry was $8.69 per million BTU, counting only fuel, and $4.85 when fuels used as raw materials were included. Near the other end of the scale of energy productivities were leather and leather products—$62.04 of value added per million BTU of fuel.

The average productivity of *capital* for all manufacturing industries was $1.13 of value added per dollar of fixed assets (buildings and production equipment). Among all manufacturing sectors, petroleum refining had the lowest capital productivity ($0.34 of value added per dollar of assets), followed by primary metals ($0.49), paper ($0.58), and chemicals ($0.80). The comparable figure for leather and leather products was $3.64.

The average productivity of *labor* for all manufacturing was $12.43 of value added per man-hour of production workers. In this measure of performance, the positions of the industries were reversed: Industries with high energy and capital productivities generally tend to have a low labor productivity. Petroleum refining had the highest labor productivity of all sectors of manufacturing ($28.43), followed closely by the chemical industry at $27.75. Leather and leather goods were near the other end of the scale: $6.25 of value added per man-hour.

Thus, compared with other sectors of manufacturing, petroleum refining and the chemical industry, which together approximate the petrochemical industry, yield remarkably little economic value (measured by value added) relative to the amounts of fuel and capital that they use and the employment opportunities that they generate. If it is important to society to maximize the productive output that is gained from the investment of energy and capital, and to enhance employment opportunities, then in comparison with all other major industrial sectors the social value of the petrochemical industry is very low.

Nevertheless, it could be argued that petrochemical products are worth manufacturing because they provide for needs that cannot be met in any other way. One could hardly complain, for example, that a unique life-saving drug ought not be produced because it yields relatively little economic return or jobs relative to the consumption of energy and capital.

Are petrochemical products unique in their uses, so as to justify their rather low social value as compared with other manufactured goods? A standard work on the chemical industry lists all the end-uses of products that are made from ethylene, the major secondary starting material for petrochemical products. Here, for example, are the end-uses of plastic products, made from ethylene, that are classified as household goods: furniture, upholstery, flooring, wall coverings, curtains (shower and otherwise), tablecloths and place mats, clothes hangers, garden hose, phonograph records, toys, stationery supplies, sporting goods, tools and hardware, raincoats, baby pants, credit cards.

These items are remarkably non-unique: After all, even before most plastics were invented, let us say in the 1930s, furniture was upholstered; walls, floors, and tables were covered; showers were curtained; and babies wore waterproof pants. All of these tasks can be met with materials other than plastics: natural fabrics, leather, paper, wood, and natural rubber, for example. Of 41 ethylene end-uses of all kinds cited in the text, only 3 could not be met by other products: high-fidelity phonograph records, dry-cleaning fluids, and an additive for military jet fuels.

Of course, some of the new plastic objects have secondary advantages over the older ones, while others have secondary disadvantages. A plastic shower curtain is likely to give better service than a rubber one (which may crack) or a canvas one (which may become mildewed). On the other hand, a natural-rubber garden hose is likely to be more serviceable than most plastic ones, some of which often crack in cold weather. In my own experience, a metal pail used out of doors invariably lasts longer than a plastic one, which is likely to crack in the weather and to be nibbled by country mice. A more serious disadvantage is that the common plastic polyvinyl chloride may gradually give off vinyl chloride, a compound which has recently been found to cause cancer. Thus, apart from minor secondary advantages and disadvantages, with relatively few exceptions a typical plastic product is a substitute for a pre-existing one made of some other material, both performing more or less the same function.

It is sometimes argued that plastics and other synthetic materials are needed because supplies of comparable natural materials are insufficient to meet demand. It is true that the amount of cotton and wool produced at this time would not be enough to satisfy all the demand now being met by synthetic fabrics and plastics. But the reason is not that the world has run out of land for growing cotton and raising sheep. Rather, cotton farmers and wool growers have been forced out of the market by the low price of the competing petrochemical products. They could readily increase production and recapture most of the lost markets—if the price were right and they were not so dependent on high-priced fertilizers and pesticides that the petrochemical industry sells them. In the case of detergents (which have captured about 85 percent of the market once held exclusively by soap since they were introduced in 1945), replacement is possible even now. As soap was driven off the market, the oils and fats previously used to manufacture it were exported. The oils and fats that the United States now exports could replace the total amount of detergents now used.

All this leaves us without an explanation for the most puzzling thing about plastics and other petrochemical products: Why have they swept into the marketplace with such force as to surround us at home, at work, in transit, and at play with a bewildering variety of synthetic objects? Why do a few styles of wooden pencils and metal pens give way to hundreds of different kinds of plastic writing instruments?

One reason, of course, is the remarkable plasticity of plastics; unlike leather, wood, or paper, they can be molded into almost any reasonable shape, extruded into rods and sheets, or blown into bottles. Lunch-counter sandwiches used to be held together by wooden toothpicks, which came in just two styles: flat or round. Now a sandwich is likely to arrive pierced by a miniature sword, spear, or trident molded out of plastic in any of a dozen different colors. Another reason is that since the molds or dies from which plastic objects are produced are expensive, the manufacturer must make an enormous number of objects to recoup the original cost of the production machinery. As a text on the plastic industry points out:

> For this reason, if you asked a craftsman to make you a special pair of candlesticks he would be delighted; if you asked for two million pairs he would be appalled; yet if you asked a plastics molder for one pair of candlesticks *he* would be appalled, but delighted if you asked for two million pairs.

The production of plastic goods is profitable *only* in enormous quantities. This explains why any new plastic product is likely to burst upon us in a sudden flood. In a few months every loaf of bread has added to its long-used wax-paper wrapping an outer plastic sack closed with a little slab of slotted plastic.

Profitability helps explain why plastics can so readily drive competitive material off the market. Regardless of the initial motivation for a new productive enterprise—the entry of synthetics into the fabric market, of detergents into the cleaner market—it will succeed relative to the older competitor only if it is capable of yielding a greater return on the investment. At times this advantage may be expressed as a lower price for the new goods, an advantage which is likely to drive the competing ones off the market. At other times this advantage may be translated into higher profits, enabling the new enterprise to expand faster than the older one —and once more driving the competition off the market. The remarkable tendency for energetically inefficient petrochemical products to push energetically efficient competitors out of the marketplace is an example of a powerful driving force in the energy crisis—the relative rate of economic return, or, in more common terms, the chance of increasing profit.

The profitability of the production of plastics is closely related to the basic economic structure of the industry. Costs of materials, fuel, and capital investment are high, and labor costs are low; the cost of materials is generally about three to ten times the cost of wages paid to production workers. These economic relationships reflect the distinctive design of the chemical process industries, in which automated flow systems predominate and labor is held to a minimum. A petrochemical plant is typically a vast network of pipes and vessels, with a few workers monitoring control valves and making repairs.

Profitability in industry is closely related to *labor productivity* (value added per man-hour), which, as we have seen, is very high in both the petroleum industry and the chemical industry. Thus, although the petrochemical industry is very inefficient in its use of fuel and capital, it is remarkably efficient in its use of human labor, and therefore highly profitable.

Here we can begin to see the source of the peculiar tendency of plastic goods to proliferate. The key is that petrochemical production is based on the never-ending flow of materials. In a continuously flowing system a by-product cannot simply be ignored; it too has to go somewhere. Most petrochemical by-products—for example, propylene, a by-product of ethylene production from refinery ethane—are combustible. Therefore they can always be gotten out of the way by burning, either usefully to provide heat where it is needed, or wastefully as one of those huge torches that light up the sky over a refinery. Disposed of by useful burning, a by-product such as propylene has the economic value of a corresponding amount of ordinary fuel, and can lessen the cost of producing ethylene by that much. However, sold as a raw material for further manufacture, propylene can fetch a price well above that of a fuel, reducing the cost of producing ethylene (and its further products) even more. Under this kind of economic lure, a way is usually found to convert the by-product into a new, salable synthetic material. For example, instead of being burned, propylene can serve as a raw material in the manufacture of acrylonitrile, which is then used to produce acrylic fiber, which is finally made into rugs. This lowers the cost of ethylene and therefore reduces the cost of making the originally intended product, polyvinyl chloride. It also thrusts acrylic fibers into the rug market at a price that is low enough to drive wool out of it.

What is crucial in these relationships is that an end-use be found for the by-products yielded at each stage in a petrochemical process. This significantly cuts down the most expensive item in the production of a petro-chemical—the cost of raw materials. So, by its own internal economic logic, each new petrochemical pro-cess generates a powerful tendency to proliferate fur-ther products and displace pre-existing ones.

This explains why new petrochemical products seem to take us by surprise, pressed upon us before we are aware that we need them. For years, ordinary grass served baseball diamonds and football fields quite well. Then, with the construction of the Houston Astro-dome, which for the sake of shielding the field from rain also excluded the light that grass must have, a substitute was needed. Enter Astroturf, a green plastic parody of grass. But, typically, once the petrochemical pipes were set up to emit this product, they could not afford to stop. Astroturf was sold so cheaply that it has been inflicted on fields naturally open to the sky, where —unlike the Astrodome—the plastic sod was exposed to sunlight, often becoming uncomfortably hot. The footsore outfielder has become victim to the predatory invasiveness that is built into the very design of the petrochemical industry. It is an industry that tends not so much to serve social needs as to invent them.

A more familiar example of the displacement of a natural material by a synthetic petrochemical is the substitution of plastics in the manufacture of articles such as purses and shoes. In this case, a direct com-parison of the several productivities can be made, since the Department of Commerce's statistical tables happen to include an industrial category exclusively devoted to the production of leather, and another to plastics. The comparison is striking: The energy productivity of leather production is 3.7 times that of plastics, and its capital productivity is 3.4 times greater. As expected, the labor productivities are reversed: 2.3 times greater in plastics than in the manufacture of leather.

When changes in production technology that worsen

energy and capital productivities occur *within* an industry, the situation can be rectified—if that social decision is made—by readjusting the inputs while the output remains the same. So the few farmers in the Corn Belt who have opted to turn away from heavy petrochemical inputs remain farmers, producing essentially the same crops that they did before. In the same way, if we had the wisdom to restore and electrify the U.S. railroad system, it would rebuild an existing industry, enhancing its output and providing new employment opportunities.

Unfortunately, the situation is very different and much more difficult when, as in the case of petrochemicals, the change in production technology creates a whole new industry. Then there is no way to restore the energy productivity involved in the production of textiles, for example, without favoring the production of cotton and wool by agriculture and cutting back on the output of synthetics by the petrochemical industry. It is regrettable but true that there is no way to improve the low social value of the petrochemical industry short of reducing its level of activity. By its very design, the industry is *inherently* inefficient in its uses of energy and capital; it cannot be reformed, it can only be diminished.

What would be the practical advantages—apart from aesthetic ones—in reducing, let us say, the flood of plastics? If most plastics were withdrawn from the marketplace and their functions were restored to the products that they have displaced, we would experience appreciable reductions in air and water pollution and in trash accumulation; known and potential risks of cancer and other diseases would be reduced; there would be appreciable savings of fuel; capital would be saved; and job opportunities and payrolls could be increased.

Obviously, there would be little sense to a blanket ban on plastics. Some of their uses *are* unique and important—for example, in artificial heart valves, shatterproof glass, phonograph records, and certain electrical and mechanical equipment. But such uses represent only a small part of the billions of pounds of plastic produced in the United States each year. For the rest—the spongy plastic coffee cups; the once-used plastic utensils; the plastic skins that encase thousands of dime-store items; the throwaway plastic pens; the plastic coverings for walls, furniture, car seats, tables, and people—there are replacements, at a price. China cups and metal utensils will need to be washed and re-used; dime stores will need more salespeople (the real purpose of using plastic to seal a one-inch electric plug onto an eight-inch card is to make shoplifting that much harder); metal implements will require more hand labor in the manufacturing process; land will need to be returned to the growing of cotton and wool.

Thus the overall design of the petrochemical industry —or even the design of a specific petrochemical process—is not merely the reflection of thermodynamics, chemical properties, and other purely technical matters. It also carries the heavy imprint of economic considerations. In particular, the design of a process is likely to reflect the requirement that it produce a short-term profit that competes favorably with profits available from other enterprises, even though the latter may be more sound on ecological or other social grounds. This means that the transfer of a petrochemical process from its country of origin to another country with a different economic system may require a thorough re-examination of the design of the process and even of the utility of the process as a whole. The wholesale transfer of a petrochemical process (which most likely has been developed under private-enterprise, profit-oriented economics) to a nation operating under, let us say, socialist economics might well turn out to be incompatible with the social values of the latter nation. Such considerations are particularly relevant to the transfer of petrochemical processes to developing nations, especially in the tropics. The inherent properties of the petrochemical industry appear to be especially unsuitable for such countries. The industry is capital- and fuel-intensive rather than labor-intensive and competes with the use of materials of biological origin. In developing tropical countries capital and fuel are in much shorter supply than labor, and materials of biological origin are relatively plentiful. However "modern" and, in the short run, profitable, the petrochemical industry would appear to be a particularly poor investment for a developing country, or for any country that preferred long-term social values to short-term profit.

In sum, the petrochemical industry confronts us with a basic problem that appears to be a common consequence of the post-war energy-mediated transformation of production technology: We shall need to consider whether, in deciding what is produced and how to produce it, we are to be governed by the goal of maximizing social value or of maximizing private profit.

8

THE PRICE OF POWER

THIS ACCOUNT of the energy crisis began, it will be recalled, with the assertion that it is part of a complex set of crises not only in energy but in the environment and the economic system as well. The interconnections among them suggested that all three crises were symptoms of some common fault that lay deep within the design of the system that governs how wealth is produced, distributed, and used in the United States. Energy, it was suggested, was a valuable way to illuminate this root problem, to uncover it, and to define it—so that possible solutions can be sought. We have now considered how energy is produced and used in the United States. An effort has been made to relate the various energy problems to the production and economic systems. It would be useful, now, to review what has been said about them, so that we can gather together the separate strands and look for a common origin that may reveal where this basic fault lies.

As we have seen, nearly all the energy produced in the United States today is derived from fossil fuels—oil, natural gas, and coal. These are limited, non-renewable sources of energy, and our nearly total dependence upon them is a blatant violation of the essential principle that the production system—if it is to survive—must be self-sustained, regenerating the resources that it uses. The unhappy consequence of this fault is especially apparent in the production of petroleum and natural gas. Despite a good deal of confusion, it is now clear that the oil and gas resources of the United States are not so depleted as the oil companies would have us believe. Nevertheless, the basic fact that oil is a non-renewable resource means that every barrel taken out of

198

the ground makes the next barrel more costly; the law of diminishing returns is at work. As petroleum reserves are consumed, the amount of capital needed to support deeper drilling and more elaborate extraction processes rises sharply, so that the amount of oil produced per dollar of invested capital (the productivity of capital) falls.

The result is an apparent absurdity: As the rate of production increases, the petroleum industry becomes correspondingly less able to generate enough capital to supply its own needs. The economic behavior of the petroleum companies then becomes understandable. In order to acquire more capital, they want larger profits; in order to get the larger profits, they demand higher prices and more tax benefits. This is what the industry means by "investment incentives." In the U.S. free-enterprise system, the oil companies are at liberty to invest their capital in whatever enterprise appears to offer the highest rate of profit. They have made considerable use of that freedom, and so long as they retain it the oil companies cannot be relied upon to produce domestic petroleum under economic conditions which are unacceptable to them. Conditions that would be acceptable to the oil companies would involve an increase over their current rate of profit and a sharp rise in the already high price of fuel.

If coal is to replace the massive use of petroleum in transportation, it must be converted into liquid or gaseous synthetic fuels. This would increase nearly tenfold the capital costs needed to acquire a given amount of energy from coal. Once more, the intensified exploitation of this energy source—which has recently been proposed by the Ford administration—would inevitably reduce the productivity of invested capital. Any attempt to counteract that trend by increasing the return on investment will raise the price of fuel well beyond its present level.

The outstanding feature of nuclear power is that, because it represents an extravagant case of "thermodynamic overkill" (using, as it does, an energy source with an inherent "temperature" that is many thousand degrees above that needed to produce steam), and is

therefore an extremely complex, unreliable, and potentially very dangerous technology, capital costs are
high and rising fast. The increasing capital costs of
nuclear power have already made the entire $11-bil-
lion breeder program economically obsolete. Rising capital costs have now become the dominant factor in the
price of nuclear power; because these costs are increasing much faster than the capital costs of coal-fired
plants, sometime in the next ten to fifteen years nuclear
power will become more expensive than coal-fueled
power. The entire nuclear-power program will then
lose its only reason for existing—its present cost advantage over coal-fired power—and is then (or sooner)
likely to collapse. As long as the nuclear-power program continues, it will contribute significantly to the
rapidly rising cost of electricity, and to the demand for
scarce investment capital.

Thus, the sources of nearly all the energy that we
now use—petroleum, natural gas, coal, and nuclear
power—suffer from the same basic flaw: Because they
are either non-renewable, or overburdened with unnecessarily complex technology—or both—they demand progressively larger investment of capital,
become increasingly costly to produce, and—in the
free market of the private-enterprise system—higher in
price. So long as we continue to rely on these sources
and on an economic system of that design, even if the
rate of energy production should remain constant,
energy will demand progressively greater capital investment and higher selling prices. The present energy
system has a built-in propensity toward inflation and,
if it continues, is bound to have a growing inflationary
impact on the economy as a whole.

This is already evident in the overall economic trends
of total U.S. energy production. For every dollar invested in energy production in 1960, 2,250,000 BTU
of energy was produced; by 1970 this figure had
dropped to 2,168,000 and in 1973 to 1,845,000—a
decrease of 18 percent in the productivity of capital in
energy production in only thirteen years. (These data
are cited in terms of 1973 dollars to eliminate the effect
of inflation.) Between 1970 and 1973 the capital

needed to support energy production amounted to about 24 percent of the capital invested in U.S. business as a whole. Estimates of the capital needed to produce energy in the 1975–85 period range up to $1000 billion, and are likely to demand a third or more of the total capital needed by private business. The situation is most acute in electric utilities, where it has been intensified by the shift from conventional to nuclear power plants. If they follow their present course, in the next ten years electric utilities are expected to spend $350–500 billion (in 1970 dollars), more than three times the amount spent in the decade before that.

Most of the needed capital must come from borrowed funds, for it has become apparent that the energy industry's own income will not meet its need for capital, even though the price of energy and the industry's profits have sharply increased in the last few years. According to a recent review, the U.S. energy industry will need some $900 billion over the next ten years, "nearly half of which will have to be raised externally." This means that the expected retained earnings from energy production will fall 50 percent short of providing the capital needed to continue the industry's planned production. The problem is worldwide. According to the Chase Manhattan Bank, the petroleum industry, worldwide, will need $1.8 trillion of investment capital between 1970 and 1985. But, as already noted, in the first four years of that fifteen-year period, despite the huge increase in income due to the price rise instigated by the 1973 oil crisis, the industry had earned, as profits, only 7 percent of the needed amount.

Thus, despite the rising price of energy, the costs of producing it are increasing so fast as to exceed the ability of the energy industries to raise the needed capital out of their own earnings. Their demand for "external capital" will significantly reduce the availability of capital for business as a whole—not to speak of capital needed by ordinary citizens to finance the purchase of a home or an automobile. This trend means not only higher energy prices, but also higher interest

rates for all borrowed capital. It is a relatively simple
empirical rule of economics that an increased demand
for capital relative to the supply will result in a higher
price for capital—that is, higher interest rates. When
this happens, all costs and prices are increased. Thus,
if the energy industry is to earn enough to support its
own growing need for capital, the price of energy must
increase. On the other hand, if the price does not increase enough to generate the needed capital, and the
industry must borrow it, interest rates will tend to rise.
Either outcome, or any combination of them, can only
lead to inflation.

It is at the economic level that the energy crisis is
linked to the environmental crisis. It is now widely recognized that energy production is responsible for a
major part of environmental pollution. There is a
built-in conflict between the biology of the ecosystem
and the thermodynamics of the present energy sources.
Fossil fuels generate energy only when they are burned,
producing temperatures that are not otherwise encountered (except for occasional volcanoes) in the
earth's natural systems. The substances that are produced at these abnormally elevated temperatures—such
as sulfur dioxide from coal-burning plants, and nitrogen oxides from automobiles as well as power plants—
are not normal constituents of the environment and
therefore tend to be incompatible with the living things
that have become adapted, through evolution, to that
environment. (Similarly, nuclear power is a potential
source of exposure to ionizing radiation at levels that
living things do not encounter in nature, and to which
they are poorly adapted.) These hazards are therefore
unavoidable in the use of present energy sources, and
the effort to control them increases the capital cost of
producing energy without adding to the energy output.
This further reduces the productivity of the invested
capital and worsens the industry's inflationary impact.

Because of the high inherent temperatures of all the
present sources of energy, they are not well matched,
thermodynamically, to many of the energy-requiring
tasks for which they are used. This thermodynamic
mismatch accounts for the extraordinarily poor ef-

ficiency with which energy is used in the production system. From Second Law efficiencies it appears that about 85 percent of the work available in the energy presently consumed is not applied to the work-requiring tasks of the production system—it is wasted. The extremely high proportion of waste in the use of energy greatly intensifies demand and worsens by that much the effects of energy production on the economic system.

In sum, we are relying on precisely those sources of energy—fossil fuels and uranium—which, with alarming consistency, violate the essential requirements of the ecosystem, the production system, and the economic system. Because the present energy sources are non-renewable and technologically complex, they demand progressively more capital; because the demand for capital grows faster than energy production itself, this vital sector of the production system has lost its capability to regenerate, through its sales, sufficient capital to sustain itself. Whether this difficulty is met by raising prices, increased borrowing, or both, it will result in worsened inflation.

Meanwhile, we are failing to draw upon the one source of energy which is renewable; is not subject to diminishing returns; is technologically simple; is compatible with the environment; and is economically capable of counteracting the inflationary effect of conventional energy production—the sun. Unlike present energy sources, solar energy is wholly unaffected by the law of diminishing returns. The future availability of solar energy is not reduced by its present use, for the ultimate source—the huge nuclear reaction deep in the sun's interior—will continue to send enormous amounts of energy toward the earth regardless of what its inhabitants choose to do with it. Compared with conventional sources, the technology of solar-energy production is remarkably simple; it is therefore free of the kind of unexpected technical difficulties that have so rapidly increased the capital cost of nuclear power. Finally, again in contrast with present energy sources, solar energy is virtually free of the environmental and health hazards that require expenditures which have further decreased the productivity of capital invested in conventional energy production.

For all these reasons, the economic relations of solar energy are precisely the reverse of those characteristic of conventional energy sources. Unlike conventional energy production, the use of solar energy does not automatically increase its future costs and the demand for capital. Solar energy can therefore be produced without imposing on the economy the inflationary effects of rising energy prices and rates of interest. Indeed, an investment of capital in solar energy now is a hedge against future inflation, for it eliminates the need to buy fuel at a constantly inflating price. By reducing the demand for conventional fuels, solar energy, developed on a sufficiently large scale, could in fact even reduce the price of conventional energy and soften its inflationary impact. Solar energy is more than a superior economic alternative to conventional energy sources; it is also an antidote to their catastrophic economic effects.

If the rapid and accelerating production of energy has generated these environmental and economic difficulties, it is, after all, in response to a *demand* for energy. This demand arises in the production system; and either the system's increasing activity or a change in its design—or both—must somehow account for the accelerating demand for energy.

Does the rising rate of annual energy consumption —which has more than doubled since 1950—reflect a comparable rise in the production system's output? The value of this output (as gauged by the GNP, expressed in fixed dollars to account for inflation) increased somewhat faster than energy consumption between 1950 and 1970, but the trend has since then begun to reverse. (This general trend probably reflects the rapid post-war growth of service industries, which, when measured against production industries, use comparatively little energy relative to their economic output.) From the point of view of economics, this might seem to be satisfactory evidence that the production system is using more energy because it is producing more economic value. On the other hand, from the viewpoint of thermodynamics we would want to answer a different question: Is the rising consumption of energy matched by a comparable increase in that which gives energy its only real value —the accomplishment of work-requiring tasks? To answer that question, we need to look at the amount of energy (or better—in keeping with the Second Law— the amount of available work that it represents) that is used to accomplish a task. This calls for an evaluation of the performance of a production process in terms of *productivity:* the tasks accomplished (output) per unit of energy used (input).

As pointed out earlier, ideally this would require a total productivity analysis of at least the major sectors of the production system. Unfortunately, we are not yet that well informed about the huge productive machine that makes the United States the wealthiest country in history. Separate segments of the needed information are, however, available and they can give us, at least in outline, an indication of how the use of energy relates to the real (as distinct from the monetary) output of the production system.

The earlier discussion of agriculture, transportation, and the petrochemical industry showed that there has been a general decline in energy productivity in these sectors of the production system. In agriculture this has come about through the substitution of fuels and energy-intensive chemicals for solar energy. As a result, although farm output has increased in the last thirty years, the amount of energy used to produce it has increased faster; it takes more energy than it used to to produce a bushel of corn or a bale of cotton.

In transportation, the modes that are low in energy productivity (trucks, private cars, and airlines) have increasingly displaced the forms with relatively high energy productivities (railroad freight and passenger traffic; trolley cars). The net result is that although freight transportation and passenger travel have increased (by 38 percent and 49 percent, respectively) between 1960 and 1970, the amount of energy used in transportation has increased faster (by 51 percent in that same period).

However, much of the present passenger travel, particularly by automobile, is done not for its own sake, but as a necessary means of accomplishing a task, such as getting to and from work. As we have seen, the great urban diaspora has considerably increased the distances that must be covered to accomplish such essential tasks. Hence, in these instances we need to be concerned not only with the energetic efficiency of travel but also with the efficiency with which travel is used to accomplish the *actual task*. (In this sense, a black laborer in the Pittsburgh area who—given his difficulties in finding a suitable home and place of employment—has to travel 32 percent farther than a comparable white laborer to and from work is using travel less efficiently to accomplish the essential task of working.) Keeping this more meaningful measure in mind, it would appear that the energetic efficiency of accomplishing those tasks for which transport is necessary has been more sharply reduced than the passenger-mile/energy data would indicate. Thus, although people in the United States, on the average, travel per capita about twice as many miles by car per year as they did in 1945, the tasks accomplished by that travel have not increased proportionally.

The same kind of situation affects the use of energy to transport goods. For example, the amount of transport (and therefore the amount of energy) needed to accomplish the task of moving food from the farm to the city has increased sharply as small-scale operations have given way to large, geographically concentrated ones. Between 1939 and 1972 the average distance traveled by a ton of railroad freight increased from 351 to 511 miles. These changes exemplify a centralizing tendency which has made the production system more dependent on transportation. Amplified by the reduced productivity of the energy used in transportation, this has further increased the disparity between the amount of energy that we use and the good that we get out of it.

An interesting example of the consequences of centralization for both environmental pollution and the waste of energy is in the bottling industry. Twenty-five or thirty years ago the bottling of soft drinks was quite decentralized; it was not uncommon to find, in a fairly small town, a local enterprise under franchise to a large company, bottling its product in an ordinary store. Small-scale breweries were also more common then. In both cases, the bottles were not widely dispersed and were readily refilled and recycled. Now, with the elimination of such local bottling plants, shipping distances have increased considerably between plant and the point of sale, and it has become too costly to ship returnable bottles for refilling. This is one reason why throwaway bottles and cans are now used almost exclusively in the industry, leading to the familiar litter problem and to a several-fold increase in the amount of energy used to bottle and deliver a unit of beverage.

The rapid growth in the typical size and cost of production units is one reason for the heavy demand for capital to support the new production technologies. This is particularly evident in the energy industry: a typical modern petroleum refinery costs $500 million or more; a nuclear power plant costs about $1–2 billion; and a breeder reactor (if it is ever built) will cost $3–5 billion. Costs of this size can be borne only by huge companies. They tend to concentrate their production facilities, increasing the distances over which their goods are shipped. The growth in size and in economic power of the giant corporations that dominate U.S. industry is a major result of the post-war transformation of production technology. Their economic power is in good part based on the inefficient use of energy to transport goods over unnecessarily long distances.

The petrochemical industry exemplifies the trend toward reduced energy productivity. It not only takes a large share of the nation's energy, but uses it at a very low efficiency, and its rapid growth has been achieved not by adding to the capability of the production system to accomplish needed tasks, but chiefly by displacing earlier means of accomplishing existing ones. Finally, with a curious and pernicious precision, almost every product which the petrochemical industry has displaced has been particularly efficient in its use of energy. As plastics have displaced leather in the production of handbags and shoes, the energy required to produce the average handbag or shoe has increased; as synthetic fibers have replaced cotton, the energy required to produce a shirt has gone up; as fertilizer nitrogen has displaced manure and legumes in the maintenance of soil fertility, the energy required to produce a bushel of corn or a bale of cotton has increased.

One reason why the petrochemical industry is so successful in invading the territory of other sectors of the production system is that, by its own internal logic, it tends to lower the cost of its products as it invents new ones. The industry can therefore readily invade a market, undersell its competitors, and drive them out of production. This has been the fate of cotton, wool, natural rubber, leather, soap, manure, and the grass that used to grow on playing fields.

Thus, out of the massive post-war changes in the production system there has emerged a dominant industrial complex, founded on the intensive use of conventional sources of energy—petroleum, natural gas, coal, and uranium—both as fuel and as raw material. One branch of this complex, the petroleum and natural-gas industry, produces fuel, chiefly for transportation and, to a lesser extent, for residential and industrial use. Another branch produces fuel, chiefly coal and uranium, for electric-power production by utilities. The transportation and electric-power industries depend most directly on these two fuel-producing branches, but ultimately the whole of the production system depends on them as well. Parallel to the fuel-producing arm of the complex, and intimately entwined with it, is the arm that uses energy sources (largely petroleum and natural gas and, to a slight extent, coal) as raw materials—the petrochemical industry, which in turn encompasses a very large and growing sector of the chemical industry as a whole.

This energy/chemical complex—petroleum and natural gas; coal mining; nuclear-fuel production; transportation; and a large part of the chemical industry—dominates the U.S. production system. It owns $181 billion in assets, or 29 percent of the assets (and sales) of the 500 largest corporations in the U.S. The sales of these companies represented 18 percent of the total gross national product in 1974. All of this wealth is in the hands of some twenty corporations with average assets of $9.1 billion each. It is the most dynamic, economically powerful sector of industry, and—if nothing is changed—it is likely to determine the future behavior of the entire production system. The interlocking activities of these corporations—many of which have substantial holdings in all energy resources—tend to reduce competition among the different sources of energy, therefore forcing higher prices. We can thank Senator James Abourezk of South Dakota for helping an energy-corporation executive make this fact quite clear. In a recent Senate hearing the following exchange took place:

> SENATOR ABOUREZK: Would you tell your coal subsidiary —or would you permit your coal subsidiary—to undersell your oil subsidiary?
> MR. HARDESTY [of the Continental Oil Co.]: No, sir, under no circumstances.

It is useful at this point to consider the general ways in which energy, capital, and labor are interrelated in the production system. Capital represents the cost of the machines that are used in the production process and the factories that house them. As technology advances, machines tend to become larger, more complex, and more costly. The added capital cost is acceptable because the new technology is expected to reduce the costs of other inputs, to increase the value of the output (or both), and thereby enhance the overall economic returns. Energy is required to run the machines, so as the latter become larger and more complex, the cost of the energy required to operate them typically increases as well. Thus, as production technology is transformed, we can expect the inputs of capital and energy to increase together (as we shall see, the empirical data support this expectation).

The intensified use of capital equipment, and of the energy needed to run it, typically results in an increased output of goods. However, the increased output is not necessarily proportional to the increased inputs of capital and energy. Indeed, particularly with the development of modern technology, the added costs for capital and energy may well yield a proportionally smaller increase in output: capital productivity (output/capital) and energy productivity (output/energy) would then decrease.

Obviously, if nothing else changed, it would make less and less economic sense to introduce more costly, more energy-intensive capital equipment. But something does change: the productivity of labor (output/man-hours), which, in contrast to the productivity of capital and energy, typically *increases* as new technology is introduced. Indeed, the expectation of increased labor productivity is normally the chief motivation for introducing new technology into a production enterprise.

As a result of these general relationships, we might expect the productivities of capital and energy of different industries to vary in parallel and the productivity of labor to be inversely related to both of them. The productivities of energy, capital, and labor in industrial production can be ascertained from statistical data on the twenty-one standard classes of manufacturing industries (using the latest comprehensive compilation for 1971). Among these twenty-one industries, energy productivities range from a low value of $5–10 of value added per million BTU of energy (for petroleum; primary metals; paper; stone, clay, and glass; and chemicals) to a high of $100–125 (for clothing manufacturing and printing and publishing). Capital-productivity values range from a low of $0.34–0.80 of value added per dollar of fixed assets (for the same five energy-intensive industries) to high values of $3.64 (leather) and $4.40 (clothing manufacturing) of value added per dollar of fixed assets. For all twenty-one industrial sectors, energy productivity is proportional to capital productivity. The proportionality is highly significant mathematically, with a correlation coefficient of 0.82. (1.00 means a perfect correlation; a coefficient of 0.82 is indicative of a good one. It means that 67 percent of the variation among the productivities of the different industries can be accounted for by the proportionality of energy and capital productivities.) Hence, as a general rule, a low efficiency in the use of energy relative to output may be interpreted as indicative of a correspondingly low efficiency in the use of capital.

The relationship between the productivity of labor and the productivities of capital and energy is somewhat more complicated by the actual design of the production equipment. However, as a group, the five industries that have the lowest energy productivities also have capital productivities that are significantly lower, and labor productivities that are significantly higher, than the industrial average. These industries—petroleum; primary metals; paper, stone, clay, and glass; and chemical manufacturing—make up a major segment of U.S. industry.

Viewed in terms of productivity, it becomes apparent that there have been sweeping changes in the technology of argicultural and industrial production in the last thirty years. Striking reductions in the productivity of both energy and capital (usually accompanied by an *increase* in the productivity of labor) have occurred in the post-war switch from natural to synthetic materials; from railroads to trucks, cars, and airplanes; from small low-compression car engines to large high-compression ones; from manually operated manufacturing machines to automated ones; from natural, balanced agricultural methods to the heavy use of chemicals.

What has changed is largely the *means* of production, rather than the final use value of what is produced. Before the post-war transformation in production technology, food was grown and eaten, shirts, shoes, and handbags were manufactured, freight was moved, and people washed dishes and clothes—all in amounts, per capita, that are about the same as they are now. But the methods were different: farms used manure rather than chemical fertilizers; shirts were made of cotton instead of synthetic fibers; shoes and handbags were made of leather rather than plastics; freight and people were carried chiefly by railroads and small, low-powered cars instead of by trucks, airplanes, and large cars; dishes and clothes were washed with soap made out of natural fat rather than with synthetic detergent made out of petroleum. The amount of energy and capital needed to accomplish the same task has increased; the amount of labor used to produce the same output has decreased; the impact on the environment has worsened.

Here we can begin to sense the deeper, hidden meaning of the energy crisis. It is a symptom of a profound change in the design of the production system, which has taken place, almost unnoticed except for its outward products, in the last thirty years. And these changes, which surfaced first as the chief cause of the environmental crisis and later of the energy crisis, have a much deeper, and more immediate, *economic* meaning. They have seriously affected the relationship between the output of the production system and two major economic inputs: capital and labor. The two effects are diametrically opposed: Most of the newly introduced production technologies have reduced capital productivity (i.e., output/dollars of capital invested) and have increased labor productivity (i.e., output/man-hours of labor used). Energy links the two effects, for it is used to run the new, more capital-intensive machinery that produces goods with much less participation of labor than before. As new production technologies have displaced the older ones, energy has displaced human labor.

Recall, now, that if the economic system is to survive, it must regenerate its essential resources. One of these is capital, which is needed to build new productive machinery. Hence, in order to sustain itself, the economic system must set aside from its current output sufficient capital to support the future rate of production. However, if the productivity of capital falls, so that more and more of it must be used to maintain the same rate of output, this capability is threatened. At the same time, if progressively less labor is required for a given rate of output, the ability of the economic system to regenerate jobs is also threatened. These considerations suggest that unless some countervailing force intervenes, the post-war transformations in production technology will tend to generate a shortage of both capital and jobs.

In considering these implications of the declining productivity of capital and the rising productivity of labor, it is useful to cast the problem into a somewhat different framework. Rather than thinking of the manufacture of leather or plastics—to return to this example —as a process for producing shoes or handbags, let us regard these enterprises as alternative means of producing capital and employment opportunities. As pointed out in the preceding chapter, capital productivity is very low in the plastics industry and high in the leather industry, while their relative labor productivities are the other way around. In this sense, of the two alternatives, the manufacture of plastics is a much poorer technique for generating both capital and jobs. The displacement of leather by plastics, then, does much more than change the kinds of handbags and shoes that are found in the store. It also increases the demand for capital and reduces the availability of jobs. As the petrochemical industry becomes increasingly dominant, the entire production system becomes less able to replenish its capital or to employ the people to whose welfare it is presumably devoted.

This much is theory. What about the facts? The facts about the shortage of jobs are only too well known: Unemployment has been chronic in the United States, in the last few years rising to levels unprecedented since the Depression. Apparently there has been no economic force sufficiently strong to counteract completely the effects of the changes in production technology on the availability of jobs.

The facts about the shortage of capital are less well known but just as real. In recent months there have been reports and analyses prepared by various business organizations, all calling attention to the growing shortage of capital in the most urgent terms. In September 1974 a New York Stock Exchange report claimed that U.S. business will lack some $650 billion of the approximately $4700 billion of investment capital needed in the next ten years. According to a more recent Chase

Manhattan Bank report, the shortage in that period is likely to amount to $1500 billion in a total need for $4100 billion. A recent issue of *Business Week,* devoted to an extensive analysis entitled "The Capital Crisis," projects a capital demand in that same period of $4500 billion, and, while refraining from estimating a total shortage, the study asserts:

> The obstacles to raising that kind of money in the economic environment that is likely to prevail in the next decade, and distributing it to where it will be needed, are formidable, perhaps insurmountable.

According to the *Business Week* review, in the previous decade the supply of capital rose at an annual rate of 6.7 percent; but the amount produced in the next decade will have to increase at an annual rate of 8.7 percent in order to meet the demand. Investment in production machinery, which has increased at an 8.9-percent annual rate in the last decade, will need to increase at an annual rate of 11.5 percent in the next. According to the survey: "To finance that spending, given an expected 5% to 6% inflation rate, companies will have to spend some $1.9 trillion in the next decade against $670 billion in the past decade."

Some economists have criticized these reports, denying that there is, or will be, a capital shortage. The critics usually do not deny that there is an increased demand for capital, but they contend that the economic system is capable of meeting that demand, and thereby of preventing a shortage. In effect they deny the question by claiming that it can be answered. Thus, a recent Brookings Institution study, while agreeing that capital demands will be very high, asserts that there will be no "shortage" because the economy can adjust to the demand (providing employment is high) by government action involving ". . . a significant shift toward larger government budget surpluses." In other words, they expect the demand for capital to be relieved by reduced government expenditures. or by increased taxes. This is one way to provide public funds to support new industrial investment, in the manner of the $100-billion energy corporation recently proposed by Mr. Ford. Such a move would relieve the capital shortage by finding the missing capital in the tax-payers' pockets. A recent analysis by the Bureau of Labor Statistics also agrees that capital demand will increase sharply—for example, that "real investment for each new member of the labor force between now and 1985 would have to equal about $84,000, an amount three-fourths greater than the average during the past two decades." The study claims that there will be no shortage—provided that corporate investment-tax credits and capital depreciation allowances are increased and the corporate income tax is reduced.

In sum, there is no disagreement on the basic fact that the demand for capital will increase sharply, and that it can be met only if there are very large shifts in the present disposition of the nation's wealth. As we shall see, the economic shifts that would be required to eliminate the impending shortage of capital are so severe as to require a corresponding change in the social goals that the economic system is supposed to serve. If the capital shortage is to be denied, then these social changes must become real.

The reasons for the capital shortage that are commonly advanced in such analyses are that business needs a rising amount of capital and that profits are not expected to be large enough to generate the needed capital through retained earnings and business savings. For example, a New York Stock Exchange report (June 1975) analyzes the ability of U.S. industry to supply its own needs directly from the capital which industry itself produces. In 1950–55 industry was able to supply an average of about 70 percent of its total capital needs from its own profits; by 1970–74 it was able to supply only an average of about 26 percent from that source. In the past, the remainder has been supplied largely by the investment in industrial corporations of savings by private consumers, often in the form of funds accumulated by insurance companies and private and public pension and retirement plans and by foreign investors. According to the Stock Exchange analysis, even the considerably increased reliance on such external funds will not meet industry's total need for capital in the next ten years, so that unless some new steps are taken, an overall shortage will develop.

It would appear, then, that the tendency toward diminished capital productivity that is inherent in modern production technology has not been effectively overcome by opposing economic forces. That the decreasing productivity of capital plays a dominant role in the shortage of capital is strongly suggested by the fact that the shortage is most acute in the industrial sector in which, as we have seen, declining capital productivity is likely to be most pronounced—the energy industries. Energy production represents the most rapidly growing demand for capital among all sectors of industry. The most immediate and intense expression of the capital shortage is in the electric-power industry. For example, according to the Bureau of Labor Statistics study of the demand for capital by a series of major industrial sectors, the utilities are expected to demand a much-increased share of total private investment capital—50 percent more in 1985 than in 1965–70. In the last few years a considerable number of planned installations, particularly of nuclear power plants, has been canceled for want of sufficient capital. Lacking sufficient customers for its capital-intensive wares, the largest U.S. manufacturer of nuclear power plants recently called on the government, which has a large supply of capital, to buy them. If the energy industry's demand for capital continues to grow at the present rate, it may take up so much of the available capital as to interfere with the capital requirements of the rest of industry. The energy industry would then be in the absurd situation of interfering with the growth of its own customers.

It is worth noting that none of the reports on the capital shortage makes any serious effort to relate the problem to the effects of the sharp reduction in capital productivity that has accompanied the transformation of production technologies. For example, the *Business Week* analysis provides a series of charts showing the growth in the demand for capital; the concurrent decline in the funds available to industry from its own earnings; the corresponding need for outside funds (tripling between 1967 and 1975); the projected rise in borrowing and the resultant high interest rates. Amid all this economic detail, the only reference to the possible origin of the capital shortage from changes within the production system is the brief comment that ". . . the pollution and safety laws have increased the amount of capital required for a given level of production. And, finally, there are signs that it is now taking more and more dollars' worth of capital to produce one dollar's worth of output."

This is typical of the present analyses of the capital shortage. They regard it as a purely economic problem, and ignore its origin in changes in the production system—which, after all, is the source of the wealth that takes the form of capital. The shortage of capital is a sign that the economic system is having trouble reproducing its capital resource, at least in part because of the falling productivity of capital. By failing to recognize the relation between the capital crisis and this change in the character of production technology, the conventional analyses tend to foreclose the option of curing the problem at this basic level.

It has been my purpose, in this chapter, to re-examine the range of problems that have so gravely affected the production and use of energy in order to learn whether, as suggested by their interconnections, all of them arise from some common fault. It does seem clear, at this point, that the problems in energy, the environment, and the economic system are so intimately and fundamentally connected that there must be somewhere in this nest of interlocking crises a common, germinal fault. Where does this fault lie: in the ecosystem, the production system, or the economic system?

One current view would locate the fault in the ecosystem; it would hold that the basic problem, to which all the others are connected, is that the world is running out of resources—of raw materials, energy, and environmental quality. The proponents of this "limits to growth" approach argue that the supplies of essential resources have already been so far depleted as to set off a series of physical and social stresses that must be relieved by reducing not only the amount of goods that people consume, but the number of people as well. They point to the supposed evidence of an "oil shortage" and its spreading economic and political effects as an example of how the physical exhaustion of resources gives rise to all the rest of our troubles. According to the main author of this approach, Dr. Jay Forrester, these include "drug addiction, kidnapping, aircraft high-jackings, sabotage, revolution and a returning threat of atomic war."

Certainly with respect to energy there is no evidence that our present problems stem from a shortage in that resource. There is enough petroleum in the United States to meet all our needs for at least the next fifty years. There is no evidence that physical limitations on our ability to produce cotton and wool have led to the production of synthetics that consume petroleum resources so wastefully; or that we are forced to use chemical fertilizers because we have reached the ecological limits of growing legumes; or that we must produce detergents because there is not enough fat to make all the needed soap. All of these changes have only the *appearance* of a response to the constraints brought about by the "limits to growth" imposed by the ecosystem. In each case, they were brought about not by some abstract, mindless force called "growth," but by deliberate human actions, motivated by an *economic* factor—the desire to maximize profits.

Even in the most immediate and pressing resource issue—the need for food sufficient to support the world's growing population—all the evidence shows that we now have and will have ten years from now enough food-producing capability in the world to provide all of the earth's inhabitants with an adequate diet. Every recent scientific analysis of the food-production problem shows in fact, if not in the overlaid political interpretations, that people go hungry not because the world cannot produce enough to feed them but because they are too poor to afford it. To claim that many people go hungry and cold in the world because there is not adequate food and fuel has no more basis in fact than the claim that some people in the United States are poor because there is not enough wealth to go around. The basic fault that gives rise to these calamitous problems is the unequal distribution of wealth—between rich countries and poor ones, and, within each country, between rich people and poor people. Their origins will not be found in the earth's ecosystem or in the present state of its available resources.

There are grave faults in the present design of the production system that are the immediate cause of most of our difficulties with the production and use of energy and with environmental degradation. However, these faults have not arisen, autonomously, from *within* the production system. Rather they have been imposed on it from without by economic considerations. Consider the electric trolley. It was once recognized as a valuable part of the production system and was extensively and successfully developed as an effective means of transportation. The trolley car did not disappear because of some *inherent* fault. (Although overhead wires were cited as an environmental eyesore, they were blithely exchanged for the bus's smog and smells.) It was deliberately destroyed by the transportation industry—for profit. Trolley cars did not sicken and die, they were killed—sacrificed on the altar of profit.

As we have seen, there are many other examples of how economic considerations have governed the postwar transformation of the production system. On the testimony of the oil companies themselves, we know that purely economic reasons (the need for what they regard as adequate profits, or "incentives") led them to reduce domestic production in favor of foreign operations. On the testimony of Mr. Kissinger and Mr. Ford, we know that they have worked to maintain the high price of energy in order to help provide these "incentives" and to ensure that investments in new fuels, such as shale oil, will yield a satisfactory profit.

It seems evident, then, that the fault which lies at the root of the three interlocked crises will be found in the realm of economics. What we have learned so far about the origins and effects of the energy crisis does not identify that fault. The main clues that we have as to its nature are the links between energy problems and the economic system: capital, labor, profit. Since these are all basic attributes of the economic system, the fault is likely to be found on that same fundamental level.

When engineers want to test the strength of a mechanical system, they stress it until it breaks and thereby reveals where it is weakest. The energy crisis is such an "engineering test" of the economic system. The stress it has imposed on that system is the threatened shortage of energy—the inevitable result of our short-sighted dependence on non-renewable and technically unreliable sources of energy, and our grossly inefficient ways of using it. Modern production technology has transmuted that stress into a shortage of capital and jobs. This is an ominous metamorphosis, for it signifies that the economic system is unable to regenerate the essential resource—capital—which is crucial to its continued operation, or to serve the people in whose name it was created. What is now threatened is the economic system itself. This may be the true price of power.

9

THE POVERTY OF POWER

WE NOW DEPART from the realm of energy, taking leave of such matters as thermodynamics, oil reserves, nuclear hazards, the inefficiencies of furnaces and corn-fields, the gaudy iniquities of plastics, the toxic embrace of petrochemicals, and the shameful murder of the trolley car. We now know from an analysis of the energy crisis that the operative fault—and therefore the locus of any remedy—lies in the design of the economic system.

Clearly, the economic system, whch governs how wealth is produced and distributed, encompasses vastly more than the matters that I have discussed in this book, and there are many reasons other than energetic inefficiency or environmental degradation to find fault with it. For example, one reason for the wasteful expenditure of energy for passenger travel in the United States is that racial discrimination has forced some blacks to live at greater distances from their place of work than whites with comparable incomes. But surely there are other, more direct and meaningful reasons to deplore racial discrimination and its economic effects. Energy considerations tell us how the development of synthetics drives natural cotton and rubber off the market; this has greatly intensified the economic inequities which impoverish developing countries, for these countries are particularly well suited to produce such natural materials and thereby gain a position in world trade. But we hardly need to invoke the thermodynamic follies of the petrochemical industry to find evidence of the terrible consequences of colonialism. We have seen that, in modern production technology, energy replaces human labor, tending to worsen unemployment. But clearly the relationship between the worker and the job encompasses a range of issues much broader than this scant statement: the unquestioned humane value of using machines to supplant labor in dangerous and unhealthy work; the worker's dissatisfaction with the insecurity of his job, with the wages and conditions of work; the importance of *meaningful* work in one's life.

In moving into this more general realm, then, it is not my intention to transform economics into a branch of thermodynamics, or the relationship between entrepreneur and worker into a branch of ecology. Rather, I intend to pursue the economic leads arising out of the earlier consideration of energy problems wherever they may take us. In particular, I wish to explore the contradictory effects on the productivity of capital and labor that are revealed by the economic behavior of the new, energy-intensive sectors of the production system. The object of this quest is to discover what fault in the economic system can account for the complex of problems that has been the concern of this book.

(This pursuit will trespass into a field that lies outside my own professional training, but, as I have said in an earlier work, if those of us who have some knowledge of the scientific and technological features of this knot of problems fail to make contact with its economic facets, then the burden of establishing this essential link will fall on economists, who may be no better prepared to cope with the technical matters. Both sides need to make the effort, accepting the risk of error as a duty that we owe to a deeply troubled society.)

In tracing the origin of the energy crisis, and its relation to the crises in the environment and the economy, we have found that these crises arise from some as yet unspecified fault in the economic system which may be so basic as to suggest that the system is self-contradictory and fated to collapse. However, one obvious and inescapable fact casts considerable doubt on the reality of this fault and therefore on the value of any further effort to identify it.

The U.S. economic system has not in fact collapsed.

Obviously, other economic factors have successfully countered the self-contradictory effects of the system's tendency toward increased labor productivity (leading to fewer jobs) and decreased capital productivity (leading to a shortage of capital). Moreover, a very wide and presumably well-qualified body of opinion—including some academic economists, nearly all businessmen, and many government officials—holds that the U.S. economic system is ". . . the envy of the rest of the world. . . . We have the strongest economy in the world by far, and we can win any economic battle that we determine to win."

While the force of this particular statement might be questioned because of its origin (a speech on inflation, delivered on July 25, 1974, by Richard Nixon), more current and less clouded representatives of this point of view can be readily cited as well. For example, Mr. Nixon's immediate successor, President Ford, has said essentially the same thing, albeit in his own idiom:

> . . . our greatest danger today is to fall victim to the more exaggerated alarms that are being generated about the underlying health and strength of our economy. We are going to take some lumps and we're going to take some bumps, but with the help of Congress and the American people we are perfectly able to cope with our present and foreseeable economic problems.

Here are some other representative opinions on this matter. C. Howard Hardesty (executive vice-president, Continental Oil Co.):

> The United States has the strongest economy in the world. In most circles this nation is the most envied. We owe a good deal of that advantage to the years of cheap and abundant energy provided by the petroleum industry. . . . The petroleum industry has served the country well. Historically petroleum products have been the most stable element of our economy.

Barry M. Goldwater (Senator from Arizona):

> [T]he competitive-enterprise system is the best system available in this imperfect world of ours.

Alfred Schaefer (chairman, Union Bank of Switzerland):

> [America is] the one nation where capitalism seems safe for the next one or two generations.

This opinion is somewhat clouded by Mr. Schaefer's second statement, made some four months after the previous one:

> If we are realistic we must conclude that permanent inflation will lead to the downfall of the free-market economy and the social system that goes with it.

Discounting political fervor and other sources of exaggeration, clearly these enthusiasts for the U.S. economic system must have reasons for their optimism. What are they? What economic forces have staved off the trend toward economic collapse that the growing shortage of capital appears to threaten? (A recent advertisement by the ITT Corporation carries the caption, "What happens to capitalism if we run out of capital?")

It seems evident that the most effective countervailing factor which has thus far stabilized the economic system is growth—the rise, with time, in the annual output of the production system. It could be argued, for example, that increased output can be relied upon to overcome the effects of the declining productivity of capital and the rising productivity of labor, and to generate sufficient capital and jobs to maintain a stable economy. The argument might proceed along the following lines: Capital available from the production process represents some fraction of the overall output. Therefore, the total amount of capital produced by the economic system will increase as the total output of the production system rises. Hence, even if the productivity of capital falls (that is, progressively more capital is needed to maintain the same output), it should be possible to counteract this effect simply by using more capital than before—which is obtainable from the increased output. In the same way, it could be argued that even though labor productivity rises, so that the number of jobs that need to be filled to achieve a given level of production declines, the total number of jobs can be maintained by overall growth in the rate of production.

This is the meaning of the principle developed by economist Arthur M. Okun, which is described in a recent *New York Times* article on "Okun's Law" as follows:

> The law starts from the basic premise that it takes about 4 percent real growth in the gross national product just to keep unemployment from rising—and much more than that to bring it down. . . . On average, it takes that much of a rise in activity to keep the jobless rate from rising as new workers enter the labor force and as productivity improves.

Thus, Okun's Law asserts that as labor productivity increases and the need for labor, relative to output therefore declines, growth in production must exceed some minimum value in order to keep unemployment from rising. And, according to this approach, growth rather than redistribution of income is counted on to relieve poverty—the inevitable result of unemployment —which, according to official classification, now afflicts some 24 million U.S. citizens. For example, according to William Simon, Secretary of Treasury:

> Thus capital is a key factor in economic growth, and increased production. It is growth that enables our citizens to enjoy rising real incomes. And it is growth that permits the shares of the less privileged to rise without requiring the shares of others to fall.

However, that increased investment of capital and increased employment are in conflict is also clear from his statement:

> New [capital] investment helps increase productivity, that is, it makes it possible for the same number of workers to produce a greater amount of goods and services.

One can hardly escape noticing the sharp contrast between the way in which I have used the term *pro-*

ductivity and the way in which this same word is used in the foregoing quotations. In conventional usage, of which these quotations are typical examples, although the qualifying phrase does not appear, the unadorned term *productivity* always means *productivity of labor*. Apparently most conventional observers have become so transfixed by the alluring notion that rising labor productivity will sustain a continuing increase in total production output that, in their usage, labor productivity has become synonymous with total productivity.

But elimination of the qualifier has a significance that goes far beyond semantics or matters of usage. By itself, "productivity" is a wholly positive thing: the production of more goods from the available resources. High productivity is good and low productivity is bad. Thus, when this unqualified term is used to describe what is in reality *labor* productivity, it gives an aura of undiluted good to a process which, if it were more explicitly described, might well be regarded by a worker as not entirely in his best interests. With the adjective in place, a worker might well see that higher "productivity" is not simply a high-minded improvement in the effectiveness of the production process, but also involves a loss of jobs.

This is made evident in an article in *Business Week,* published in 1970, shortly after Mr. Nixon appointed a National Commission on Productivity because it was noticed that the steady rise in labor productivity had begun to slacken a bit (it fell by 1.0 percent between 1968 and 1970). Despite its unconditional title, this commission had nothing to do with the productivity of capital, of energy, or of any other resource. In the words of the *Business Week* article, its mission was only to "help find ways to boost output per manhour —which has been on a ragged decline since the fourth quarter of 1968."

Now, although a rise in labor productivity can be regarded as a way to increase output without additional labor, it can also be regarded as a way to reduce the number of workers that need to be employed to produce a given amount of output. Constant output with less labor is usually in the employer's interest, but not necessarily in the workers'. In practice, this is what is often achieved. As the article, citing a textile manufacturer, puts it: "The long-run solution [to the need for higher labor productivity] is capital investment that will reduce the number of workers." The president of one corporation which was unable to make new capital improvements reported that labor productivity was "slipping" because, as he said, "I don't know how to make people work faster. A speed-up will cause the labor unions to get upset."

This is a strange, purblind approach to a concept as fundamental to the economy as productivity, on the part of the nation's industrial executives, not to speak of the Secretary of Treasury. It may well account for the fact that while the pace of the rise in labor productivity is minutely scrutinized by the business community, the concurrent decline in *capital* productivity, especially in certain key industries such as energy production, goes almost unnoticed. What *has* been noticed and loudly proclaimed is the shortage of capital. But despite all the attention given to this calamitous phenomenon, astonishingly (to my knowledge), apart from a single sentence in the *Business Week* survey cited earlier, no discussion of it has analyzed the relationship that the intensive use of capital, relative to output, might have to the shortage of capital.

A case in point is a recent report published by the U.S. Chamber of Commerce, which on page 43 takes note of the broader meaning of productivity:

> The most widely used measure of productivity for purposes of international comparisons and as the basis of economic projections and policy decisions is output per manhour—labor productivity. Yet it is worth considering whether, in an age when capital, energy, and many traditional resources are becoming increasingly scarce, other productivity measures would not provide more relevant comparisons and a better basis for policy decisions.

Yet on page 34 this same report presents a discussion of "the dilemma of capital shortage," making no reference to the possible role of declining capital productivity in the shortage.

However, the failure to take the productivity of capital into account turns out to be remarkably selective. In one crucial area the relationship between invested capital and productive output is given close attention in the recent discussions of the capital shortage. This is the matter of the effect of measures to improve workplace safety and health and environmental standards on capital productivity. Thus, Secretary Simon tells us that among the causes of the capital shortage are

> . . . the pattern of government policies . . . exercising increased influence over private investment decisions through the growing number of safety, health and environmental standards. . . . While such standards may be highly desirable, we should recognize that these investments [i.e., capital investments needed to meet standards] do not increase the nation's total productive capacity.

Apparently, capital investment in radiation safeguards for a nuclear power plant is bad because it "does not increase the nation's total productive capacity." But the investment of capital in the nuclear power plant itself is good—despite the fact that this investment greatly reduces the power-producing capacity that could have been achieved if the same capital had been used to build a coal-fired plant.

Another example of the selective attention given to productivity problems is the role of military expenditures, which represents the diversion of production capacity into uses that are obviously non-productive. One of the ironies of the current discussion of capital shortage (for example, in Mr. Simon's recent testimony) is that much is made of the need to reduce the disparity between the fraction of the real national output that is devoted to capital investment in the United States (17.5 percent) and the comparable figures for West Germany and Japan (25.8 percent and 35.0 percent). What Mr. Simon fails to notice is an important reason for this difference: that the United States now devotes nearly 10 percent of its national output to non-productive military expenditures, whereas West Germany and Japan are now using only about 1 percent. Their capital stock benefits from this level of military expenditure. Evidently, as the real issues that lie behind the capital shortage and the true state of the nation's production system come to light, we will need to confront, on these grounds alone, the long-standing inviolability of the huge U.S. military budget. Perhaps Mr. Simon's concern with the urgency of devoting more of the national output to productive investments will lead him to join with the anti-war movement in a campaign to reduce the military budget.

Wittingly or not, there has been a good deal of unnecessary confusion about the relative productivity of labor and capital. This confusion tends to obscure the fundamental flaws in the conventional view that growth in output can successfully overcome the basic contradiction between the trends in capital and labor productivity.

There are two flaws in this argument, both of them serious. First is the empirical fact that the process has not worked very well. Despite the very considerable growth in output in the post-war period (in constant dollars the GNP doubled between 1950 and 1970) the two phenomena that it might be expected to prevent—shortage of jobs and shortage of capital—have in fact developed and have worsened considerably in the last few years. The second flaw is that the very way in which the production and economic systems interact sets up a contradictory relationship between the production of capital and the creation of jobs which cannot indefinitely be overcome by growth in output.

Recall that growth in output is now very largely due to the rise in *labor* productivity. The doubling in production output between 1950 and 1970 is largely accounted for by the doubling of labor productivity in that time. The productivities of all other factors that contribute to production—of capital, energy, raw materials, and other resources—have either declined or have remained relatively constant during the post-war technological transformation, especially in those sectors of production which use a great deal of capital (and energy). As progressively larger amounts of capital are invested the output of the production system increases but the amount of labor that is used does not keep pace with the rising output. As a result the following relations emerge: Rising labor productivity is largely responsible for the increase in overall output; increased output is the source of the added capital needed to combat the effect of its falling productivity; the investment of increasing amounts of capital in new labor-saving machinery causes labor productivity to rise. It follows, then, that production of capital is being maintained at the expense of a declining need for labor relative to capital. The capability of the production system to regenerate capital at a rate sufficient to sustain itself is achieved by using less labor relative to output.

As they have just been described, these relationships are, of course, not universally characteristic of each part of the production system. As seen in the preceding chapter, they do, however, seem to fit the behavior of the industries that make up the energy/chemical complex. Since these industries now play a dominant role in the economy as a whole, we can expect these relationships to at least have a significant effect on overall economic trends. It is also true that one of the tenets of conventional economics is that there are self-adjusting mechanisms at work in the economic system that can counteract tendencies such as the replacement of labor by capital and thereby slow them down and even, periodically, bring them to a halt. For example, as capital becomes scarce and more expensive, entrepreneurs can be expected to take the rational step of reducing capital consumption in favor of other inputs, such as labor. However, the fact is that the trend toward intensive use of capital appears to continue unabated, so that although such compensatory mechanisms exist and may have been effective in the past, they do not seem to work very well now. In the last few years a number of economists have made a point of calling attention to the failure of the economic system to behave as expected. The recent statement by Arthur Burns (Chairman of the Federal Reserve Board), in commenting on continued high unemployment and inflation, is typical, if stark: ". . . our economic system is no longer working as we once supposed." Thus, while it is clear that the self-contradictory trend toward the displacement of labor by capital is, in this sense, "irrational," it does seem to be under way, and, even in the absence of an explanation of the process, it does seem reasonable and prudent to recognize that it is in fact taking place.

Thus, the post-war transformations in the production system have created a contradictory link between the two tendencies which are the chief economic outcome of these transformations—the rising productivity of labor and the falling productivity of capital. Increased labor productivity has become a means of meeting the intensified demand for capital—a way of counteracting the tendency of the falling productivity of capital to create a shortage of capital. As a result, unemployment has become a prop to support the supply of capital, a way of preventing a shortage. But since capital thus acquired is being used to finance increasingly capital-intensive production, the process is inherently self-defeating and must eventually fail. And we now know that it *is* failing—that despite growth in output and a still-rising labor productivity (and excessive unemployment) the U.S. economy will need more capital in the next ten years than it knows how to produce.

Thus, the hope that these basic faults in the interactions among the ecosystem, the production system, and the economic system might be overcome by a rising level of production output turns out to be an illusion. It was based on the ephemeral idea that by operating fast enough the system could somehow outrun its inherent faults. However, these faults are themselves worsened by the same factors that increase the rate of production: the creation of capital- and energy-intensive means of production in order to increase labor productivity and therefore total output. A picture comes to mind: We are fleeing as fast as we can out across thin ice in the hope of outrunning the spreading cracks that are created as we run. A plunge into the deep, cold waters of reality is inevitable.

One chilling reality is that the rate of profit has been falling. Despite periodic fluctuations, the overall trend since World War II is clearly downward, and the decline has accelerated since 1966. Thus, according to a recent Bureau of Labor Statistics report, the profits (before taxes) of non-financial corporations, expressed as percent of their gross output, fell from an average of about 20 percent in 1948–52 to about 16 percent in 1966, and then dropped precipitously to about 10 percent in 1970. Profits rose slightly between 1970 and 1973 (largely due to the windfall profits occasioned by the nation's travail with the energy "shortage"), but now seem to have resumed their downward trend.

Especially in the modern, capital-intensive industries, the rate of profit is largely dependent on the rate of return on capital, and this too is trending downward. According to a 1972 report in the *Survey of Current Business,* the rate of return on net capital stock (the value of the capital representing the corporation's total investment in production, before taxes) for non-financial corporations averaged 15.9 percent in the period 1948–50, and despite fluctuations followed a general decline, reaching an average of 8.2 percent in the period 1969–71.

The falling rate of profit expresses, in a more fundamental way, the same phenomenon that the business community has brought to our attention as the "shortage of capital." However, the falling rate of profit is a real, historical phenomenon, and—unlike shortages of capital that are projected over the next decade—cannot be dismissed as guesswork or propaganda. The rate of profit depends on the ratio of the amount of profit to the amount of invested capital. As capital productivity falls—and progressively larger amounts of capital are needed to obtain the same output—the denominator of this ratio will increase and the ratio itself will shrink. The problem is fundamental because it involves the feedback, or recycling, mechanism that keeps the economic system going—the reinvestment of part of its output in new production. Under the precepts of private enterprise, what generally governs investment decisions is the expected rate of return on the investment—the rate of profit. The falling productivity of capital has a telling effect on this essential process, reinvestment, through its influence on the rate of profit:

As the rate of profit falls, the "incentive" to invest weakens, and so long as the continued functioning of the production system depends on reinvestment that is thus motivated, the system appears to be headed toward serious trouble in sustaining itself.

However, according to Mr. Simon, the fundamental fact that the rate of profit has been in a long-term decline is not well known, even within the business community, *because it has been concealed:*

> A good part of the erosion in profits in recent years has been concealed by what might be called "public relations bookkeeping." It has been hidden from shareholders and often from management itself by accounting practices which in times of major inflation fail miserably to reflect real earnings.

This astonishing admission is amply confirmed in a recent article by a leading accountant, who asserts:

> Present financial accounting does not reflect economic reality. Worse than that, it creates an illusion of enormous profits where often no true profit exists. . . . Our economic system is floundering from a severe lack of real profits essential to capital formation and preservation. Profits need enhancement, not trimming.

One can, of course, dismiss such claims simply as a greedy reach for a larger share of the wealth that the production system yields. However, what is more important than the motivation is the fact. And this seems to be attested to not only by the proponents of business, but by highly competent economists. Thus, a very detailed analysis of the problem by William D. Nordhaus begins with the flat assertion: "By most reckonings corporate profits have taken a dive since 1966," and after a searching mathematical analysis of the trend he concludes:

> The basic facts of this rather complicated argument are not in dispute. Over the post-war period the share of measured profits has declined in a dramatic way. Even after a number of corrections to obtain a conceptually cleaner definition and to adjust for cyclical factors, the

share of net capital income in net corporate income shows
a drop, albeit one less striking than the uncorrected figures
display.

From what we now know about the changes in the
production system since World War II, especially in
the energy-producing industries and in the energy-intensive sectors of production that depend on them,
there is good reason to believe that this trend is beginning to intensify. For example, the falling productivity of capital that is inherent in present energy-
production technologies means that the output of energy
produced per dollar of invested capital will fall, so that
unless there is a rise in prices, the rate of profit is
bound to fall. If, in order to maintain the rate of profit,
the price is increased, then the use of energy will, of
course, claim more of the consumer's wealth, transferring more of it to the energy industries, where it can
be accumulated as capital. The *symptom* of this situation—industry's demand for higher prices to offset the
tendency toward a falling rate of profit—provides a
handy target for protests against commercial greed and
the widening economic gap between the rich and the
poor. But more deeply perceived, such symptoms suggest a more serious and radical response—that the
economic system is so basically faulted that the relief
from them will need to be achieved by correcting their
cause.

Another of the chilling realities is the theme, ur-
gently stated, in all of the recent reports on the capital
shortage, and echoed in a crescendo of statements by
the Secretary of the Treasury and a number of in-
dustrialists: *Consumption must be reduced in the
United States*.

In very general terms, we can regard the output of
the production system as serving two ultimate economic purposes: (a) <u>consumption</u>, in which goods are
literally used up, in the economic sense; (b) capital,
representing goods which become instruments of new
production and which therefore contribute to new output. Thus, an automobile used to deliver newspapers
represents capital because it participates in a productive

process. On the other hand, if the same vehicle is used for personal activities or by the military, it yields no productive output and represents consumption rather than capital. Both guns and butter are consumption, not capital.

Obviously, then, one way to improve the supply of capital is to increase the proportion of output that goes into investment. But the only way to get more capital out of a given amount of production is to reduce consumption. This explains a veritable chorus emanating from the business community calling for reduced consumption. A few typical examples:

> Essentially, the task of accumulating enough capital means that people must save more and consume less. In a society accustomed to perhaps more than its share of material self-indulgence, that suggests a reversal of form approaching the revolutionary. [James J. Needham, president, New York Stock Exchange]

> Perhaps the most significant aspect of our three decades of post-war life was our dedication to a consumer society. . . . [Now] we lack the conviction that it is sufficiently important to forgo some of our precious consumer goods. . . . We have to face the fact that excessive emphasis on consumer spending is as harmful to our society as is excessive use of alcohol or tobacco. [Gaylord Freeman, chairman of the board, The First National Bank of Chicago]

> The critical problem seems to be that certain economic policies now create considerably stronger incentives to consume than to save and invest. [Council on Trends and Perspective, U.S. Chamber of Commerce]

There is in these recent statements a noteworthy lack of attention to the most obvious drain on capital —the enormous cost of the war in Southeast Asia. The cost of that war has been estimated, according to evidence recently provided by Senator Mansfield, at about $352 billion—most of it resources consumed and therefore unavailable for investment as capital. This is more than half the capital shortage predicted by the New York Stock Exchange for the 1975–85 period. If the ongoing "normal" U.S. military budget is added to this amount (about $112 billion in 1976), it becomes apparent that military expenditures represent the largest single drain on capital, and that even partly eliminating it could go a long way toward preventing the anticipated shortage of capital. Here is a prime target for "reduced consumption."

When the cool, professional term *consumption* is translated into the language of real life, the demands to reduce it mean that the people of the United States would be called upon to reduce their expenditures for food, clothing, housing, household goods, education, health, and recreation. It means that the government would be required to spend less on schools, hospitals, social security, welfare, and the military. Given that the proponents of reduced consumption show little sign of applying the principle to the nation's huge military budget, it becomes clear that what they have in mind is that less of the output generated by the U.S. production system should be devoted to the welfare of its people.

In his article on the falling share of profits, Professor Nordhaus asks: "[D]oes the declining share of profits portend the euthanasia of the capitalist class, and indeed of capitalism itself?" There seem to be good grounds for asking this question. One need not resort to the intricate mathematical tools of modern economics to notice a very serious and possibly fatal flaw in the position taken by the leaders of the U.S. business community in seeking a way to solve the capital crisis. They fervently appeal for more profits and less consumption. But suppose that the appeal were heard, and people consumed less. Who then would purchase industry's output, and generate sufficient sales to yield a profit large enough to feed the production system's growing demand for capital? This "solution" is reminiscent of a scheme for perpetual motion.

Economists and other students of capitalism will recognize that the basic ideas I have discussed in this chapter are among those first put forward by Karl Marx. What Marx called the "law of capital accumulation," as summarized by his colleague Frederick Engels, holds that

[C]apital is not merely reproduced; it is continually increased and multiplied. . . . However, owing to the progress of machinery . . . fewer and fewer workers are necessary in order to produce the same quantity of products. . . . They form an industrial reserve [which] is irregularly employed, or comes under the care of public Poor Law institutions.

Engels says of Marx's contributions in writing *Capital*,

The most original is the attempted proof that side by side with the concentration and accumulation of capital, and in step with it, the accumulation of a surplus working population is going on. . . . The productivity of the machine is measured by the extent to which it replaces human labor-power.

Marx believed that as capital accumulated, the amount of its fixed forms (productive machinery)—which is related to what he called the "organic composition of capital"—would increase. This is the denominator in the profit equation, and Marx believed that as this denominator grew, the rate of profit would fall. To counteract this trend, the capitalists would need to make increasing inroads on the share of production output that goes to the workers. The working class would become increasingly impoverished, and the growing conflict between capitalist and worker would lay the grounds for the revolutionary change that is the political outcome of the Marxist analysis. According to Marxist theory, this would lead to the creation of a socialist economy—in which the means of production would be socially rather than privately owned and governed—to replace the failed capitalist economy. Marx also wrote about the alienating effects, on the lives of the workers, of the relationships (especially to work itself) imposed on them by capitalist economics; he expressed a preference for more humanistic relations in society. However, the main thrust of his critique was that capitalism has deep-seated, inherent faults that must eventually lead to its failure as a viable economic system.

Marx's expectation that industrial capitalism would

fail because of the inevitable conflict between the economic roles of capital and labor has, of course, not
come about as predicted. Instead, the main industrialized economies of the world have survived, and since
his time have grown enormously—as capitalist systems. The extensive political development of states
founded on socialism—in the multifarious and to some
extent conflicting forms that it has now taken—began
in a largely agricultural country, Russia, and has more
recently spread to relatively poorly industrialized countries such as China, Cuba, nations of the Third World,
and to a few industrialized ones such as East Germany
and Czechoslovakia.

That the economic collapse of capitalism predicted
by Marx has not materialized has of course strongly affected attitudes toward the validity of his economic
analysis. A recent article in *The Washington Monthly*
on the capital shortage is so impressed by the parallel-
ism between Marx's analysis and Mr. Simon's recent
statements as to caption one page "Why Bill Simon and
Karl Marx Think There's a Capital Crisis." This article
suggests that the claims about a shortage of capital are
unwarranted and merely a new ploy to enhance corporate profits. In support of the view that neither Karl
Marx nor Mr. Simon is right about the critical state of
the capitalist system, the article suggests that

> . . . those who share Marx's view that the crisis of capital-
> ism is structural and irreparable . . . should keep in mind
> the disappointing experience of several generations of
> leftists, who have passed their entire lives waiting in vain
> for the imminent demise of capitalism.

In a curious way, an explanation of why Marx's
prediction failed to materialize—that is, until now—
emerges from the improved understanding of economic processes that is one product of the recent concern
with the environment. One of the questions that arose,
as the enormous extent of the environmental pollution
generated by modern production technology became
clear, was why this obviously harmful process could be
allowed to happen. In answer, it was pointed out that

pollution is "external" to the operation of the market-place transactions that govern a capitalist economy. In such a transaction an exchange takes place—a mutually beneficial transfer of commodities undertaken voluntarily between the parties. But pollution is neither voluntary nor mutually beneficial; as a result, the marketplace exchange takes no account of it, and there is no way of charging the cost of pollution to any party in the exchange. Since no one has to pay for it, there is nothing to keep pollution from happening. And, as we now well know, the cost is borne by society as a whole. As I pointed out in *The Closing Circle*, "A business enterprise that pollutes the environment is therefore being subsidized by society; to this extent, the enterprise, though free, is not wholly private." I pointed out as well that this arrangement leads to

> . . . [a] temporary cushioning effect of the "debt to nature" represented by environmental degradation on the conflict between entrepreneur and wage earner, which, as it now reaches its limits, may reveal this conflict in its full force. . . . In this sense, the emergence of a full-blown crisis in the ecosystem can be regarded, as well, as the signal of an emerging crisis in the economic system.

In 1971, when these words were written, there was little sign of an economic crisis in the United States: unemployment was close to its "normal" level of 4 percent; industrial capacity had been operating at 85–90 percent for several years; personal income and expenditures, industrial output, and the gross national product were all at historic highs. There were no complaints from the business community or government officials about a shortage of capital; nor were they asking the U.S. people to consume less so that more of the nation's wealth could be accumulated as capital.

Since then things have turned around dramatically. Mr. Simon and representatives of the business community like to blame some of the current capital shortage on the "unproductive" expenditures forced on industry by the country's unflagging insistence on environmental improvement. However, it seems likely that the more powerful cause of the capital shortage has been not the environmental externality, but another, closely related one represented by energy.

We can define an externality as a cost of a productive enterprise which is borne by society because it is not taken into account by the conventional mechanism of marketplace exchange. This definition applies quite well to the transactions in the oil industry that led to a situation in which ". . . a high percentage of the petroleum resources of the United States is immobilized" (in the words of the National Petroleum Council, cited earlier, in Chapter 3). Clearly the nation is paying a huge social cost for the decision by the major U.S. oil companies to abandon the full development of domestic petroleum resources in favor of more profitable adventures in the Mideast. The disruption of life during the 1973 oil crisis is the smallest part of that cost. The rest of it is the huge increase in the price of fuel, which has triggered an unprecedented rate of inflation and suddenly turned the course of the U.S. economy around and sent it skidding into a serious decline. Like the fumes emitted by the oil industry's refineries, this huge and still-spreading economic disaster was in no way anticipated or accounted for in the ordinary marketplace operations of the U.S. capitalist system. "Project Independence" is proof of that. This declares as a "national goal" that the United States should become free of imports for its energy supply. Clearly this social purpose did not form a natural part of the operation of the free-enterprise system as practiced by the large oil companies. Quite the contrary: The abandonment of the proper development of the domestic oil supply, the nation's inevitable dependence on foreign oil, and the ensuing economic problems were a natural outcome of the operation of the free-enterprise marketplace. Thus, like the environmental crisis before it, the energy crisis illuminates a fundamental fact about the way in which the capitalist system seems to work in these areas: it appears to be singularly incapable of responding, by its own internal mechanisms, to social needs such as a livable environment or a reliable petroleum resource.

By the same criterion, the U.S. private-enterprise system has also been unable to meet a whole series of essential social needs that have been discussed here: development of energy resources that are renewable and non-polluting; of agricultural, transportation, and manufacturing production technologies that use energy efficiently and minimize environmental impact; of production processes that are sparing in their demand for capital and provide rewarding and safe opportunities for employment.

One reason for this failure has already been illustrated: In the development of each new production technology, the operative decision has not been the social need that some task—keeping a home warm, moving people to and from work, feeding and clothing them—should be accomplished at least cost in energy, capital, and environmental degradation, and in a way that provides meaningful employment. Rather, in every instance the governing principle has been maximum profitability, which seems so frequently to contradict these goals. Of course, laws have been passed to correct environmental pollution and some have been proposed to conserve energy, but these laws have failed to get at the root of the environmental problem—the faulty design of production technology—and, despite great efforts, only minor progress has been made. In the context of the private-enterprise system, all of these socially desirable ends are "externalities" and suffer the neglect that is their common fate in that system.

Another reason why the capitalist economy is unable to meet many social needs is that it is based on the exchange of commodities—privately owned goods that are produced for profitable exchange in the marketplace. In the energy sector what is produced is oil, coal, and uranium; power plants, furnaces, and air-conditioners; automobiles, trucks, and airplanes. The *social need* is for a system that efficiently applies energy toward a suitable task, but this need is met solely by thrusting these commodities into the marketplace and hoping for the best. A furnace is not manufactured and sold as the manufacturer's most effective contribution to the social need that people's homes shall be maintained at 70° in the winter. If the manufacturer's purpose were defined by that thermodynamic task, then what would be sold would not necessarily be a furnace at all, but perhaps a heat pump or a solar collector. In the absence of such a task-oriented, *social* motivation, we have been provided with the wrong kinds of heating and cooling devices, the wrong kinds of automobiles and freight carriers, the wrong kinds of power plants, the wrong kinds of fuels. No society, however wise or disciplined, can readily make a rational *system* for the efficient production and use of energy out of such inappropriate ingredients. These goods have not been foisted on us out of malice, or even—in most cases—out of personal greed. These inappropriate, wasteful, and sometimes harmful commodities have been produced and sold as the logical embodiment of the accepted principle which in a capitalist economy governs what is produced—the maximization of profit.

In the last thirty years many thousands of production decisions have been made in the United States. They have determined that automobiles shall be large and sufficiently powerful to travel at a rate of 100 mph; that electricity shall be produced by nuclear power plants; that we shall wear synthetic materials instead of cotton and wool, and wash them in detergent rather than soap; that baseball shall be played on plastic rather than grass; that the beneficent energy of sunlight shall go largely unused. In every case, the decision was made according to the "bottom line"—the expectation of an acceptable profit. More precisely, as we have seen from the behavior of U.S. oil companies, such decisions are based on the marginal difference between existing rates of profit and hoped-for, larger ones. It would have been a fantastically improbable statistical accident if most or even a small fraction of these thousands of decisions, made on the basis of a hoped-for marginal increase in profit, happened neatly to fit into the pattern of a rational, thermodynamically sound energy system. Such an energy system is a social need, and it is hopeless to expect to build it on the basis of production decisions that yield commodities rather than the solutions to essential tasks; that produce goods which are maximally profitable rather than maximally useful; that accept as their final test private profit rather than social value.

Thus, the energy crisis and the web of inter-related problems confront us with the need to explore the possibility of creating a production system that is consciously intended to serve social needs and that judges the value of its products by their use, and an economic system that is committed to these purposes. At least in principle, such a system is socialism.

There has, of course, been a long-standing political taboo against casting the issues of current policy in terms which question the capability or usefulness of the capitalist system, let alone suggest that it be openly compared with so "foreign" an alternative as socialism. However, it has become increasingly difficult to discuss any serious issue of national policy without raising questions which touch so deeply on the capitalist system's basic faults as to become—even if they are not so intended—a criticism of the system itself.

For example, if, as industrial leaders claim, the rate of profit in the oil industry and other major sectors of production must be *increased* if they are to survive as viable economic enterprises, then criticism of increased profits can be regarded as an attack on private enterprise itself. And—again taking business leaders at their word that the capital which is essential to the survival of capitalism cannot now be accumulated unless the people of the United States "consume less"—then any quite non-revolutionary protest against this policy is likely to be interpreted as a commentary on capitalism itself. If it is in fact true that U.S. capitalism is in such straits that it must give up its long-standing claim to produce both good profits for the capitalist and the good life for the worker, then it would seem only prudent to acknowledge this state of affairs and to recognize that a proposal merely to reform capitalism will become a threat to replace it.

It has often been argued that the U.S. economic system has failed to exhibit the distinctive faults of capitalism which form the basis, in Marx's analysis, for the theory of socialism, and that the socialist reorganization of that system is therefore uncalled for. However, now its proponents have themselves acknowledged that the U.S. economic system has in fact experienced a falling rate of profit (albeit obscured by "public relations bookkeeping") which seems to be closely related to the displacement of labor by capital. Moreover, their proposed solution is to reduce "consumption," a measure which surely would also reduce the share that workers receive of the wealth that the system produces. These are in fact precisely the diagnostic faults that Marx attributed to capitalism. And, as we have seen, the effect of these faults has been minimized until now by temporary "externalities." But the environmental and energy crises signal that these expedients are no longer effective and that the inherent faults of the capitalist system will now appear in full force. Although economists can, of course, provide alternative explanations for these phenomena, their general similarity to the faults which are the substance of the socialist critique of capitalism suggests that there are grounds to at least consider the possibility that the pervasive and seemingly insoluble faults now exhibited by the United States' economic system can best be remedied by reorganizing it along socialist lines.

Some will argue that the U.S. capitalist system has served us long and well, and that the present difficulties should require only a temporary adjustment rather than a reorganization that alters the basic principle of private enterprise. However, there is growing evidence that, in response to the failing supply of capital, the system is *already* being reorganized—by the private entrepreneurs themselves. Once again, the energy industry, and public utilities in particular—where, as we have seen, the capital shortage is most acute—are leading the way. Unable to raise their own investment funds, some private utility companies are taking the unprecedented (and possibly illegal) step of acquiring capital by charging their customers for it. For example, in Missouri the Union Electric Company has just received approval from the Public Service Commission to charge the capital cost of constructing a nuclear power plant to its present customers (although they will receive no power from this plant, which is due to be completed in 1983, if then). Since the utilities' capital is the base on which the customers' electric rates are computed, the customers will be paying the utilities a return on capital which they themselves have furnished. As a letter to the local newspaper put it, ". . . what we have here is a case of socialism for Union Electric and private enterprise for its customers." In California, utilities are asking that their customers pay the costs of options to purchase Alaskan natural gas when and if it becomes available in about ten years. And, of course, the Ford administration's proposal to use $100 billion of public funds to guarantee private investments in synthetic fuels and other profit-motivated adventures into new energy sources is a similar maneuver. These instances are real, empirical evidence that at least in the energy sector there *is* a shortage of capital; that private entrepreneurs are unable to meet capital requirements out of their own earnings; and that they are not so devoted to the ideology of private capital as to reject *social* capital—when they need it. In this sense the economic reorganization of the utilities has already begun. The question that arises is whether their expanding social economic base will be reflected in some form of public, social control, so that the production and use of their power can be governed by social values rather than by private profit.

It will be argued, as well, that a socialist economy is necessarily rigorously planned, highly centralized, and therefore incompatible with the individual freedom that is the foundation of U.S. democracy. It has been forcefully argued that it would be disastrous to give up this cherished political freedom for the dictatorial rule that has accompanied the establishment of socialism in other countries. History has demonstrated the reality of this danger. (At the same time, current history—in the form of the scandalous revelations of Watergate and the Congressional investigations of the FBI and the CIA—also demonstrates that political freedom is endangered in the United States, often on the pretense of countering real or imagined critics of its economic and political systems.) However, there appears to be nothing in basic socialist theory that *requires* the establishment of a totally centralized economy, or of political repression to enforce it. There is now a sharp divergence, even within the Communist left, regarding the political forms that are appropriate to a socialist economy. This is evident in the basic disagreement between the two largest and most powerful socialist states—the U.S.S.R. and the People's Republic of China. More relevant to the issue in the U.S. are the policies recently adopted by several European Communist parties. Thus, according to a recent report in the *New York Times:*

> The two largest Communist parties in Western Europe, the Italian and the French, agreed in an unusual joint statement today [November 16, 1975] that the way to power was through the democratic systems of their countries. . . . In their statement, the two parties pledged themselves to guarantee "freedom of thought and expression and freedom of the press and religious freedom." They also backed "the plurality of political parties" and "the right of existence and activity of opposition parties."

To underscore their position, the Italian party newspaper said that the refusal of the Soviet government to allow the dissident physicist Andrei Sakharov to leave the U.S.S.R. to receive the Nobel Peace Prize "confirms the existence of an unresolved problem in the life of the Soviet State: the problem of dissent."

It seems unrealistic, then, at this moment in history, to categorically reject a socialist economy on the grounds that its political form is necessarily repressive and therefore abhorrent to the democratic freedoms that are the foundation of political life in the United States. That no existing example of a socialist society —whether the U.S.S.R., China, or Cuba—is consistent with both the economic democracy of socialism and the political democracy inherent in U.S. tradition means that wholly new political forms would need to be created. It is appropriate, in 1976, to remind ourselves that such radical political innovation is a 200-year-old, if long-neglected, tradition in the United States.

All this suggests that it may be time to view the

faults of the U.S. capitalist economic system from the vantage point of a socialist alternative—to debate the relative merits of capitalism and socialism. Such a debate is now the central issue of political life in Europe, and it is perhaps time for the people of the United States to enter into it as well.

There are signs that the process has already begun. For example, at the recent National Democratic Issues Convention, organized by the liberal wing of the Democratic Party, in Louisville, Kentucky, leading economists debated the merits of a position paper that proposed measures not usually regarded as compatible with private enterprise. These included public ownership of corporations in energy, transportation, and defense; employee management and ownership of other corporations; and economic planning by local community councils. The authors of this paper, economists Gar Alperovitz and Jeff Faux, point to recent opinion polls indicating that a considerable segment of the public recognizes that the economic system is not working and is interested in radical alternatives to it. According to a Washington *Post* report of the meeting:

> John Kenneth Galbraith told the Louisville session no thinking person can dismiss their paper out of hand. Their analysis points vividly to flaws in the present system—flaws that both parties have been attacking with classic methods and without much success.

Indeed, Galbraith has himself given cogent reasons why, in the United States today,

> for unduly weak industries and unduly strong ones—as a remedy for an area of gross underdevelopment and as a control on gross overdevelopment—the word socialism is one we can no longer suppress.

The entry of such debates into the political life of the nation may have some immediate benefits. They may help to alleviate, or at least to explain, the dismal floundering, uncertainty, and self-contradictory arguments that have marked the attempt to create an "energy policy." Administrators and legislators in

Washington may have perceived that there is a very short political distance between questions of energy policy and the profound and very disturbing faults in the economic system to which they are connected. Only a few years ago *nationalization* was a term that brought averted eyes or nervous titters in Washington. Now, out of necessity, it is regarded—in a very gingerly fashion, it is true—as one possible way to deal with the problems of the railroads and even of the energy industry. It is as though those who are wrestling with energy policy have begun to suspect that they are only flirting with a symptom of a basic, radical issue. They may have become fearful of probing too deeply lest, in the process, the radical issue be thrust explosively upon a nation that is not yet prepared to discuss it rationally.

A distinguished journalist, John B. Oakes, of the *New York Times,* has recently written movingly about the deepening anguish of America: "[H]ave our concepts of government and society kept pace with the technological progress of mankind?" He then describes what we must do to confront that question:

> The new era requires new leadership, new creativity, a willingness to evaluate new ideas and new concepts and new relationships with the kind of courage and conscience that our history and our heritage have bestowed upon us.

We will not know how best to answer this question until we have the collective courage to ask it; we will not have the "willingness to evaluate new ideas" until we have the wisdom to evaluate old ones.

HERE WE COME to the end of the blind, mindless chain of events that transformed the technologies of agricultural and industrial production and reorganized transportation; that increased the output of the production system, but increased even more its appetite for capital, energy, and other resources; that eliminated jobs and degraded the environment; that concentrated the physical power of energy and the social power of the resultant wealth into ever fewer, larger corporations; that has fed this power on a diet of unemployment and poverty. Here is the basic fault that has spawned the environmental crisis and the energy crisis, and that threatens—if no remedy is found—to engulf us in the wreckage of a crumbling economic system.

Now all this has culminated in the ignominious confession of those who hold the power: That the capitalist economic system which has loudly proclaimed itself the best means of assuring a rising standard of living for the people of the United States, can now survive, if at all, only by reducing that standard. The powerful have confessed to the poverty of their power.

No one can escape the momentous consequences of this confession. No one can escape the duty to understand the origin of this historic default and to transform it from a threat to social progress into a signal for a new advance.

NOTES

Chapter 1
THE PROBLEM

Page 1
Clashing efforts to solve crises separately: Many examples can be found in the newspapers. Particularly striking examples are in newspaper advertisements of oil companies, especially during the 1973 oil crisis, claiming that their efforts to produce domestic oil were being impeded by "environmentalists." A current example is that the AFL-CIO in California is opposing a legislative initiative that would place certain additional requirements, relative to safety, on nuclear power plants, on the grounds that a slowdown in construction of such plants would cost jobs. I have discussed the apparent conflict between jobs and environment in an article, "The Workplace Burden," in *Environment,* vol. 15, 1973.

Page 3
Lightly disguised threats to invade oil-producing countries: The following appeared in an Associated Press story (St. Louis *Post-Dispatch,* January 4, 1975): "Secretary of State Henry A. Kissinger 'did reflect the President's views' when he said the United States would consider using military force in the Middle East 'in the gravest emergency.' In an earlier interview with *Business Week* Kissinger had said in response to a question as to whether he had considered military action in response to the elevation of oil prices by Mideast producers: 'I am not saying that there's no circumstance where we would not use force. But it is one thing to use it in the case of a dispute over price, it's another where there's some actual strangulation of the industrialized world.'" Earlier an article in *Newsweek,* October 7, 1974, had quoted a "top U.S. official" as saying that "If the oil-producing nations drive the world into depression in their greed, the West might be forced into a desperate military adventure." The article is accompanied by sketches illustrating an airborne attack on oil fields.

Chapter 2
THERMODYNAMICS, THE SCIENCE OF ENERGY

Page 6
Bridgman, quotation: This statement is taken from P. W. Bridgman: *The Nature of Thermodynamics* (Cambridge: Harvard University Press; 1943), p. 3.

Pages 8–9
Time irreversibility; motion pictures running backward: For a further discussion of this topic, see Richard Feynman: *The Character of*

Physical Law (Cambridge: MIT Press; 1967). This is a remarkable book by a remarkable scientist—a marvelous combination of deep scientific insight and lucid explanation. It is based on a series of public lectures and the language is straightforward and readily accessible to the non-scientist. In writing this chapter, I have relied a good deal on some of Feynman's ideas.

Page 10
The experiments of Count Rumford: These are described in S. W. Angrist and L. G. Helper: *Order and Chaos: Laws of Energy and Entropy* (New York: Basic Books; 1967), pp. 10–15.

Page 12
The perpetual-motion ship: See Hans Thirring: *Energy for Man* (New York: Greenwood Press; 1968), pp. 19–20. Thirring's book is an excellent account of the basic physics of energy production, if somewhat dated (and overly optimistic) in the area of nuclear energy.

Page 19
Second Law of Thermodynamics, quotation: G. N. Lewis and M. Randall: *Thermodynamics*, second edition (New York: McGraw-Hill; 1961), p. 92.

Pages 19–20
Probability of a spontaneous upward leap: See G. N. Lewis: *The Anatomy of Science* (New Haven: Yale University Press; 1926), p. 145. In this book, G. N. Lewis, a physical chemist with a rare and wide-ranging grasp of science, exhibits these gifts in a lively, readable way.

Pages 20–21
Wiener, quotation: This statement is from Norbert Wiener's book *The Human Use of Human Beings* (New York: Doubleday; 1954), p. 21.

Pages 22–23
Carnot's pamphlet: See Nicolas Léonard Sadi Carnot, *Réflexions sur la Puissance Motrice du Feu* (Paris, 1824; reissued in Librairie Scientifique et Technique, Paris: A. Blanchard; 1953). Dover Press has published an English translation, but it is out of print.

Page 24
Quotation, Second Law of Thermodynamics: This statement appears in R. P. Feynman, R. B. Leighton, and M. Sands, *The Feynman Lectures on Physics* (New York: Addison-Wesley; 1963), Vol. 1, pp. 44–13.

Page 25
Entropy: The only rigorous way to define this term is mathematically: If an amount of heat is added, reversibly, to a system at a given temperature, then the resultant *change* in entropy is equal to the amount of added heat divided by the temperature. Although entropy is an abstract concept, it can be related mathematically to the more concrete thermodynamic factors that have been discussed in this chapter: order, probability, and information. For example, as Feynman puts it (see *Feynman Lectures*, Vol. 1, pp. 46–7): "We measure 'disorder' by the number of ways that the insides [of a

system] can be arranged, so that from the outside it looks the same. *The logarithm of that number of ways is entropy.*"

Page 25

The laws of thermodynamics, in general: Anyone interested in a deeper understanding of thermodynamics will find, as I have, that there is a bewildering variety of approaches to the subject which end up at the same place from different starting points. Obviously, the description provided in this chapter is far from rigorous or complete. I have tried only to provide some understandable points of contact between the main principles of thermodynamics and the more or less concrete experiences of ordinary life. Perhaps the best place to find a mathematical but understandable explanation of thermodynamics is in Chapters 44, 45, and 46 of Volume 1 of the *Feynman Lectures.* My colleague Professor Ron Lovett was kind enough to review an early draft of this chapter and to point out some of my specific blunders. Since he also gave me a cogently reasoned argument for an approach to the whole subject quite different from the one that I have adopted, it should be clear that, despite his greatly appreciated help, he should in no way be regarded as responsible for any remaining errors, whether specific or general. I am also grateful to him and to several other colleagues—in particular, Professor Sam Weissman, Professor Herbert Yaris, and Professor Tom Sandell—for enlightening discussions about thermodynamics, among other subjects, during many pleasant lunches.

Page 26

BTU of energy: The abbreviation stands for British Thermal Units. Both the scientist and the lay person have a bewildering choice of energy and related units. I have tried to use only a few familiar ones in this book: BTU, kilocalorie (3.97 BTU) and kilowatt-hour (3413 BTU); all of these are units of energy. The BTU, while a familiar unit, is a very small one, so that it frequently becomes necessary to speak of trillions of them. The only unit of power (energy flow per unit time) used in this book is watts and kilowatts (1000 watts). It is useful to think of a kilowatt as a kilowatt-hour divided by hours (and thus energy per hour).

Chapter 3
THE FOSSIL FUELS: OIL

Page 30

Automotive, petrochemical, and petroleum industries make up nearly one-fifth of the total U.S. economy: The estimate is based on data taken from the *Survey of Current Business,* August 1975. Total sales of the following industries were added together to provide a rough estimate of the portion of the economy that is devoted to these sectors. Total sales = $286.5 billion (20.5 percent of 1974 GNP). Industries included are: transportation equipment, chemicals and allied products, petroleum and coal products, rubber and plastics products, and sales of utility gas. Some oil is used to produce electric power.

Page 31

Recession in the auto industry: In 1973 the auto industry employed an average of 1,891,000 workers. The 1974 average fell to 1,786,000 and reached a low of 1,556,000 in February 1975. Total production of vehicles was 20.4 percent lower in 1974 than in 1973, implying a similar reduction in plant-capacity utilization. These data are from the August 1975 issue of the *Survey of Current Business,* Department of Commerce, Washington, D.C.

Page 31
Public-opinion polls: St. Louis *Globe-Democrat,* September 23, 1975; article describing the results of a poll by Cambridge Reports, Inc.

Pages 31–32
Available amounts of petroleum products: See K. Shea, "Oil: The Glut Worsens," *Environment,* September 1974, p. 4.

Page 32
Informative but rarely discussed reports: The most important and revealing of these reports is *U.S. Energy Outlook: Oil and Gas Availability* (Washington, D.C.: National Petroleum Council; 1973), an enormously detailed analysis of the projected capability of domestic energy production in the period 1971–85 carried out by a committee of the National Petroleum Council. The NPC occupies a strange and powerful position in the Federal government. It is described as ". . . an officially established industry advisory board to the Secretary of the Interior," but until the recent establishment of the Federal Energy Administration it was in fact the main source of the government's own information about petroleum, gas, and other energy resources. When, in January 1970, the NPC was asked by the Assistant Secretary of the Interior to appraise the availability of domestic energy sources, it responded by setting up "a committee structure of over 200 representatives of oil, gas, coal, nuclear and other energy-related fields, as well as a number of financial experts." The composition was not exactly "representative" since it included only specialists from major energy companies and related corporations, a few members of the NPC staff, and one or two specialists from the Geological Survey and the Atomic Energy Commission. Not one university professor or any other specialist who might be regarded as independent of the energy industries was included. The study therefore represents industry's view of the nation's energy problem. The enormous amount of detailed information in the report, which far outweighs that available from the regular government agencies, is direct proof of the frequently voiced allegation that the government's own knowledge of fossil-fuel resources is based on what the industry provides. The report's main conclusion, as concisely expressed in the NPC chairman's letter of transmittal (see the Summary Report, December 1972, p. 330), asserts flatly that there would be no shortage of energy in the United States, provided that Federal policies were changed to meet the industry's financial demands:

U.S. energy supplies, including oil and gas, are not expected to be limited by potentially discoverable [domestic] resources during the 1971–1985 period. If federal policies are designed to encourage large expenditures by private industry for new supplies and for improved recovery from producing and prospective areas, including public lands onshore and offshore, then the potential exists for significant expansion of U.S. oil and gas reserves and production, possibly even beyond the amounts projected in this report. Prompt improvements in federal policies could result in expanded domestic supplies of energy; such improvements are essential before vast sums are committed to more expensive energy alternatives.

A good deal of the more recent government documentation—for example, by FEA—is based on the NPC study. Even now the government—and the people of the United States—must depend on the industry for most of the information about fossil-fuel resources, much of which is Federal property. What is remarkable about the NPC study and the subsidiary documents is that they contain so much of the raw data that are needed to develop one's own understanding of what the industry, in concert with the government, has done that has resulted in the present state of affairs, in which (to quote one of their own reports cited in the note for p. 53) ". . . a high percentage of petroleum resources in the United States is immobilized."

Page 34
World and U.S. per-capita oil consumption: For consumption data, see: *Energy Perspectives,* U.S. Department of the Interior (Washington, D.C.: U.S. Government Printing Office; 1975). This is an excellent reference for general data on the overall patterns of energy production. Data on U.S. population come from the *Statistical Abstract of the U.S.,* U.S. Bureau of the Census (Washington, D.C.: U.S. Government Printing Office, 1971 and 1974 editions used). Data on world population come from the Population Reference Bureau, 1775 Massachusetts Avenue, Washington, D.C., 1974.

Page 34
How petroleum fuels are used: The data are U.S. averages for 1968 and are taken from Stanford Research Institute: *Patterns of Energy Consumption in the United States,* Report for the Office of Science and Technology (Washington, D.C.: U.S. Government Printing Office; January 1972).

Pages 35–36
First and Second Law efficiencies: See *Efficient Use of Energy,* APS Studies on the Technical Aspects of the More Efficient Use of Energy, edited by K. W. Ford *et al.* (New York: American Institute of Physics; 1975), pp. 4, 32, 35. This is an extremely important study which, it is to be hoped, will mark a historic turning point in the proper evaluation of the U.S. energy system. The importance of Second Law (in contrast to First Law) computation of energy efficiency had been earlier recognized by physicists and engineers; in particular see Charles Berg's paper, "A Technical Basis for Energy Conservation," in *Technology Review,* February 1974, p. 14; and J. H. Keenan *et al.,* "The Fuel Shortage and Thermodynamics," in *Proceedings of the MIT Conference* (Cambridge, Mass.: MIT Press; 1973). However, the APS study was the first effort to delineate in a comprehensive way what thermodynamics tells us about how to compute the efficiency with which energy is used and to apply the procedures to a wide range of typical energy processes. The study is a good example of how experience in a purely "aca-

demic" field (in this case, physics) can be used to achieve important results when that experience is applied, in a fundamental way, to issues that arise in society rather than in the laboratory. An excellent summary of the APS study will be found in *Physics Today*, August 1975, p. 23.

Pages 38–39
The origin of the atmosphere: This is discussed in my earlier book *The Closing Circle* (New York: Alfred A. Knopf; 1971), pp. 17–21. For a detailed description of the process, see L. U. Berkner, and L. C. Marshall, "History of Major Atmospheric Components," *Proceedings of the National Academy of Sciences,* Vol. 53 (1965), p. 1215 ff.

Page 39
Past and anticipated rates of world fossil-fuel consumption: See M. K. Hubbert's article, "Energy Resources," in *Resources and Man,* National Academy of Sciences (San Francisco: W. H. Freeman and Co.; 1969).

Page 39
Total amount of carbon deposited: I wish to thank Professor Ron Lovett for carrying out this computation.

Page 39
Maximum depth of coal seams: This information was provided by the Peabody Coal Company, St. Louis, Missouri.

Page 39
Total world coal supplies and their longevity: See S. S. Penner and L. Icerman: *Energy: Demands, Resources, Impact, Technology and Policy* (Reading, Mass.: Addison-Wesley), Vol. 1 (1974), pp. 123, 126.

Page 40
Eight out of ten exploratory wells are "dry holes": See *Petroleum Facts and Figures* (Washington, D.C.: National Petroleum Council; 1971), p. 26. (Data for 1968.)

Page 41
Oil recovery rate: Data regarding the trend in this rate are given in *U.S. Energy Outlook* (cited above), p. 48. The higher value cited is extrapolated from this trend.

Page 41
Decline in petroleum reserve after 1967: See *Petroleum Facts and Figures,* 1971 (cited above), p. 110, for trends in the size of the reserve.

Page 42
Decreasing rate of finding oil: See *Petroleum Facts and Figures,* 1971 (cited above), p. 110, for yearly data on this rate.

Page 42
Oil imports: See *ibid.* and *Monthly Energy Review* (FEA) (January 1975), p. 9, for these data.

Page 42
Mr. Kissinger's belligerent comment: See note for p. 3.

Page 45
Oil-company estimates of recoverable oil: These are tabulated in
Energy Perspectives (cited above), p. 84.

Page 45
Offshore-oil estimates: See Penner and Icerman, Energy, Vol. 1
(cited above), p. 113.

Page 46
M. K. Hubbert, quotations: From "Degree of Advancement of
Petroleum Exploration in the United States," West Texas Geological
Society Symposium on Economics and the Petroleum Geologist
(Midland, Texas: October 1966), pp. 138, 161.

Page 47
Zapp's technique for measuring rate of oil discoveries: This was
originally described in A. D. Zapp: "World Petroleum Resources
in Domestic and World Resources of Fossil Fuels, Radioactive
Minerals, and Geothermal Energy: Preliminary Reports Prepared
by Members of the U.S. Geological Survey for the Natural Resources Subcommittee of the Federal Science Council, Nov. 28,
1961" (unpublished). Cited by Hubbert—see reference in preceding
note.

Page 47
Hubbert, quotation: See p. 161 reference in note for p. 46.

Page 47
National Academy of Sciences report: Mineral Resources and the
Environment, a report prepared by Committee on Mineral Resources
and the Environment (COMRATE), Commission on Natural Re-
sources, National Research Council (Washington, D.C.: National
Academy of Sciences; February 1975).

Pages 47–48
Reason for decline in oil found per foot of exploratory well: This
issue has been raised by S. Fred Singer in Science, Vol. 188: 4187
(May 2, 1975), p. 401. The basic issue here is that Hubbert prefers
to draw a smoothly declining curve through the Zapp plot, whereas
in fact the plot shows that the finding rate per foot of exploratory
well drilled falls in several abrupt drops and—most important—has
remained essentially constant in the last twenty years. Hubbert
argues that the failure of the rate to drop as he would expect in
this time is a result of especially rich finds in Louisiana, but this
argument runs counter to his basic position that we are "running
out" of easily findable oil.

Pages 48–49
Declining exploration: For data on trends, see Energy Perspectives
(cited above), p. 124; and Geophysics, 22:1 (1957), pp. 59, 105;
and 38:2 (1973), p. 410.

Page 49
Potential oil reserves: See Future Petroleum Provinces of the United
States (Washington, D.C.; National Petroleum Council; July 1970).

Page 50
Quotations: See Future Petroleum Provinces (cited above), p. 113
and pp. 1–2.

Page 51
Profitability of U.S. petroleum companies: See the article by H. W. Blauvelt, vice-president of the Continental Oil Company, "How to Become a Foreign Oil Company," in *Exploration and Economics of the Petroleum Industry* (Houston, Texas: Gulf Publishing Co.; 1966), p. 273.

Pages 51–52
Blauvelt, quotations: See his article, cited above, pp. 268–9, 272, 275.

Page 52
That total national demand for oil for the next 50–60 years could be met by domestic production: The crucial policy question here is to estimate the amount of oil that we can expect to produce in the future from domestic sources. This amount is the sum of the present existing recoverable reserves and the amount of recoverable oil (that is, the amount that can actually be taken out of the ground) which is as yet undiscovered but which we might expect to find in the future. In 1974 the existing recoverable reserves came to about 35 billion barrels of crude oil. At that time about 110 billion barrels had already been taken from the ground, so that about 145 billion barrels of recoverable oil had already been found. Determination of the amount of future discoveries is generally made by estimating the *total* amount of recoverable oil that will eventually be found and subtracting 145 billion barrels from that figure. The estimates of total recoverable oil vary a great deal, from Hubbert's figure of about 175 billion barrels to Zapp's value of 600 billion barrels. Estimates of about 450 billion barrels have been made in several government reports and by a study of the National Petroleum Council, *Future Petroleum Provinces of the United States* (cited above). As pointed out in this chapter, the higher estimates are the more reliable ones because they are based on an evaluation of the depletion process that takes into account the voluntary curtailment of exploration by the oil companies. According to these higher estimates, then, some 300 billion barrels of recoverable oil remain to be found. Together with present reserves (about 35 billion barrels) this comes to about 335 billion barrels available for future use. Since the present rate of total oil consumption in the United States (that is, of domestic and imported oil) is about 6.3 billion barrels per year, at this rate the potentially available supply would last fifty to sixty years. (For data on consumption, see *Energy Perspectives,* cited above, p. 91.)

Page 53
Cost of producing available domestic oil: See *Oil: Possible Levels of Future Production,* Final Task Force Report, Project Independence, FEA (Washington, D.C., November 1974). The specific data referred to in this discussion will be found on pp. IV-2 and IV-21 of that report. The values for capital productivity of oil production and the cost of oil over the period 1975–88 were computed from data provided for 1974, 1977, 1980, 1985, and 1988, for the production of and capital investment in oil.

Page 54
Price of oil in early 1975: The price cited ($7 per barrel) represents the average price of oil at the refinery as given by the *Monthly*

Energy Review, FEA, August 1975, converted to 1973 dollars using the inflation index given in *Survey of Current Business.* Here and elsewhere in the book, prices are given in "uninflated dollars" in order to compare the price of the same material in two or more different years in a way that eliminates the effect of inflation. The general procedure is based on tables of "implicit price deflators" published by the U.S. Department of Commerce. These give the value of different classes of expenditures (such as the GNP, personal expenditures, or wholesale prices) for various years relative to the value in some base year. Thus in this case, the price of oil in 1975 was "deflated" to what it would cost if purchased in 1973 dollars by determining the ratio of prices in 1975 to those in 1973 from the table of deflators for consumer prices published monthly in *Survey of Current Business.* This ratio measures the effect of inflation of general commodity prices over that period of time. It will be noticed that in different places in this book different base years (in the above case, 1973) are used in computing the deflated value, rather than, in every instance, converting the values to a common base (such as 1958, which is often used in economic computations). This procedure was adopted in order to depart as little as possible from the base lines used in the source materials themselves (which of course varied), thereby minimizing manipulation of the original data.

Page 55
Quotations on rate of return: See *U.S. Energy Outlook* (cited above), p. 71. In the quoted statement, the word *price* is enclosed in quotation marks because it is computed and not real. However, since the publication of this study the high "prices" that it projects have become real enough.

Page 57
Quotation: This is from the FEA Task Force report *Oil: Possible Levels of Future Production* (cited above), p. 1.

Page 57
Purchase of the Montgomery Ward mail-order business by the Mobil Oil Company: "Mobil Oil Corporation announced its $800 million acquisition of controlling interest in MARCOR has been completed," *Wall Street Journal,* September 25, 1974, p. 8.

Page 57
Tendency of oil companies to invest their capital in chemicals: See *Chemical and Engineering News,* January 6, 1975, p. 7.

Page 58
Quotation: John J. Dorgan, executive vice-president, Occidental Oil Corp., quoted in *Newsweek,* August 11, 1975, p. 3.

Page 58
G. C. Hardin, quotation: "Economic Parameters in Prospect Evaluation," West Texas Geological Society Symposium on Economics and the Petroleum Geologist (cited above), p. 90.

Page 59
Quotations from Oil and Gas Journal *article:* Issue of August 18, 1975, p. 29.

Page 59
Current return of oil companies: See *Business Week* Quarterly
Profits Survey, 2nd quarter, 1975.

Page 59
Petroleum companies' return on stockholders' equity 1951–71: See
E. W. Erickson and R. M. Spann, "The U.S. Petroleum Industry"
in *The Energy Question,* Vol. 2, E. W. Erickson and L. Woseman,
eds. (University of Toronto Press; 1974), pp. 8–10. The petroleum
industry figure is the average for the eight largest corporations, which
dominate the industry.

Page 59
Gulf Oil official quotation: Oil and Gas Journal article cited above,
p. 33.

Page 59
Capital need for world petroleum production: See *How Much Oil—
How Much Investment,* Energy Economics Division, Chase Man-
hattan Bank, March 1975.

Chapter 4
THE FOSSIL FUELS: COAL

Page 61
Coal reserves: See, for example, M. K. Hubbert's article "Energy
Resources" in *Resources and Man,* National Academy of Sciences
(cited above).

Page 61
The U.S. exports rather than imports coal: In 1974 U.S. exports of
coal were $2.5 billion, according to *Survey of Current Business,*
August 1975, p. S-23.

Page 62
$100-billion government energy corporation: This proposal is de-
scribed in the St. Louis *Post-Dispatch,* October 5, 1975, p. 1-B.

Page 63
Coal consumption in the U.S.: See *Patterns of Energy Consumption
in the United States* (cited above), p. 26.

Page 63
Second Law efficiencies of coal use: See *Efficient Use of Energy*
(cited above), p. 50.

Page 63
Second Law efficiencies of space heat and hot water: See *ibid.,* p. 84.

Page 63
Percent of coal-fired electricity used for space heat and hot water:
See *Patterns of Energy Consumption in the United States* (cited
above), p. 26.

Page 64
Efficiency of combined electric/heat systems: See *Efficient Use of
Energy* (cited above), p. 87.

Page 66
Capital productivity of coal mining: See *U.S. Energy Outlook: Coal Availability* (Washington, D.C.: National Petroleum Council; 1973), p. 38.

Page 67
Reclamation and health costs of surface coal mines: See G. E. Dials and E. C. Moore: "The Cost of Coal," *Environment,* 16:7 (September 1974), pp. 30–31, 35.

Page 67
Compensatory payments for black-lung victims: See *ibid.,* p. 30.

Page 68
Water requirements of coal mining and synthetic-fuel production: See *Project Independence Blueprint,* "Task Force Report—Coal," p. 55; and "Task Force Report—The Potential Future Role of Oil Shale: Prospects and Constraints," p. 50; FEA, U.S. Department of the Interior (Washington, D.C.: U.S. Government Printing Office; November 1974).

Page 68
In the United States, 75–80 percent of the cancer incidence is due to environmental agents: For a further discussion of this problem, see J. L. Steinfeld (Surgeon General of the U.S. Public Health Service): "Environment and Cancer: Detecting and Eradicating Hazards in our Environment," in *Environment and Cancer,* papers presented at the twenty-fourth annual Symposium on Fundamental Cancer Research, 1971 (Baltimore: Williams and Wilkins; 1972), p. 43. I have summarized the present state of the problem and possible approaches to solving it in several articles in *Hospital Practice:* February 1975, p. 43; March 1975, p. 82; October 1975, p. 138.

Pages 68–69
Cancer rates near chemical plants: See R. Hoover and J. F. Fraumeni, Jr., *Environmental Research,* Vol. 9 (1975), p. 196.

Pages 68–69
National Cancer Institute Survey: See T. J. Mason *et al.: U.S. Cancer Mortality by County: 1950–1969,* National Cancer Institute DHEW Publication (NIH) 74–615 (Bethesda, Md.; 1974).

Page 69
Output of different compounds from coal-hydrogenation plant: See R. J. Sexton: "The Hazards to Health in the Hydrogenation of Coal," *Archives of Environmental Health,* Vol. 1 (1960), p. 181. The quoted passages are from this article.

Page 70
Cancer of the scrotum in Scottish shale-oil workers: This phenomenon was first described by B. Bell, *Edinburgh Medical Journal,* Vol. 22 (1876), p. 135.

Page 70
Shale oil and tumors of the skin in mice: See A. Leitch, "Paraffin Cancer and Its Experimental Production," *British Medical Journal,* ii (December 9, 1922), p. 1104.

Page 70
FEA's report on shale oil: "The Potential Future Role of Oil Shale: Prospects and Constraints" (cited above).

Page 72
Capital productivity of coal and synthetic-fuel production: These data were compiled from two sources. The capital investment required to produce one ton of coal was obtained from *U.S. Energy Outlook* (cited above), p. 38. The capital investment required to produce different synthetic fuels was obtained from the *Project Independence Task Force Report on Synthetic Fuels from Coal*, p. 35, and also the *Task Force Report on Oil Shale*, p. 65 (full citation for Task Force reports is given above).

Page 73
Price of synthetic fuels: Business Week (August 11, 1975, p. 19) states that "Estimates of the cost of synthetic fuels now range from $14 to $24 per barrel, well above current world oil prices." Prices as high as $26 per barrel have been quoted more recently.

Page 73
Kissinger, quotation: This statement appeared in the St. Louis *Globe-Democrat*, February 4, 1975.

Page 74
Report of Paris meeting quoted: See *New York Times*, March 21, 1975.

Page 74
Coal conference, quotation: See *Electrical World*, August 1, 1975, p. 58.

Chapter 5
NUCLEAR POWER

Page 76
Projections of nuclear-power growth: See Nuclear Fact Sheet, FEA 169-A, Washington, 1975. The projections represent a 40- to 50-percent reduction from estimates made by the AEC in 1970 (*Business Week*, November 17, 1975, p. 99).

Page 76
McCormack, quotation: See *Energy Finance Week*, July 30, 1975.

Page 77
Eisenhower, quotation: This statement is from the President's address before the U.N. General Assembly, December 8, 1953, *The Atom for Progress and Peace* (Washington, D.C.: U.S. Government Printing Office; 1953).

Page 77
AEC statutory responsibility: Quoted from the Atomic Energy Act of 1946. The AEC ended its existence in January 1975, and its functions were taken over by the Energy Research and Development Administration (ERDA) and the Nuclear Regulatory Commission (NRC).

Page 78
The structure of the uranium atom: There is an excellent, beautifully written book that explains, in understandable terms, atomic structure and its relation to nuclear fission: Selig Hecht, *Explaining the Atom* (New York: Viking; 1964).

Pages 78–79
Thirring, quotation: This statement is from Thirring's book *Energy for Man* (cited above), pp. 323–24.

Page 79
The fission process: For a more detailed but understandable description, see John Fowler, *Energy and the Environment* (New York: McGraw-Hill; 1975). This book is an excellent source of scientific information on energy problems generally.

Page 83
Radioactivity and toxicity of a nuclear power plant's wastes: This information is from Thirring, *Energy for Man* (cited above), pp. 336 and 357. His figure is an "equilibrium" value, based upon the production and decay values of waste products in the reactor. The yearly amount of waste produced depends on how often the core is changed.

Pages 83–84
Zarb, quotation: This remark occurs in Zarb's speech *Nuclear Power —A Time for Decision* (Washington, D.C.: Federal Energy Administration; July 1975).

Page 84
A. M. Weinberg, quotation: This statement appeared in Dr. Weinberg's interesting article, "Social Institutions and Nuclear Energy," in *Science,* Vol. 177 (1972), p. 27.

Page 84
The latest report on the nuclear power industry: The Nuclear Industry, 1974, U.S. Atomic Energy Commission, Document WASH 1174–74 (Washington, D.C.; November 1974).

Page 85
Nuclear expert, quotation: This statement was made by D. J. Rose in his article, "Nuclear Eclectic Power," in *Science,* Vol. 184 (1974), p. 351.

Page 85
Antarctic waste storage: This idea was proposed by E. J. Zeller *et al.* in "Putting Radioactive Wastes on Ice," *Bulletin of the Atomic Scientists,* 24:1 (January 1973), p. 4.

Page 85
Experts on waste disposal, quotation: See A. S. Kubo and D. J. Rose, "Disposal of Nuclear Waste," in *Science,* Vol. 182 (1973), p. 1205.

Pages 86–87
Dimensions of reactor containment vessel: See *1000-MWE Central Station Power Plants Investment Cost Study,* Vol. 1, AEC, Document WASH-1230 (Washington, D.C.: U.S. Government Printing Office; June 1972), plate 5.

Page 87
Increases in nuclear-reactor costs: These data are in *Power Plant Capital Costs: Current Trends and Sensitivity to Economic Parameters*, AEC, Document WASH-1435 (Washington, D.C.: U.S. Government Printing Office; October 1974), p. 19.

Page 87
1957 report on reactor accidents: Theoretical Possibilities and Consequences of Major Accidents in Large Nuclear Power Plants, AEC, Document WASH-740 (Washington, D.C.: U.S. Government Printing Office; 1957).

Page 87
AEC memorandum, quotation: This memorandum was written by N. M. Staebler for the Steering Committee Meeting on the revision of Document WASH-740, December 21, 1964. The memorandum is printed as Appendix C in H. W. Kendal and S. Moglewer *et al.: Preliminary Review of the AEC Reactor Safety Study* (San Francisco–Cambridge: Joint Review Committee, Sierra Club–Union of Concerned Scientists; November 1974), p. C-5.

Page 88
Rasmussen report: The full title of this report is *Reactor Safety Study: An Assessment of Accident Risks in U.S. Commercial Nuclear Power Plants*, AEC, Document WASH-1400 (draft) (Washington, D.C.: U.S. Government Printing Office; August 1974). The final version, which appeared late in 1975, makes only trivial modifications of the draft, despite a good deal of intervening criticism.

Page 88
Union of Concerned Scientists report: This report is cited above, note for p. 87.

Page 88
American Physical Society calculations: These are described by Frank von Hippel in "A Perspective on the Debate," *Bulletin of the Atomic Scientists*, 31:7 (September 1975), p. 37.

Page 92
Available supplies of uranium: This estimate was made by M. Benedict in the *Proceedings of the National Academy of Sciences*, Vol. 68:8 (1971), p. 1923.

Pages 92–93
AEC reactor-research policy: For a further discussion of this topic, see J. M. Vernon: *Public Investment Planning in Civilian Nuclear Power* (Durham, N.C.: Duke University Press; 1971).

Page 92
Cost of developing the first experimental breeder: A *New York Times* article on nuclear reactors, March 30, 1975, quotes a $10.7-billion estimate for development of the breeder. (See also note for p. 98.)

Page 93
The breeder and nuclear fuel cost: These estimates were made by Manson Benedict in "Electric Power from Nuclear Fission," as reprinted in *Perspectives on Energy: Issues, Ideas, and Environmental Dilemmas*, L. C. Ruedisili and M. W. Firebaugh, eds. (New York:

Oxford University Press; 1975), p. 203. This book is an excellent place to find some of the more conventional scientific and technical treatments of the energy problem.

Page 94
Hazards of radioactivity: For an excellent discussion of the general problem, and of the specific hazards of the nuclear-power program, see Virginia Brodine: *Radioactive Contamination* (New York: Harcourt, Brace; 1975), one of a series of useful books published by the Scientists' Institute for Public Information. For an early analysis of nuclear-plant hazards, see Sheldon Novick: *The Careless Atom* (Boston: Houghton Mifflin; 1969).

Page 94
Hazards of a "plutonium economy": For a detailed analysis of this problem see *The Plutonium Economy: A Statement of Concern,* submitted to the National Council of Churches of Christ in the U.S.A. (475 Riverside Drive, New York, N.Y.), September 1975.

Pages 94–95
Carcinogenicity of plutonium: This estimate was made by J. W. Gofman in *Estimated Production of Human Lung Cancers by Plutonium from World Wide Fallout* (Dublin, Calif.: Committee for Nuclear Responsibility; July 1975). Dr. Gofman and his colleague Dr. Arthur Tamplin have challenged the over-optimistic approach of the AEC to radiation hazards in a remarkable series of scientific analyses carried out while they were employed by the AEC. For this courageous and important service to society, they were rewarded by losing their positions.

Page 95
Plutonium supplies with the breeder: T. B. Cochran has estimated that breeders alone will produce 130 million pounds of plutonium by the year 2000. See *The Liquid Metal Fast Breeder Reactor* (Baltimore: Johns Hopkins University Press; 1975).

Page 95
Present incidence of cancer in the U.S.: See *1975 Cancer Facts and Figures* (New York: American Cancer Society; 1975).

Page 95
Experiment at the Lawrence Radiation Laboratory: For an account, see D. P. Geesaman in *Energy and Human Welfare—A Critical Analysis,* Volume 1: *The Social Costs of Power Production,* edited by B. Commoner, H. Boksenbaum, and M. Corr (New York: Macmillan; 1975), p. 167. This book is a useful source of information on the environmental hazards associated with power production.

Page 96
Homemade plutonium bomb: For a fascinating account of Dr. Taylor's efforts to explain this problem, see John A. McPhee: *The Curve of Binding Energy* (New York: Farrar, Straus and Giroux; 1974). For a detailed analysis of the problem of safeguarding plutonium, see Mason Willrich and Theodore M. Taylor: *Nuclear Theft: Risks and Safeguards* (Ballinger; 1974).

Page 97
Explosive potential of plutonium reactor fuel: For a further discus-

sion, see T: B. Cochran: *The Liquid Metal Fast Breeder Reactor* (cited above). This book is an excellent source of information about the breeder problem generally.

Page 97
Reported Soviet breeder explosion: For a brief account of this explosion, which has been denied by the U.S.S.R., see *The Economist,* March 9, 1974, p. 88.

Page 98
Editor of Science *magazine, quotation:* This is from an article by A. L. Hammond in *Harper's,* January 1973, pp. 30–34.

Page 98
Escalation of breeder-reactor costs: For a discussion of the implication of these cost increases, see I. C. Bupp and J. C. Derian, "The Breeder Reactor in the U.S.: A New Economic Analysis," *Technology Review,* July-August 1974, p. 26.

Pages 98–99
ERDA report: See *Nuclear Fuel Cycle,* Energy Research and Development Administration, Document ERDA-33 (Washington, D.C.: U.S. Government Printing Office; 1975).

Page 99
ERDA report, quotation: See page ix of the report cited above.

Page 100
Morton, announcement: This change in policy was announced at a press conference held by the Secretary. See Rogers C. B. Morton, Secretary of Commerce, Transcript of News Briefing (Arlington, Va.: Federal Data Retrieval Systems; June 9, 1975), pp. 1–4.

Page 101
Delay of plutonium recycling: The Nuclear Regulatory Commission originally called for a three-year delay while the Generic Environmental Statement on Mixed Oxide Fuels (GESMO) was rewritten. (Order issued on May 8, 1975, as reported by Sheldon Novick in *Environment,* 17:5 [July-August 1975], p. 21.) Then on November 12, 1975, the NRC, apparently in response to considerable pressure from the nuclear-power industry, announced procedures designed to cut this delay to eighteen months (*Weekly Energy Report,* November 12, 1975, p. 1).

Page 101
Relative cost of fuel in nuclear-power production, 1966: See the analysis of future projections of the cost of nuclear power in R. E. Scott, *Projections of the Cost of Generating Electricity in Nuclear and Coal Fired Power Plants* (St. Louis: Center for the Biology of Natural Systems, Washington University; December 1975). Details regarding data on cost trends cited in this discussion will be found in this report and in I. C. Bupp *et al.:* "The Economics of Nuclear Power," *Technology Review,* February 1975, p. 15. This article is based on an earlier report, *Trends in Light Water Reactor Capital Costs in the United States* (Cambridge: Center for Policy Alternatives at the Massachusetts Institute of Technology; December 18, 1974).

Page 101
Confirmation of the commitment to breeder technology: See *Civilian Nuclear Power: The 1967 Supplement to the 1962 Report to the President,* AEC (Washington, D.C.: Government Printing Office; February 1967).

Page 102
Study of nuclear costs by Bupp's group: For references, see note for p. 101.

Page 106
Reports by Bupp and Scott: Both are cited above in note for p. 101. These analyses necessarily represent extrapolations of future expectations from past data. This is not a rigorous, precise procedure. Nevertheless, past experience with similar problems suggests how it can be done. For example, an engineer can predict a car's gasoline mileage quite accurately—provided he knows in advance the speed at which it will be driven (since gasoline mileage is strongly affected by speed). However, even if he does not know how fast the car will be driven on a particular trip, he can make useful predictions by assuming a certain reasonable range of speeds and then making separate predictions for each of the assumed speeds. In this way, the predictions form a set of guidelines that can tell the user what to expect under different circumstances. The analyses carried out by Bupp's group, and Scott's modifications of them, are based on this general approach. A series of assumptions, hopefully within a reasonable range of expectations, is made about the future changes in the factors that influence that cost of producing power. Computations are then carried out to define the time trends for uranium- and coal-based operations.

Page 107
Nuclear plant capacity factors: See the analysis by D. D. Comey, *Nuclear Power Plant Reliability: A Report to the Federal Energy Administration* (Chicago: Business and Professional People in the Public Interest; September 1974). Comey reported an "average capacity factor of 54.0% for commercially operating nuclear power plants greater than 100 MW [electric capacity]. An AEC hypothesis that a design capacity factor of 80% will be achieved after a 3 to 4 year break-in period is contraindicated." The Scott study assumed a generous figure of 60 percent average capacity factor for nuclear plants. It also assumed that coal-fired plants are more reliable and will be able to achieve the design capacity factor for base load power of 75 percent.

Page 109
Quotation from The Economist: From an article on breeder reactors, March 9, 1974, p. 88.

Page 110
Bupp, quotation: See Bupp *et al.,* cited above.

Page 110
Westinghouse plans to break uranium contracts: This was reported in the *Wall Street Journal,* September 9, 1975. For a recent discussion of the growing crisis in the nuclear-power industry, see the

article "Why Atomic Power Dims" in *Business Week*, November 17, 1975, p. 98.

Page 111
Government guarantees for new enrichment plant: This statement appeared in the *New York Times*, June 19, 1975.

Page 111
Financing the next enrichment plant, quotation: This remark appeared in an article in *Energy Finance Week*, June 9, 1975.

Chapter 6
THE SUN

Pages 113–114
Daniels, quotation: This statement appeared in Farrington Daniels: *Direct Use of the Sun's Energy* (New York: Ballantine; 1974), p. 3. This book is probably the best introduction to solar energy, its background and potential, available at present. Farrington Daniels was a gifted scientist who, with very little encouragement, did a great deal to advance research on solar energy in the United States.

Page 114
Solar energy largely ignored in current energy debate: The Nixon and Ford administrations consistently ignored solar energy, and until a few years ago there was little interest in Congress. However, beginning in 1974 there has been a remarkably increased appreciation of solar energy in Congress which has been reflected in a number of new bills. As a result, Federal agencies have been required by Congress to pay more attention to solar energy. But the overall effort is still very small compared to that directed toward nuclear power and similarly "high-technology" processes such as shale oil and coal conversion.

Pages 114–115
The nature of solar energy: Much of this information appears in B. J. Brinkworth, *Solar Energy for Man* (New York: John Wiley and Sons; 1972).

Page 117
Fraction of the sun's energy falling on the earth: At the earth's orbit, the sun's energy is falling on a sphere with an area of 100×10^{15} mi^2 (sphere of radius 93 million miles). A cross-section of the earth (radius of 4000 miles, is 50×10^6 mi^2. Therefore the fraction of the sun's energy falling on the earth is $\frac{1}{2} \times 10^{-9}$ or one-half billionth of the original.

Pages 119–120
Value of solar energy reaching the earth: The solar power reaching the earth's stratosphere is about 180 trillion KW (see F. Daniels, *Direct Use of the Sun's Energy*, cited above). If we assume that 15 percent of this amount reaches the earth's surface; that 10 percent of the latter is converted to electricity (the current efficiency of solar photovoltaic cells); that electricity is worth one cent per KWH; then the value of the electricity would be $648 billion.

Page 120
Quotation from U.S. Energy Outlook: See *U.S. Energy Outlook: New Energy Forms* (Washington, D.C.: National Petroleum Council; 1973), p. 79.

Pages 123–124
Nicholas Georgescu-Roegen: This idea is mentioned in his article in *Southern Journal of Economics,* 41:3 (January 1975), p. 347. This article summarizes ideas regarding the relationship between economics and entropy originally put forward in his book *The Entropy Law and the Economic Process* (Cambridge: Harvard University Press; 1971), which discusses the philosophical implications of entropy and the failure of conventional economics to take them into account.

Page 124
Collector temperatures: See W. E. Morrow's informative paper "Solar Energy: Its Time Is Near" in *Technology Review,* December 1973, p. 31.

Page 125
Incident solar power: The basic figure is taken from W. E. Morrow, *ibid.;* it is based on December averages in order to be descriptive of the worst conditions that will be encountered in supplying space heat. The data for the power requirements of a typical household are derived from *Patterns of Energy Consumption in the United States* (cited above). Morrow provides a similar analysis based on a hypothetical household and its requirements for energy during the worst time of the year. Using his calculations, the total collector area would be 1300 square feet, which is about the roof area of the average home.

Page 126
Land requirements of solar-power generation: These estimates were made by W. E. Morrow in *Technology Review* (cited above).

Page 127
Aluminum and glass needed for solar collectors: The amount of glass used in making beverage bottles was reported in "Glass Recycling Makes Strides," *Environmental Science and Technology,* 6:12 (November 1972), p. 988. Consumption of aluminum for throwaway cans was reported in *Modern Metals,* June 1971, p. 25. The quantities of aluminum and glass required to build solar collectors were published in the *Project Independence Solar Energy Report,* Federal Energy Administration (Washington, D.C.: U.S. Government Printing Office; November 1974).

Page 127
Morrow's understatement: See W. E. Morrow's article cited above, p. 41.

Page 127
National energy requirements for space heat, hot water, and electricity: The data are from *Patterns of Energy Consumption in the United States* (cited above).

Page 128
Hydrogen hazards, quotation: Quoted from S. S. Penner and L. Icer-

man: Energy, *Vol.* 2 (Reading, Mass.: Addison-Wesley; 1975), p. 121.

Pages 128–129
Fuel-cell efficiency: Penner and Icerman (*ibid.*, p. 284) state that "Theoretically-achievable efficiencies now exceed 80 percent, although practically-available fuel-cell systems for electricity generation have been limited to overall efficiencies of less than 60 percent."

Pages 129–130
Power from ocean temperature differences: For an example of the design of such units see J. H. Anderson and J. H. Anderson, Jr.: *Mechanical Engineering,* Vol. 88 (1966), p. 41.

Page 130
Zener on the energy potential of the Gulf Stream: See his interesting article in *Physics Today,* Vol. 26 (1973), p. 48.

Page 130
Examples of different kinds of solar devices: These examples are given by Farrington Daniels in *Direct Use of the Sun's Energy* (cited above), pp. 6–8. In the last few years, as interest in solar energy has increased considerably, there has been a very rapid proliferation of writings about existing and potential solar devices. *The Energy Primer: Solar, Water, Wind and Biofuels,* written by the Portola Institute (Fremont, Calif.: Fricke-Parks Press; 1974), is a general catalogue of source materials and basic information. *The Solar Energy Digest* is a monthly newsletter (P.O. Box 17776, San Diego, Calif. 92117). Wilson Clark's *Energy for Survival: The Alternative to Extinction* (Garden City, N.Y.: Anchor Books; 1975) is a particularly informative book not only about solar energy but about other aspects of the energy problem as well. These sources should be consulted for some of the solar energy techniques, such as the production of methane from manure, not discussed here.

Page 131
Energy research budget: Funding for research and development in the 1973 fiscal-year budget is outlined in J. H. Holloman, M. Grenon, et al.: *Energy Research and Development* (Cambridge: Ballinger; 1975), p. 108. The volume is a useful source of information about energy research generally.

Page 131
Overall price of energy in the U.S.: The increase was computed from data in *Survey of Current Business* for 1970 and 1975 (pp. 5–8; 5–9).

Page 132
Dixy Lee Ray's report: The Nation's Energy Future: A Report to Richard M. Nixon, President of the United States, U.S. Atomic Energy Commission, Document WASH-1281 (Washington, D.C.: U.S. Government Printing Office; December 1973).

Page 133
Report of Solar Subpanel IX: Alfred J. Eggers, Jr., Chairman: "Solar and Other Energy Sources," National Science Foundation, October 27, 1973 (photocopy obtained from the AEC public-documents room). Prepared for the Chairman of the U.S. Atomic Energy

Commission in support of her development of a comprehensive Federal energy research and development program to be recommended to the President on December 1, 1973.

Pages 133–134
Estimates of potential solar energy: These were calculated by the Scientists' Institute for Public Information in testimony regarding the AEC's *Draft Environmental Statement on the Liquid Metal Fast Breeder Reactor Program* (New York: SIPI; April 1973). The calculations are based on data contained in the Subpanel IX Report.

Page 135
Subpanel IX, quotation: Subpanel IX report, p. 141.

Page 137
Bernard Yudow's study of solar hot-water heating: These data are from Mr. Yudow's interesting master's thesis: "Engineering Design and Economics of Solar Domestic Hot Water Heating in St. Louis," Sever Institute of Technology, Washington University, St. Louis, Mo., August 1975.

Page 140
Ali Shams's study of the economics of solar space heat: As part of the CBNS research program on the economic implications of the energy crisis, Mr. Shams has developed a mathematical analysis of the relationship between the cost of space heating and the relative proportions of solar and conventional energy used for that purpose. The system costs are for a hot-air device, and the calculations take into account the fact that home finance charges are tax deductible, which lowers the effective interest rate to about 7.5 percent. This analysis is described in his report *Cost/Benefit Analysis of Solar Heating* (CBNS, February 1976). The data cited here are preliminary estimates based on this analysis. I am indebted to Mr. Shams for his review of the material on solar energy and for a number of helpful discussions of economic problems.

Chapter 7
THE USES OF POWER

Page 145
Second Law efficiencies of different sectors of the national energy budget: The efficiencies are from the APS study cited above, and the proportion of the energy budget devoted to various tasks is from *Patterns of Energy Consumption in the United States,* also cited above. These figures are national averages, taking into account the variety of devices used.

Page 147
Energy productivity analyses: Some of the more important of these studies are those of Bruce Hannon and R. A. Herendeen (summarized and additional references given in Bruce Hannon's paper "Options for Energy Conservation" in *Technology Review,* February 1974, p. 25); Charles A. Berg's studies, which introduce the concept of Second Law computations (see his paper "A Technical Basis for Energy Conservation" in *Technology Review,* February 1974, p. 15), and Eric Hirst's studies, especially in the area of transportation (see

Energy Intensiveness of Passenger and Freight Transport Modes 1950–1970 [Oak Ridge, Tenn.: Oak Ridge National Laboratory; 1973]).

Page 148

Report on energy consumption, quotation: This statement appears in *Patterns of Energy Consumption in the United States* (cited above), p. 1, and the quotation which follows appears on p. 19.

Page 150

Increased farm production: The data referred to here are taken from the U.S. Department of Agriculture's basic summary, *Agricultural Statistics—1972* (Washington, D.C.: U.S. Government Printing Office; 1972). Unless otherwise indicated, the data relative to agriculture discussed in this chapter will be found in this volume and in the corresponding volume for 1974.

Page 151

National Academy of Sciences report, quotation: This statement appears in *Agricultural Production Efficiency* (Washington, D.C.: National Academy of Sciences; 1975) pp. 47–48.

Page 151

Professor Woodruff's question: The statement is quoted from his presentation at a 1975 meeting of CBNS.

Page 151

Carbon and nitrogen cycles: For a more detailed description see Chapters 2 and 5 of B. Commoner: *The Closing Circle* (cited above).

Page 154

Legume seed production: The data relate to seeds of clover, vetch, alfalfa, and lespedeza and are from various editions of *Agricultural Statistics* (cited above).

Page 156

Energy inputs in farming: See Pimentel *et al.*, "Food Production and the Energy Crisis," in *Science*, Vol. 182 (1973), p. 443. Cited as reprinted in P. H. Abelson, ed.: *Energy: Use, Conservation and Supply* (Washington, D.C.: American Association for the Advancement of Science; 1974), p. 41.

Page 156

Energy used in corn production, Illinois: These data are derived from B. Commoner, M. Gertler, R. Klepper, and W. Lockeretz: *The Effect of Recent Energy Price Increases on Field Crop Production Costs*, Center for the Biology of Natural Systems (CBNS-AE-1) (St. Louis, Mo.: Washington University; December 1974). (See table, p. 67 of this report.) I am indebted to Dr. Lockeretz for his review of this and other material pertaining to agriculture.

Page 156

Nitrogen fertilization efficiencies: The energy required to produce inorganic nitrogen fertilizer was computed from data included in Commoner *et al.*, *ibid.*, p. 11. The energy cost of seeding vetch is from Pimentel *et al.*, *ibid.*, p. 44.

Page 158
Relation between corn yield and rate of fertilizer application: See Pimentel *et al.* (cited above).

Page 158
Nitrogen fertilizer productivity: See *Agricultural Production Efficiency* (cited above).

Page 159
Capital per worker—petroleum industry: This figure is from *1971 Annual Survey of Manufactures* (industry profiles), U.S. Bureau of the Census (Washington, D.C.: U.S. Government Printing Office; 1973).

Pages 160–161
Rising prices of agricultural inputs: See Commoner *et al.* (cited above), pp. 26–27.

Page 161
Colonization of rural America: I developed this point more fully in an address before the National Conference on Rural America, Washington, D.C., April 17, 1975 (available as a CBNS report, *Energy and Rural People*).

Page 162
Earl Butz, quotation: Mr. Butz made this remark on a "Meet the Press" television and radio interview, NBC, December 12, 1971. Quoted in *What They Said in 1971: The Yearbook of Spoken Opinion,* Alan F. Pater and Jason R. Pater, eds. (Beverly Hills: Monitor Book Co.; 1972), p. 123.

Page 163
Comparison of conventional and organic farms: See W. Lockeretz *et al.: A Comparison of the Production, Economic Returns, and Energy Intensiveness of Corn Belt Farms That Do and Do Not Use Inorganic Fertilizers and Pesticides,* Center for the Biology of Natural Systems (CBNS-AE-4) (St. Louis, Mo.: Washington University; July 1975).

Page 164
Transportation, petroleum, and chemical corporations: Data on the twenty corporations that comprise this sector of U.S. industry were obtained from the 1974 "Fortune Directory of the 500 Largest Industrial Corporations," *Fortune,* May 1975. These corporations also represent the "energy/chemical" complex which is referred to later in this chapter.

Page 165
Number of railroad accidents: See *Summary and Analysis of Accidents on Railroads in the U.S. Subject to the Interstate Commerce Act for the Calendar Years 1964 and 1972,* U.S. Departments of Commerce and Transportation (Washington, D.C.: U.S. Government Printing Office).

Page 165
Recession in the auto industry: See note for p. 3.

Page 165
Automobile petroleum consumption: See E. Hirst, *Energy Intensive-*

ness of Passenger and Freight Transport Modes (cited above). This report, a pioneering study of the energetic efficiency of various modes of transportation, contains most of the basic data on this subject that are discussed in this chapter.

Page 167

U.S. production statistics: An effort to analyze almost any aspect of the role of energy in industrial production is, of course, absolutely dependent on the basic facts regarding the amounts and kinds of goods produced, their value, and the nature and value of the various relevant inputs. The basic sources of such data are: *The Census of Manufactures* (published every five years) and *The Annual Survey of Manufactures* (published in the years not covered by the Census), U.S. Department of Commerce (Washington, D.C.: U.S. Government Printing Office). General data on the economy are published annually in the *Statistical Abstract of the U.S.* (cited above). J. W. Kendrick's *Postwar Productivity Trends in the United States, 1948– 1969* (New York: for the National Bureau of Economic Research by Columbia University Press; 1973) is one widely recognized economic text on this topic, although his primary focus is labor productivity (he combines all other production inputs under the term "capital"). A valuable source of basic data on economic trends is *Long-term Economic Growth, 1860–1970,* U.S. Department of Commerce, Bureau of Economic Analysis, 1973.

Page 169

Energy productivities of inter-city transportation: These data are from Eric Hirst's report cited above.

Page 169

Productivities of transportation: These data on capital, labor, and other productivities of transportation were first prepared by Robert E. Scott and myself in connection with testimony which I gave to the U.S. Senate Transportation Subcommittee Hearings on "The Future of the Highway Program" on July 30, 1975. The data required to compute these productivities came from the following sources: U.S. Department of Transportation (DOT): *Capital Stock Resources for Transportation* (Washington, D.C.: U.S. Government Printing Office; December 1974); DOT: *1972 National Transportation Report* (Washington, D.C.: U.S. Government Printing Office; July 1972); DOT: *National Transportation Statistics, Summary Report* (Washington, D.C.: U.S. Government Printing Office, November 1974); *Statistical Abstract of the U.S.* (cited above). Details regarding the methods used to compute the various productivities can be found in the testimony referred to above.

Pages 172–173

Improving the thermodynamic efficiency of the passenger car: See the APS study *Efficient Use of Energy* (cited above), p. 99.

Page 174

Revenues from passenger traffic on European railroads: These values were computed from data in *A Brief Survey of Railroads of Selected Industrial Countries* (New York: Union Pacific Railroad Company; April 1973).

Page 175
Railroad freight traffic: These data are from *The Yearbook of Railroad Facts* (Washington, D.C.: Association of American Railroads; 1973) and Eric Hirst's paper (cited above).

Page 176
Transportation-industry profits: Data on the profits of major corporations, classified by their activities, are published in *Business Week* at quarterly intervals, and yearly profits are published in March following each of the calendar years covered. The results reported here are computed from the *Business Week* surveys for the years indicated.

Page 177
Trolley trip of Tateh and his daughter: See E. L. Doctorow's fascinating novel *Ragtime* (New York: Random House; 1975).

Page 177
Dismantling of U.S. trolley systems: See Bradford C. Snell: *American Ground Transportation: A Proposal for Restructuring the Automobile, Truck, Bus and Rail Industries,* as printed for the Subcommittee on Antitrust and Monopoly of the Committee on the Judiciary, U.S. Senate (Industrial Reorganization Act, Appendix to Part 4) (Washington, D.C.: U.S. Government Printing Office; 1974). The data regarding the numbers of streetcars in service in Los Angeles and nationally are also from this source.

Pages 177–178
General Motors counsel's statements: Ibid., p. A-30.

Page 178
Snell, quotation: Ibid., p. A-32.

Page 178
Transportation specialist, quotation: Statement of Professor G. Hilton of the University of California, Los Angeles, quoted in Snell: *Ibid.,* p. A-32.

Pages 178–179
Photochemical smog in Los Angeles: For a description of this classic example of the origin of pollution, see B. Commoner: *The Closing Circle* (cited above), Chapter 4.

Page 179
Reorganization of the Northeast railroads: The latest version of the government's reorganization plans will be found in *Preliminary System Plan* (Washington, D.C.: U.S. Railway Association [USRA]; February 1975). For data regarding the cost and freight capabilities of the reorganized system, see Vol. 1, p. 13, of this report; data regarding traffic to be shifted to trucks will be found on p. 342.

Page 180
Railroad reorganization and NEPA: I have written an account of the relationship between the reorganization of the Northeast railroads and their environmental impact and energy productivity in *Harper's,* December 1973. For a more recent account, see the article "Thinking the Unthinkable about U.S. Railroads," *National Observer,* August 9, 1975.

Page 181
Effect of proposed reorganization on energy consumption: For details, see article in *Harper's* referred to above.

Page 181
Quotation, DOT environmental impact statement: See U.S. Department of Transportation, *Draft Environmental Impact Statement on the Northeast Railroad Restructuring Act* (May 1973).

Page 181
Union Pacific study: For reference, see note for pp. 172–173.

Page 183
Energy used by the chemical industry: Data on the consumption of fuels are from the *Annual Survey of Manufactures* (1971), cited above, and from the *Census of Manufactures* (1972). Data on fuel consumed as a raw material come from the *1972 Minerals Yearbook,* U.S. Bureau of Mines (Washington, D.C.: U.S. Government Printing Office; 1973).

Page 184
Numbers of organic compounds: The latest available listing of known organic compounds is in the 1975 edition of *Chemical Abstracts* (Cleveland: Chemical Rubber Publishing Company). The list contains over seventy different compounds of the formula $C_6H_{12}O_6$, among them ordinary grape sugar, glucose. The figure for the total number of organic chemicals was derived from information in M. J. S. Dewar *et al.: Computer Compilation of Molecular Weights and Percentage Compositions for Organic Compounds* (New York: Pergamon Press; 1969).

Page 185
Toxicity of organic chemicals: These data are based on a survey of toxicities carried out at CBNS in connection with my paper "The Environmental Impact of the Chemical Industry," presented before the American Chemical Society meeting in Charleston, S.C., on November 8, 1973. The survey covered those commercial chemicals listed in the pattern of production of the chief petrochemicals (each representing at least $10 million in value and in the aggregate comprising about two-thirds of total petrochemical production) shown in *Chemical Origins and Markets: Flow Charts and Tables* (Palo Alto, Calif.: Stanford Research Institute; 4th edn., 1967). The toxicities (classified as "zero," "slight," "moderate," or "high") of each of the listed compounds were then determined from N. Irving Sax's standard handbook on toxicity, *Dangerous Properties of Industrial Materials* (New York: Van Nostrand Reinhold; 1963).

Page 187
Production of synthetic organic chemicals: The data on production of synthetic fibers and detergents come from the *Census of Manufactures* (1972); on production of plastics from the *Survey of Current Business* (1973); on pesticide production from the 1974 edition of *Agricultural Statistics.* All of these are cited above.

Page 187
Article on "The Synthetics Age": See R. Houwink's article under that title in *Modern Plastics,* Vol. 43 (1966), p. 98.

Page 187
Rate of increase in production: These rates were computed from data reported in *Long-term Economic Growth, 1860–1970*, U.S. Bureau of Economic Analysis (Washington, D.C.: U.S. Government Printing Office; 1973).

Pages 188–189
Productivities for sectors of manufacturing: The values for capital, labor, and energy productivities were computed from data published in the 1971 *Annual Survey of Manufactures* (cited above).

Page 190
End-uses of ethylene: The list of ethylene end-use products is taken from A. V. Hahn: *The Petrochemical Industry: Market and Economics* (New York: McGraw-Hill; 1970), Chapter 5.

Page 192
Plastics-industry text, quotation: See J. H. Briston and L. C. Goselin: *Introduction to Plastics* (Middlesex, England: Newness Books; 1968).

Pages 192–193
Ratio of materials to wages: The data cited represent the average of eight sub-divisions of the chemical industry as given in *Annual Survey of Manufactures, 1971* (cited above).

Chapter 8
THE PRICE OF POWER

Page 199
Coal-conversion costs: See the discussion in Chapter 4.

Pages 200–201
Capital productivity in energy production: These data are computed from capital estimates made in B. Bosworth *et al.: Capital Needs in the Seventies* (Washington, D.C.: Brookings Institution; 1975), pp. 27–29, and from domestic energy production as reported in *Energy Perspectives* (cited above.) The book by Bosworth *et al.* estimates that although production of energy from domestic U.S. sources will increase more slowly in 1970–80 than it did in 1960–70 (annual growth rates of 2.5 and 3.9 percent respectively), energy investment will need to increase considerably, from an annual rate of 4.3 percent in 1960–70 to 8.1 percent in 1970–80. These estimates suggest that capital productivity in energy production is likely to decline more rapidly in the 1970s than it did in the previous decade.

Page 201
Estimates of capital needed by energy industry: See Bosworth *et al., ibid.;* and also *Business Week*, special issue on the capital crisis, September 22, 1975, pp. 50–51.

Page 201
Capital requirements of world petroleum production: See "How Much Oil—How Much Investment," The Chase Manhattan Bank, Energy Economics Division (New York, March 1975), p. 7. The estimates are based on an assumed 5-percent inflation rate.

Page 204
Trend in energy consumption relative to GNP: See, for example, "How Much Oil—How Much Investment," *ibid.,* Fig. 1.

Page 205
Energy productivity in transportation: See second note for p. 169.

Page 206
Average travel by a black worker in Pittsburgh: See revealing article by James O. Wheeler, "Work-Trip Length and the Ghetto," in *Land Economics* (February 1968), pp. 107–12.

Page 206
Per capita auto travel—1945–70: These data are derived from values for total auto travel and the U.S. population as published in the 1971 edition of *Statistical Abstract of the U.S.* (cited above). According to the 1974 edition, since 1970 per capita auto travel has increased at the rate of about 5 percent per year.

Page 206
Distance traveled per ton of railroad freight: These data are derived from values for total tonnage and total distance published in *The Yearbook of Railroad Facts* (cited above).

Page 208
The energy/chemical complex: See note for p. 164.

Page 209
Senate hearing, quotation: Hearing of Subcommittee on Antitrust and Monopoly of the Senate Judiciary Committee, June 19, 1975.

Page 210
Relation between energy and capital productivities: The sources of data used in computing these productivities (for 1971) are described in notes for pp. 185 and 188–189. The correlation coefficient between capital productivity (value added per dollar of fixed assets) and energy productivity (value added per million BTU) was calculated, using the standard statistical formula, and was found to be .82.

Page 213
New York Stock Exchange report: See *Capital Needs and Savings Potential of the U.S. Economy: Projections through 1985* (New York Stock Exchange; September 1974).

Pages 213–214
Chase Manhattan Bank report: This report appeared in the form of an advertisement in the *New York Times,* April 1, 1975, p. 48.

Page 214
Business Week, *quotation:* These quotations and the figures which follow them are cited from the special issue of September 22, 1975, pp. 42 and 45.

Page 214
Brookings Institution study, quotation: See Bosworth *et al.* (cited above), p. 4.

Page 215
Bureau of Labor Statistics, quotation: This statement is from *Capital*

Formation and the Outlook for Employment, Analysis by the Special
Study Group Established by the Secretary of Labor (Washington,
D.C.: Bureau of Labor Statistics; July 22, 1975), p. 3.

Page 215
New York Stock Exchange report: See *Demand and Supply of
Equity Capital: Projections to 1985* (New York Stock Exchange;
June 1975). This is a sequel to the New York Stock Exchange
report cited earlier.

Page 216
Capital shortage in the electric-power industry: Thus, Bosworth
et al. (cited above) remark, regarding the intense demand for
capital by the energy industries as a whole, "The largest dollar
amounts are in electric utilities, with much of the growth resulting
from the more capital-intensive nuclear fuel plants" (p. 27).

Page 216
Request for government to buy nuclear reactors: See "Nuclear
Power: Westinghouse Looks to Washington for a Customer," by J.
Carter, in *Science* (July 4, 1975), pp. 29–30.

Page 217
Business Week, *quotation:* This statement appears on pp. 45 and 48
of the special issue cited above.

Page 218
Forrester, quotation: This statement appeared in an article in the
New York Times, October 21, 1975, p. 18.

Page 218
Population and food: For a more detailed discussion of this problem,
see Barry Commoner, "How Poverty Breeds Overpopulation (And
Not The Other Way Around)," *Ramparts,* August-September 1975.
This article summarizes recent data regarding the current and an-
ticipated balance between world demand and the world food supply.
An informative source of such data is *A Hungry World: The Chal-
lenge to Agriculture,* Report by the University of California, Food
Task Force (Berkeley, Calif.: Division of Agricultural Sciences;
July 1974).

Chapter 9
THE POVERTY OF POWER

Page 222
Economics as a field that lies outside my own professional training:
Among the informal sources of my education in this field are
frequent lunches during which the subject has been discussed,
generally from quite opposite points of view, by two colleagues,
Professors Hyman Minsky and Murray Weidenbaum.

Page 223
Nixon, quotation: See *Vital Speeches of the Day,* 40:21 (August 5,
1974), p. 647.

Page 223
Ford, quotation: What They Said in 1974: The Yearbook of Spoken

Opinion, Alan F. Pater and Jason R. Pater, eds. (Beverly Hills: Monitor Book Co.; 1975), p. 165.

Page 223
Hardesty, quotation: Ibid., p. 107.

Page 223
Goldwater, quotation: Ibid., p. 168.

Page 224
Schaefer, quotations: Ibid., p. 180.

Page 224
ITT advertisement: See the *New York Times,* October 31, 1975.

Page 225
Okun's Law: See the *New York Times,* July 2, 1975, p. 43.

Page 225
Poverty affects 24 million Americans: This figure comes from the *Statistical Abstract,* 1974.

Page 225
Simon, quotation: This statement and the one immediately following it are from testimony of Secretary of Treasury William M. Simon, before the House Ways and Means Committee, July 8, 1975, as reported in *Department of the Treasury News,* pp. 16–17.

Pages 226–227
Business Week *article, quotations:* See *Business Week,* July 25, 1970, p. 65.

Page 227
U.S. Chamber of Commerce, quotation: See the pamphlet entitled *Economic Growth: New Views and Issues, Enterprise in a New Economic Era,* a Report of the Council on Trends and Perspectives (Washington, D.C.: Chamber of Commerce of the U.S.; 1975). This report is an interesting effort to explain to the business community that the issues raised by the environmental and energy crises have serious economic implications. It states, for example, that "The ecological approach is not a 'non-economic' way of looking at the world. It is a broader way of looking at the traditional concerns of economics: capital, cost and productivity . . . there can be little doubt that the ecological approach will become increasingly influential as a basis for economic calculations" (pp. 22–3).

Page 228
Simon, quotation: This statement was made before the Senate Finance Committee, May 7, 1975, and published in *Department of the Treasury News,* pp. 10–11.

Page 228
Simon on capital investment in the U.S. relative to Japan and West Germany: Ibid., p. 5.

Page 229
Doubling of GNP: See the *Statistical Abstract of the U.S., 1971* (cited above), p. 224.

Pages 229–230
Relations among output and labor and capital productivity: I am

aware that this statement ignores a number of complicating factors in these relationships with which economists are very much concerned. Particularly relevant to the argument presented here is the widely held view that the economic system is capable of adjusting automatically to processes, such as the displacement of labor by capital, through the pricing mechanism. In this case it could be argued that as the demand for capital relative to the supply intensifies, its cost (for example, the interest rate) will rise and that conversely, with a rising supply of labor relative to the demand (unemployment), the cost of labor (wages) will fall. These processes would then operate to counter the tendency of capital to displace labor. As a result of this interaction, one would expect the balance between capital and labor to go through periodic fluctuations rather than exhibiting an overall trend. Such self-compensating effects do appear to operate, but it is empirically a fact that, certainly since World War II, there has nevertheless been an *overall* trend, at least within the basic manufacturing industries and agriculture, toward a progressive displacement of labor by capital. As noted in the passages that follow, one direct consequence of the displacement of labor by capital is that the ratio of profits to capital tends to fall (because the denominator rises faster than the numerator) so that the return per unit capital invested declines. There seems to be a general agreement that, despite short-term fluctuations, the overall trend in this factor is downward. For example, Bosworth *et al.* (cited above) state, "recent studies of corporate profits indicate that the rates of return on capital have been declining for some years and that the decline is not merely cyclical" (p. 4). They then discuss various factors that affect the accumulation of investment capital and which might counteract this process, but finally conclude that "While these short-run dynamic factors change the immediate outlook for capital formation, they do not imply a lasting change" (p. 6). Thus, despite short-term fluctuations, there is an overall long-term process in which capital displaces labor, leading to the simplified relationships described here. It is appropriate here to take note of my considerable debt to Dr. Robert Klepper of the CBNS staff for a number of illuminating discussions of this and related issues in economics.

Page 230
Burns, quotation: See Chairman Burns' speech given at the University of Akron (Ohio), December 14, 1975.

Page 232
Bureau of Labor Statistics report: See *Capital Formation and the Outlook for Employment* (cited above). Some experts hold that such a computation ignores the returns to capital that are represented by interest costs on corporate debt (which is not counted when before-tax profits are computed). In other words, according to this view, if part of a corporation's income is used to pay interest on debts that are incurred in order to acquire more investment capital, then these funds too should be reckoned as profit. The BLS report shows that when these earnings are added in, the profit rate still declines, although less rapidly, falling, overall, by half between 1920 and 1975 and by 30 percent since 1945 (see chart V of this report).

Page 232
Survey of Current Business *report:* See the article by John A. Gorman, "Nonfinancial Corporations: New Measures of Output and Input," in *Survey of Current Business* (March 1972), pp. 21–33.

Page 233
Simon, quotation: See the Secretary's testimony before the House Ways and Means Committee, July 8, 1975 (cited above), p. 39.

Page 233
Public accountant, quotation: This statement is from an article by Philip L. Defliese in *Business Week*, August 4, 1975.

Pages 233–234
Nordhaus, quotations: See W. D. Nordhaus, "The Falling Share of Profits," *Brookings Papers on Economic Activity*, Vol. 1 (1974), pp. 169 and 204–5.

Page 235
Needham, quotation: This statement is from p. iii of his introduction to the New York Stock Exchange report *Demand and Supply of Equity Capital* (cited above).

Page 235
Freeman, quotation: This statement is quoted from "Qualitative and Quantitative Dimensions of Our National Energy Needs" by Gaylord Freeman (Chairman of the Board, First National Bank of Chicago), remarks to the National Conference on Capital Investment and Employment, New York City, May 19, 1975, pp. 4, 20, 27.

Page 235
U.S. Chamber of Commerce, quotation: This statement appears in: *Economic Growth: New Views and Issues* (cited above), p. 38.

Page 235
Cost of the Vietnam war: Senator Mansfield's estimate appeared in the *Congressional Record*, May 14, 1975, pp. S8151–6. I wish to thank Abby Rockefeller for bringing this important point to my attention.

Page 235
1976 U.S. military budget: This estimate appeared in an article in the St. Louis *Post-Dispatch*, November 19, 1975.

Page 236
Reduced consumption: The sweeping economic and political implications of the notion that reduced consumption is necessary to increase the availability of investment capital are just beginning to emerge. Recent examples can be found in an article on p. 9 in *Weekly Energy Report* (an industry-oriented news report) for December 15, 1975, reporting on discussions at a meeting of the Atomic Industrial Forum:

> Problems with capital formation are tied to social goals. More precisely, "we have been living dangerously for many years by diverting investment funds to meet the operating costs of social objectives," according to Joe Greif, Vice-President of Finance for Exxon Nuclear. Less and less of the national output is devoted to increasing the productive base, more and more devoted

to what Greif calls "social engineering and social enrichment." The result? An economic and social climate "in which the accumulation of savings and therefore the formation of investment capital is discouraged," says Greif. . . . Put simply, things have come to the point where somebody must lose. "It's a trade-off between more attempts to redistribute income or accelerate savings. You can't do both," said Arnold Pearlman, a young economist with Chase Manhattan Bank. Income redistribution, he said, is consumption-oriented; it takes from those who save (and invest) and gives to those who only spend. "The only thing that can be done is to increase personal savings, reform the tax laws, 'give a break' to high savers—to corporations and other income groups. . . . A choice," he said, "between the advantages of income redistribution versus having a larger pool of investment capital." . . . But how, politically, to reverse the trend toward social enrichment?

These are explicit statements that the failure of the economic system to generate sufficient capital to sustain itself is to be met by reducing the share of the nation's wealth available to those people who are so poor that they cannot save and therefore "only spend." In simple terms, this proposal would further impoverish the poor in order to place more wealth in the hands of people wealthy enough to save. It would redistribute the wealth, but in the direction counter to the conventionally envisaged one.

Page 236
Nordhaus, quotation: See his article "The Falling Share of Profits" (cited above), p. 170.

Page 237
Engels, quotations: These statements appear in *Frederick Engels on Capital* (New York: International Publishers; 1974), pp. 19 and 24. In this collection of writings Engels explains Marx's basic ideas about capital and labor in a particularly lucid way.

Page 238
Washington Monthly, quotations: See D. Ignatius: "Crying Wolf on Wall Street," *Washington Monthly,* November 1975, pp. 20–21.

Page 239
The Closing Circle, quotations: See B. Commoner: *The Closing Circle* (cited above), pp. 268, 277.

Pages 244–245
Utilities' capital raised from customers: The effect of the decision by the Missouri Public Commission to allow Union Electric to recover construction costs of the nuclear power plant before the plant goes into service is described in an article in the St. Louis *Globe-Democrat* of January 5, 1976. The letter quoted appeared in the St. Louis *Post-Dispatch* of January 4, 1976. For an account of the efforts by California utilities to charge their customers for options on future gas, see *Weekly Energy Report* (cited above), December 15, 1975.

Page 246
New York Times, quotation: See issue of November 17, 1975.

Page 247
Washington Post, *quotation:* See Hobart Rowen's column, Thursday, November 27, 1975.

Page 247
Galbraith, quotation: See pp. 272–74 of *Economics and the Public Purpose* (New York: New American Library, 1975). Galbraith has written a series of important analyses of the structure of the U.S. economic system. In this book, especially in the chapter entitled "The Socialist Imperative," he marshals a comprehensive argument to show why, at least in several major sectors of the economy, socialism has become essential to adequate productive performance.

Page 248
Oakes, quotation: This statement appeared in John B. Oakes: "Conscience of the Nation," *New York Times,* November 11, 1975.

ACKNOWLEDGMENTS

A BOOK such as this cannot be written out of one person's head; no one, single-handed, can assimilate the broad range of facts and ideas that need to be taken into account in considering the interaction among the crises in the environment, in energy, and in the economic system. In this instance, I have depended for nearly all of the factual information on collaboration with the colleagues and friends who make up the staffs of the two organizations in which my own work is encompassed: the Center for the Biology of Natural Systems (CBNS) and the Scientists' Institute for Public Information (SIPI).

In addition to the individuals cited in the Notes, I owe a great deal to the staff of CBNS as a whole: for their incisive approach toward the issues that are the common subjects of the CBNS program and of this book; for the hard work—usually done under difficult circumstances—that has produced a great deal of the information conveyed in this volume; for the sharing of their ideas and for their criticism of my own.

If the facts and ideas in this book find a response among the general public, it will be largely because the members and staff of SIPI have worked so hard to create a dialogue, on these issues, between the scientific community and the larger world of which it is a part. SIPI has pioneered in many of the specific issues discussed in this work: the hazards of nuclear radiation; the environmental impact of industry, agriculture, and transportation; the importance of solar energy. Even more important, SIPI has led the way in connecting these problems to the larger economic and social issues of which they are but a part, in particular the economic implications of the environmental and energy crises. (SIPI relies heavily on individual support for its work, and readers who are looking for a way to contribute to the solution of these problems are invited to communicate with SIPI at 49 East 53rd Street, New York, New York 10022.)

In the actual writing of this book, as in many other projects, I have relied heavily on the unstinting efforts of particular individuals. Alan McGowan and Virginia Brodine have given me the immeasurable gift of their comradely concern for the ideas and hopes that I have tried to express in writing this book. Robert E. Scott has worked long, hard hours, not only to find numerous facts, but also to think about what they mean and to help work out effective ways of expressing that meaning. Vivian Eveloff Goldman, together with Robert Scott, patiently assembled the notes for this book, and in many other ways helped to keep the project going, as did Jennifer Hoppe, who did a good share of the typing. And it is fair to say that it would have been impossible to produce this book if it were not for the astonishing ability of Rosaline Broadwater to convert hundreds of handwritten pages into a readable typescript, her willingness to work long hours under the heavy pressure of time, and her personal commitment to the book's purpose.

Finally, I wish to express my gratitude to a group of far-sighted individuals who have helped to find, and themselves provide, support—not only in the form of funds but, more important, in the form of understanding and encouragement—for the research activities that have yielded much of the information contained in this work: David Hunter and the Trustees of the Stern Fund; Mary Anna Colwell, Rita and Leonard Sperry of the Laras Fund; Maryanne Mott Meynet; Daniel R. Noyes; and Archibald Gillies.

INDEX

Abourezk, James, 133, 209

agricultural chemicals, 30, 31, 145, 149, 157–8, 160–3; pollution, 157, 162; price increase, 160–1; *see also* fertilizers

agriculture, 118, 148–64, 205; capital demands, 157, 159; capital/labor ratio, 159; energy mismanagement in, 151, 153–158, 159–64; energy productivity, 155–7, 205; energy use, 156–8, 164; farm income, 150–151, 157–8, 163; farm mortgage debt, 150; farm prices, 161; labor productivity, 150–151; livestock, 149–50, 153–4; mechanization, 149, 155–6, 159; number of farms, 150, 158; organic farming, 162–4; production increase, 150, 158–159; share of national energy consumption, 156–8; single-crop *vs.* crop rotation, 149, 153–4

air-conditioning, 64, 121, 145, 148; solar-powered, 124, 142

airline industry, 165, 176

airplane industry, 176

air pollution: airplanes, 171; buses, 178; cars, 165, 171, 175, 178, 202; chemical industry, 195; coal burning, 71–2, 104–105, 107, 202; fuel oil, 72; nitrogen oxides, 91, 165–6, 202; railroads, 171, 174; smog, 165–166, 178; sulfur dioxide, 66, 71–2, 91, 105, 107, 202; trucks, 175, 181

air travel, 171–2, 175, 179, 205, 211; capital productivity, 170; energy productivity, 169, 175; labor productivity, 170–1; pollution from, 171

Allied-General Nuclear Services, 100

Alperovitz, Gar, 247

American Physical Society (APS), 88; study on efficiency, 26, 36, 37, 63, 145, 156, 172–3

American Transit Association, 178

Antarctic Treaty (1959), 85

anthracite, 66

Arab oil countries, 30–1

atom, energy state of, 115–17

atomic chain reaction, 79–81, 93

Atomic Energy Commission (AEC), 76–7, 85, 97–8, 102–103, 107–8; attitude toward solar power, 134–5; breeder reactor program, 92–3, 94, 96, 97–8, 132–3, 134; and nuclear accident risk, 87–8, 90; Ray ("Futures") report, 132–4; safety standards, 103

atomic fission, 77–81, 93–4

"Atoms for Peace" program, 76–77

automation and mechanization: displacement of labor by, 3–4, 159, 209–12, 221–2, 237; in farming, 149, 155–6, 159

automobile, 172, 175, 178–9, 205–206, 211, 212; capital productivity, 170, 172; energy productivity, 169, 172–3; gasoline consumption, 165–6, 173; pollution, 165–6, 171, 175, 178, 202

automotive industry, 30, 31, 143, 165, 176

bituminous coal, 66

black-lung disease, 67

Blauvelt, H. W., 51–2, 57

Bohr, Niels, 115

boiling water reactor, 81

bottling industry, 206–7

breeder reactor, 92–9, 100–1, 102, 104, 132, 134, 135, 200, 207

Bridgman, P. W., 6, 24

Brookhaven National Laboratory, 87

Brookings Institution, 214

BTU (British thermal unit), 26, 34

Bupp, I. C., 102, 104, 106, 110

Bureau of Labor Statistics, 215, 216, 232

burning process, 33–4

Burns, Arthur, 230–1

buses, 174–5, 177–9; air pollution, 178–9; capital productivity, 169–70, 172; energy productivity, 169, 174–5; labor productivity, 170; overall economic productivity, 172

Business Week, 214, 216, 226, 227

butane, 186

Butz, Earl, 162–3

caloric (heat concept), 10

cancer, environmental causes of, 68–70, 72, 117, 185, 190, 195; plutonium, 94–6

Capital (Marx), 237

capital accumulation, law of, 236-7

capital costs, 121, 207, 209; of coal conversion, 72–3, 200; coal-fired power plants, 105–7, 134, 140; in inter-city travel, 169–70; mechanized farming, 157–8, 159; nuclear fusion, 130–1; nuclear power plants, 101–7, 108, 110, 134, 143, 200; shale-oil production, 73; solar-energy devices, 131–2, 134–5, 137–8, 139–41, 142–3

capital investment, 228; in oil industry, 53–5, 58–60; by oil industry, diversification, 57–8, 199; return on, 232

capitalism, 224, 236–8, 240–5, 247, 249

capital/labor ratio, 159, 229–31; in agriculture, 159; future projection, 215; in petrochemical industry, 192–3; in petroleum industry, 159

capital productivity, 53–4, 143, 166–7, 189, 209–13, 216, 217, 223, 224, 226–30, 231–2; in coal industry, 66; coal conversion, 73, 199; domestic oil production, 53–4, 58–9, 143, 189, 199; in energy production, 200–1, 202–3, 216, 227–8, 234; petrochemical industry, 189–190, 193, 195; in solar energy, 143; transportation, 168–9, 170–1, 172, 174, 175, 176–7

capital shortage, 3, 58–9, 142, 143, 159, 200–2, 203–4, 212–217, 220, 223, 224, 227–9, 231, 232, 234–6, 238, 239, 244–5

carbon cycle, 38, 151–2

Carnot, N. L. S., 22–5, 28, 37, 64, 129

Center for the Biology of Natural Systems, 106, 140, 163

chemical energy, 33–4, 114

chemical industry, 159, 164, 188, 208; crude-oil consumption by, 183; productivity data, 188–9, 193; *see also* petrochemical industry

Closing Circle, The (Commoner), 239

coal, 61–75, 113, 198–200, 208; chemical make-up, 37–8, 63, 69; depth of deposits, 39, 66; energy content, 62, 65; forms of, 66; origin of, 37–9, 61; as pollution cause, 61, 66–9, 71–72, 105, 107, 202; price of, 67, 106, 107, 108–9; share of national energy market, 63; suitable uses, 63–65; sulfur content, 66, 71–2, 105; U.S. consumption, 13; U.S. reserves, 66; various uses of, 61–2, 63; world reserves, 39, 61

coal conversion, 62, 67–71, 73–75, 199; deemed uneconomical, 70–1, 72–3, 74; environmental costs, 68; Ford administration stance toward, 73–5, 108, 199, 245; gasification, 62, 67–8, 72–3; health dangers, 69–71; liquefaction, 62, 65, 67–68, 72–3

coal-fired power plants, 62, 104–109; capacity factor, 107; capital costs, 104, 105–7, 134, 140; efficiency, 63–4, 65; *vs.* nuclear power plants, 101, 104–109, 199–200; percentage of coal used in, 63; pollution problems, 105, 107

coal industry, 208; capital needs of, 66

coal mining, 66–8, 71, 72–3

consumption, 234–6, 244

Continental Oil Company, 51, 209, 223

cooking, 121; heat requirement, 145

corn production, 154–5, 158; energy use in, 155–7

corporate income tax, 215

cotton, 161, 191, 196, 205, 208, 211, 218, 221

crude oil, 31, 185–6; "in place," 41; price of, 54–6, 73, 108; *see also* petroleum

Daniels, Farrington, 113, 130
detergents, 161, 184, 187, 191, 192, 212, 218
developing countries, 221
diesel engine, 37, 62, 129, 146, 147, 172, 173
diesel fuel, 156, 186
diesel railroad, 173, 174, 175
Doctorow, E. L., 177
domestic oil, *see* oil production, domestic
Dorgan, John J., 58
dry holes, 40

economic crisis, 1–3, 27, 31, 198, 212–18, 219–20, 222–3, 239–240; *see also* capital shortage; inflation; unemployment
economic growth, 218, 224–5, 229
economic system, 2, 5, 142, 221, 222–4; defined, 2; failure of self-correcting mechanisms, 230, 240; faults in, 5, 166, 212–18, 219–20, 221–3, 225–234, 240–4, 247–9; role of energy costs in, 114, 203–4, 234
Economist, The, 109
ecosystem, 1–3, 4, 38, 151–4, 166, 185, 203, 217–19, 239; defined, 1
efficiency, 34, 145–6, 167; of agricultural energy use, 156–7; of coal uses, 63–4; diesel engine, 62, 129; of electricity, 27–8, 63–4, 148; electric power plants, 28, 63–4, 90–1, 128–9; fuel cell, 128–9; heat engines, 22–3, 27–8; heat pump, 37; in household energy use, 34–7, 64, 121–2, 136, 145, 148; in industrial energy use, 145–6, 148; measurement by Second *vs.* First Law of Thermodynamics, 26–7, 34–7, 63–5, 148; (*see also* First Law efficiency; Second Law efficiency); oil furnace, 34–6; steam engine, 22–3, 62; thermal, 62; in transportation energy use, 145, 169, 172–3, 174–6
Eggers, Alfred, 132
Einstein, Albert, 78, 117
Eisenhower, Dwight D., 76–7

electricity, 27–9, 34; average annual household use, 125; cost of, nuclear *vs.* coal-fired, 93, 101–2, 105–8, 200; convertibility with mechanical motion, 27–8; efficiency considerations, 27–8, 63–4, 148; farm use, 156; fuel-cell generation, 128–129; inefficient for heat, 28, 63–4; solar energy in combination with, in home use, 137–141; solar generation of, 125, 126, 127–8, 129, 133–6, 143; suitable uses, 28–9, 62, 64–5; unsuitable uses, 28–9, 63–4, 121–2
electricity/heat systems, 64, 65
electric motor, 28
electric power plants: capacity factor, 107; capital costs, 101–107, 108, 110; efficiencies, 28, 63–4, 90–1, 128–9; fossil-fueled *vs.* nuclear, 90–2, 93, 101, 104–9; fuel-cell based, 128–9; hydro-electric, 120, 123–4; loss of waste heat from, 63, 83, 90–1; photovoltaic, 134–5, 143, 144, pumped-storage, 129; steam-heat requirement, 121, 125, 126; and thermal pollution, 23, 83; use of waste heat of 63–4, 91, 122, 136, 173; *see also* coal-fired power plants; nuclear power plants
electric railroads, 62, 64, 65, 128, 173–4, 175, 182
electric utilities, 93, 105, 208; capital needs of, 201, 216, 244–5
electrons, 115–17
energy: ability to do work, 21–9, 121; forms of, 114; high-quality, 28, 34, 63, 122; high-quality, misuse of, 28, 29, 63–64, 121–2, 123; law of conservation of, 4, 11–12, 24–5, 26, 115; law of entropy, 25; price trends, 131, 200–1, 202, 204, 219, 234
energy conservation, 26–7; in organic farming, 163–4
energy consumption, 3–4, 5, 145–197, 204–5; agricultural, 156–158, 163; coal, 63; efficiency estimates for various uses, 145–6, 147–8, 156–7; industrial, 145–6, 183; nuclear power, 76; oil, 30, 34, 46, 52,

energy consumption (*Cont.*)
53; in transportation, 61, 145, 164

energy crisis, 1, 2–5, 27, 30–1, 52, 53, 160, 183, 240, 244; roots of, 198–202, 212, 217, 220, 221, 222

energy-mass equivalency, 78–9, 116–17

energy policy, U.S., 73–5, 76, 108–9, 131, 132–6, 219, 247–248; lack of, 31–32, 53; neglect of solar energy in, 113–114, 120, 131, 132–6; on nuclear power, 76, 94, 97–8, 99–101, 103, 104, 110–12, 131; proposed $100-billion corporation, 62, 74–5, 215, 245; on railroads, 179–83

energy production, U.S., 198–9, 204–5; capital needs, 200–2, 216; capital productivity, 214, 216, 230, 242, 249

energy productivity, 188–9, 195, 205–6, 209–12; in agriculture, 155–7, 205; in petrochemical industry, 189–90, 192, 195, 207–8; in transportation, 168, 169, 172–3, 174–6, 205–6; *see also* efficiency

Energy Research and Development Administration (ERDA), 98–100

energy research funds, 114, 131, 132–6

energy sources, 2–3, 5, 198–201, 202–4; classification by work capability needed, 28–9; coal, 63, 198–200; matching of, to task to be performed, 28–9, 36, 63–5, 121–3, 145, 146–7, 202–3; non-renewable, 37, 92, 113, 120, 198–9, 203, 220; nuclear power, 76, 199–200; oil, 30, 198; renewable, 52, 53, 113, 141, 203; *see also* fossil fuels; nuclear fuels; solar energy

energy waste, 5, 34, 28–9, 34–8, 63–4, 121–2, 123, 203, 220

Engels, Frederick, 236–7

engines, comparisons of various, 62

entropy, 25, 34, 121, 124

environmental crisis, 1, 2, 27, 198, 202, 212, 217–18, 219, 222, 244

environmental hazards, 202, 203–204, 212, 238–40, 241; coal *vs.*

oil and gas, 71; fossil *vs.* nuclear fuels, 104–5; from nuclear power plants, 81, 83–90, 94–7, 101, 102–3, 105, 109, 202; *see also* air pollution; pollution

Environmental Protection Agency (EPA), 72, 98

ethane, 186, 192

ethylene, 186, 190, 193

Exxon Company, 59

Faux, Jeff, 247

Federal Energy Administration (FEA), 32, 53, 55, 57, 70, 76, 83

Federal energy policy, *see* energy policy, U.S.; energy research funds

fertilizers, 30, 31, 145, 149, 160–163, 191, 211, 218; nitrogen, 154–5, 156, 158, 161, 208; price increase, 161

Feynman, Richard, 8, 15

Firestone Tire Company, 178

First Law efficiency, 26, 35, 36, 63, 147; of diesel engine, 62, 129; of fuel cell, 129; of oil furnace, 34–5, 36

flat-plate collector, solar, 124, 126–7

food-producing capability, world, 218–19

Ford, Gerald, 108–9, 219, 223; and coal conversion, 73–5, 108, 199, 245; and crude-oil price, 31, 73–4, 108; and $100-billion energy corporation, 62, 74, 215, 245; and uranium enrichment, 110–11; veto of strip-mining bill, 67

Ford, Henry, 165

Forrester, Jay, 218

fossil fuels, 5, 38, 113, 155, 198–199, 202, 203; consumption, 39; environmental dangers, 71–72, 90–1; non-renewable, 37, 92, 113; origin of, 37–9, 61; reserves, 39, 52, 61, 113; *see also* coal; natural gas; oil

Freeman, Gaylord, 235

friction, 10, 11

fuel cell, 128–9

fuel oil, 30, 186; sulfur-dioxide pollution from, 72

fuels, 3; defined, 33; *see also* fossil fuels; nuclear fuels; *individual kinds*

fusion reactor, 116–17

Galbraith, John Kenneth, 247
gamma radiation, 117
gasoline, 30–1, 108, 156; 186; consumption, car, 165, 173; 1973-74 shortage, 30–1, 32
gasoline engine, 62, 173
General Atomic Company, 76
General Electric Company, 100, 110
General Motors Corporation, 177–8
Georgescu-Roegen, Nicholas, 123
geothermal power, 132
Goldwater, Barry M. 223
grain drying, 155, 156, 160
gravitational potential energy, 11
greenhouse effect, 119
gross national product (GNP), 229
Gulf Oil Company, 59
Gulf Research and Development Company, 121

Hardesty, C. Howard, 209, 223
Hardin, G. C., 58
health hazards, 61, 203–4; from coal burning, 71–2; of coal conversion, 69–71; mining, 67; from nuclear power, 81, 94–6, 105, 109; of shale-oil production, 70–1; sulfur-dioxide pollution, 71–2; of synthetics, 185, 190–1, 195
heat: conversion to mechanical motion, 10–11, 12–13, 22–3, 27–8; convertibility with mechanical motion, 10, 13, 15–16, 23–5; intensity of (temperature), 13, 14–15, 24; intensity requirements of various tasks and processes, 121; nature of, 13–14, 15; solar, on earth, 118–19; suitable energy sources for, 28, 37–9, 63, 64; work potential of, 10–11, 22, 25–6, 33–4
heat content of fuels, 33–4, 36
heat engines, 129–30; basic kinds, 22, 37; efficiency, 22–5, 28
heating: electric, 28, 63–4, 121, 125, 140–1, 148; heat pump, 37; integrated systems, 64, 65; low efficiency in, 28, 36, 63–4, 121–2, 136, 145, 148; oil furnace, 34–6, 64, 122; solar, 120, 124, 125–6, 127–8, 129–30, 136–7, 140–1, 142–3
heating oil, 30–1, 34–6
heat pump, 37

herbicides, 149, 157, 162
home heating, 34–7; see also heating
Hoover Dam power plant, 124
household energy, efficiency ratings for, 34–7, 64, 121–2, 136, 145, 148
"How to Become a Foreign Oil Company" (Blauvert), 51–2
Hubbert, M. King, 45, 46–50
hydrocarbon fuels, 32–4, 38, 61, 183; advantages of, 62; energy content, 33–4, 62; reserves, 39–50, 52, 61, 62; synthetic, 62, 68–71, 72–5
hydroelectric power, 120, 123–4, 132–3
hydrogen bomb, 130
hydrogen fuel, 128–9

industrial energy use, 183; efficiency, 145–6, 147–8
industrial heat, 63, 65
industrial steam production, 63, 148
inflation, 31, 121, 142, 200, 202, 203, 204, 224, 230, 240
information theory, 20–2, 25
infrared radiation, 117, 118, 119
insecticides, see pesticides
internal-combustion engine, 62, 121
investment-tax credits, 215

Japan: investment data, 228; nuclear reactor, 109; railroads, 172, 181–2
jet engine, 62
jet fuel, 186, 190
Joint Congressional Atomic Energy Committee (JCAE), 87, 94

kerosene, 186
Kerr-McGee Corporation, 58
kinetic energy, 11, 120; conversion to heat, 15–16
Kissinger, Henry, 42, 73–4, 219

labor: displacement by energy and capital, 3–4, 159, 209–12, 221–222, 229–31, 237, 244; farm, 149–50, 159; see also capital/labor ratio; unemployment
labor productivity, 189, 210, 211–13, 223, 224–5, 226–7, 229–30, 231; farm labor, 149–151; in petrochemical industry,

labor productivity (*Cont.*)
189, 193; in petroleum industry, 189; in transportation, 168, 170–1, 174, 175, 181–2
Lawrence Livermore Laboratory, 85, 95
leather, 187, 188, 194, 207–8, 211, 213
Lewis, G. N., 19
light energy, 114–15; of sun, 117–19
light-water reactor (LWR), 92, 99
lignite, 66
Lockeretz, William, 163
Los Angeles: smog, 178; trolleys, 177

Mansfield, Mike, 235
manure, 149, 152, 153, 155, 208, 211
Marx, Karl, 236–8, 243–4
Massachusetts Institute of Technology (MIT), 87, 125, 130; Center for Policy Alternatives, 102; *see also* Bupp, I. C.
mass transportation, 165, 169–176, 179–83
McCormack, Richard, 76
mechanical motion, *see* motion, mechanical
mechanization, *see* automation and mechanization
metabolic combustion, 38, 152–3
metallurgical furnace, heat requirement of, 121
Mideast oil, 30, 51, 57, 240
military expenditures, 228–9, 235–6
mining: coal, strip *vs.* underground, 66–67; uranium, 81–2, 92, 111
Mobil Oil Corporation, 45, 57
Modern Plastics, 187–8
molecular energy state, 116
molecular motion, 14–16, 116
Morrow, W. E., 125, 126, 127
Morton, Rogers, 100
Mostert, Noël, 71
motion, mechanical, 34, 114; conversion of heat to, 10–11, 12–13, 22–3, 27–8; convertibility with electricity, 27–8; convertibility with heat, 10, 13, 15–16, 22–5; laws of, 8; suitable power sources for, 28, 64; work potential of, 28, 34; *see also* kinetic energy

National Academy of Sciences, 47, 151
National Cancer Institute, 68
National Commission on Productivity, 226
National Democratic Issues Convention, 247
National Environmental Policy Act, 97, 103, 180
nationalization, 247, 248; 181–2
National Petroleum Council (NPC), 32, 49, 53, 55, 120–1, 240
National Science Foundation, 132
National Urban Vehicle Design Competition (1973), 128
"Nation's Energy Future" (Ray report), 132–4, 135
natural gas, 32, 50, 53, 61, 71, 72, 113, 198, 208; chemical make-up, 32–3, 37–8; efficiency of uses of, 148; environmental rating, 72; exploration, 74; industrial consumption, 183; origin, 37–9; petrochemical uses, 145, 155; price controls, 31; reserves, 39–40, 61
natural resources, 217–18
Natural Resources Defense Council, 97
natural rubber, 190, 208, 221
Needham, James J., 235
Newton, Sir Isaac, 8
New York Stock Exchange, 213, 215–16, 235
New York Times, 56, 73–4, 225, 246, 248
nitrogen, 151–2, 154–5; fertilizers, 154–5, 156–7, 158, 161, 208
nitrogen fixation, 152–3, 154–5
nitrogen-oxide pollution, 91, 165–6, 202
Nixon, Richard M., 133, 223, 226
non-biodegradable substances, 185
non-renewable fuels, 37, 92, 113, 120, 121, 198, 203, 220
Nordhaus, William D., 233, 236
nuclear fission, 77–81, 92–4
nuclear fuels, 5, 77–8, 79–80, 92; cost of, 82–3, 92, 93, 99, 101–102, 104, 106, 107, 110; reprocessing, 81–2, 85, 94, 99, 100–1; *see also* plutonium; uranium
nuclear fusion, 116, 130–1, 132

nuclear power, 27, 74, 76–112, 114, 200; cost of, 82–3, 92–3, 99, 101–2, 104, 105–9, 199–200; expectations for future, 76, 92–3, 99–100, 109–12, 131–3, 135–6, 199–200; government investment in, 82, 83, 92–3, 110–12, 131–2, 133, 135–6; private sector involvement, 77, 82, 92, 99–100, 109–12; share of national energy market, 76

nuclear-power industry, 76–7, 81–3, 92, 93, 100, 109–10, 208–9; and environmentalists, 102–3

nuclear power plants, 76, 77, 82, 83, 90–109, 216; capacity factor, 107; capital costs, 101–7, 108, 110, 200, 207; vs. coal-fired plants, 101, 104–9, 199–200; efficiency considerations, 90–1, 108; environmental dangers, 81, 83–90, 94–7, 101, 102–3, 105, 109; (see also nuclear wastes); number in U.S., ownership of, 76, 82; in other countries, 97, 109; radioactive emissions, 105, 109, 202; safety standards, 103; size and capacity, 83; thermal pollution, 83

nuclear reactors, 77, 79–81, 82, 86–92, 98–9; accident risks, 87–90, 97; breeder reactor, 92–9, 100–1, 102, 104, 132, 134, 135, 200; construction costs, 102–4, 110; conventional (LWR), 79–81, 86–7, 92–3, 99, 102–4; manufacturers, 109–10; types of, 80–1, 92–3

Nuclear Regulatory Commission (NRC), 90, 100, 101, 103

nuclear wastes, 81–2, 94; disposal of, 82, 83–6, 99, 101

Oakes, John B., 248

Occidental Oil Corporation, 58

offshore oil, 31; pollution dangers, 71; reserves, 45

oil, 30–60, 61, 113, 198–9; air pollution, 72; chemical make-up, 32–3, 37–8; depth of deposits, 40; onshore vs. offshore, 45; share of national energy market, 30; unsuitable uses of, 34–5, 63; U.S. consumption, 34, 46, 52, 53; uses of, 30, 34, 63; U.S. reserves, 40–50, 52–3, 62, 198–9; see

also crude oil; fuel oil; heating oil; petroleum

Oil and Gas Journal, 59

oil based industries, 30

oil companies, U.S., 199, 219; diversification of investments, 57–9, 199; earnings of, 59; estimates of oil reserves by, 45, 47–8, 198–9; exploratory efforts of, 45–51; foreign operations, 51–2, 57, 219, 240; profits, 56, 59–60, 199; role in oil crisis, 31–2, 219; see also petroleum industry

oil-consuming countries, Paris conference of (1975), 73–4

oil crisis of 1973, 30–1, 160–1, 240; embargo, 30–1, 42, 50, 53, 56, 176

oil drilling, 40–1, 45, 48

oil exploration, 39–41, 43, 45–50; profit considerations in, 50, 51, 53–4, 56–9; U.S. statistics, 48

oil furnace, 122; efficiency of, 34–6

oil imports, 30, 42, 49, 51; Ford's tariff on, 74, 108; U.S. dependence on, 42, 43, 52–3

oil prices, 50, 54–6, 60, 73–4, 107, 108, 198–9, 240; controls, 31, 74, 108; synthetic fuel, 73, 74–5

oil-producing countries, 30, 41, 73; U.S. threats of invasion of, 3

oil production, 40–2; environmental effects of, 71

oil production, domestic, 30, 31–32, 41–2, 50–1, 52, 240; vs. coal production, 72; expansion problems, 53–60, 73; potential, 53, 54–5; profit considerations, 50–1, 52, 53–60, 219–20

oil refinery, 185, 207

oil spills, 71

oil wells, 40–1, 48

Okun, Arthur M., 225

OPEC, 73

organic chemistry, 183–5, 186

organic compounds, 38, 183–5, 186

organic farming 162–4

organic matter, 38–9, 152–3, 154, 162; potential energy in, 118, 152, 153

Organization of Petroleum Exporting Countries (OPEC), 73

oxygen, atmospheric, origin of, 38–9, 61
ozone layer, 117–18

Pan American Airlines, 165
Penn Central Railroad, 164, 179, 180
perpetual-motion machine, 6–7, 12–13, 23–24
pesticides, 30, 31, 68, 145, 149, 157, 158, 161–3, 184, 187, 191
petrochemical industry, 30, 145, 159, 160–1, 183–97, 207–9, 213, 221; by-products, 193–4; capital productivity, 189–90, 192–3, 195; energy productivity, 188–90, 192, 195, 207–8; health hazards, 185, 190–1, 195; labor productivity, 189, 193; natural products displaced by, 161, 190–2, 194, 207–8, 211–12, 218; production data, 186–7; products, 184, 186–7, 189–194, 195–6; profitability, 192–3; and social values, 189–90, 194–5, 196–7; vertical integration of, 160
petroleum, 30, 32, 164, 185; discovery rate, 41–42, 43–4, 45–50; industrial consumption, 183; non-renewable, 37; origin of, 37–9; U.S. consumption, 34; uses of, 34, 63, 145, 155, 183, 208; U.S. reserves, 40–50, 52–3, 62, 198–9, 218; world consumption, 34; see also crude oil
petroleum industry, 30, 41, 159, 164, 199, 208, 223; capital productivity, 54–5, 58, 143, 189–90, 199; capital shortage, 55, 58–60, 199, 201–2; capital/labor ratio, 159; expansion problems, 52–60, 73; labor productivity, 189–90, 193; profitability, 193, 51–2, 55–6, 56–60; see also oil companies, U.S.
photons, 115–16, 117–18, 119
photosynthesis, 38, 61, 118, 151–152, 153
photovoltaic cell, 134–5, 144
photovoltaic power plant, 134–5, 143
physics, basic laws of, 6–9
plastics, 145, 160, 161, 184, 186–188, 190–6, 207, 211, 213; vinyl, 185, 186

plutonium, 77, 81–2, 93–101; recycling, 94–6, 98–101
Plutonium-239, 79, 81, 93–6
pollution, 1, 3, 91, 202, 238–40, 241; from agricultural chemicals, 157, 162; automobile, 165–6, 171, 175, 178, 202; coal as cause of, 61, 66–9, 71–72, 105, 202; noise, 171; nuclear power, 83, 105, 202; oil spills, 71; thermal, 23, 83; from transportation, 171, 174, 175, 178–9; water, 67, 71, 195; see also air pollution; environmental hazards
polycyclic hydrocarbons, 69, 72
polyvinyl chloride, 186, 190, 193
potential energy, 11–12, 33–4; in organic matter, 118, 152
Pott, Percivall, 69
power, defined, 10
precipitators, smokestack, 72
Price-Anderson Act, 90
private enterprise system, 56, 58, 110–11, 183, 199, 200–1, 223, 232, 237–8, 240–5
probability, 15, 18–22, 25
production system, 1–3, 4–5, 146–8, 166, 183, 204–5; defined, 1–2; dominant sectors, 208–9, 211, 230; energy distribution in, 147–8; energy waste in, 5, 146–8, 203, 206–7; faults in, 212–18, 219, 230–1, 241–3; position of petrochemical industry in, 208–9, 213; position of transportation in, 164, 166, 206, 208–9
productivity, 167–8, 188–9, 205–213, 225–30; see also capital productivity; efficiency; energy productivity; labor productivity
profit motive, 51–2, 55–8, 176–9, 182, 183, 192–3, 218, 219–20, 241–3
profit rate, decrease of, 231–4, 236–7, 244
"Project Independence," 53, 240
propane, 30–1, 155, 156, 160, 161, 186
propylene, 193
pumped-storage power plants, 129

radiant energy, 114–15, 116–17, 144; thermodynamic quality of, 122

radioactive wastes, *see* nuclear wastes
Ragtime (Doctorow), 177
railroads, 61, 62, 164–5, 173–4, 175, 176, 177, 179–83, 206; capital productivity, 170–1, 174; diesel, 173, 174, 175; electric, 62, 64, 65, 128, 173–4, 175, 182; energy productivity, 169, 174, 205; Europe, 165, 172, 174, 179, 181–2; freight *vs.* passenger service, 170–1, 174, 175, 179, 181–2; Japan, 172, 181–2; labor productivity,170–1, 172, 174, 181–2; nationalization, 181–3; North-east, reorganization plan, 179–181; overall economic productivity, 172; pollution from, 171, 174
Rasmussen report, 88, 89
Ray, Dixy Lee, 88, 132, 135
Ray report ("The Nation's Energy Future"), 132–4, 135
refrigeration, efficiency of energy use in, 145, 148
refrigerator, 23, 37
renewable energy sources, 52, 53, 113, 141, 203
Rockefeller, Nelson A., 62
Rumford, Count (Benjamin Thompson), 10, 11

Santa Barbara (Calif.) oil blow-out, 71
satellites, power generation in, 134
Schaefer, Alfred, 224
Science magazine, 97–8
Scientists' Institute for Public Information (SIPI), 97–8
Scott, Robert, 106, 108
Second Law efficiency, 26, 27, 35–7, 63–65, 121, 145–6, 148, 166–7, 203; agricultural energy use, 156; of coal uses, 63, 65; defined, 35–7, 156; of existing space-heat and hot-water processes, 36–7, 63, 121–2, 136, 145; in industrial energy use, 145–6; of integrated electricity/heat systems, 64; of oil furnace, 36; in transportation, 145
shale-oil production, 62, 68, 70–71; deemed uneconomical, 70–71, 72–3, 74; environmental costs, 68, 71; Ford administra-tion stance toward, 73–5, 108, 219; health hazards, 70
Shams, Ali, 140
Shell Oil Company, 46
Simon, William, 225, 227, 228–229, 233, 234, 238, 239
smog, 166, 178
smokestack devices, 72, 105, 107
Snell Bradford C., 177–9
soap, 161, 191, 208, 212, 218
socialism, 237, 238, 243, 244–8
soil cycle, 151–5; 162
solar cell, 120, 134–5
solar collectors, 124–7, 136, 137; for home heating, 125–6, 130, 138–9, 142; materials used in, 126–7; for steam-electric gen-eration, 126
solar/electric hot-water system, 137–40
solar/electric space-heat system, 140–1
solar energy, 2–3, 5, 113–15, 116–44, 151–3, 203–4; AEC's attitude toward, 134–5; agri-culture diverted from, 153–6, 157–8, 159–60, 161; amount received by earth, 117–20; ap-plications of, 120, 124–30, 133–4, 136–41; capital costs, 131–2, 134–5, 137–8, 139–40, 142–3; concentration of, 122–125; conversion to liquid fuel, 128; electric-power generation by, 125, 126, 127–8, 129, 133–136, 143; environmental effect, 141, 203; misconceptions about, 113–14, 120–1, 138; origin of, 116–18; potential of, 113–14, 120–30, 134–6, 141–4, 203–4; renewable, 113, 141, 203; research funds, 113–114, 131, 132, 133–4, 135; storage of, 126, 128–9, 138; thermodynamic quality of, 122
solar furnace, 120, 123
solar heating, 120, 124, 125–6, 127–8, 129–30, 136–7, 140–1, 142–3
solar installations, 120, 130; eco-nomics of, 121, 137–44
solar steam plant, 143
space heating, 34, 63, 121; *see also* heating
spontaneous combustion, 33
Standard Oil Company of Cali-fornia, 49, 178
steam engine, 10; efficiency, 22,

steam engine (*Cont.*)
62; *vs.* internal-combustion engine, 62; solar, 130
steam locomotive, 61–2
steam turbine, 125
strip mining, 66–8, 71, 72–3
sulfur-dioxide pollution, 66, 71–72, 91, 105, 107, 202
sun, 116–19, 122; *see also* solar energy
Supership (Mostert), 71
Survey of Current Business, 232
synthetic fibers, 145, 160, 161, 184, 185, 187, 191, 192, 193–194, 208, 211
synthetic fuels, 62–3, 67–71, 72–75, 245; estimated price of, 73, 74; *see also* coal conversion; shale-oil production
synthetics, 161, 183–5, 186–8, 190–6, 208, 211, 218

Taylor, Theodore, 96
temperature, 13, 14–15, 24; requirements of various tasks and processes, 121–2
thermal pollution, 23, 83
thermodynamics, 4, 6–29, 33, 35, 166; First Law of, 12–13, 25, 26, 35; First Law stated, 4, 11, 25; practical applications, 21–2, 25–9, 35–7; Second Law of 4, 18–21, 24–7, 35–6, 121; Second Law stated, 13, 18, 19, 20–1, 24, 25; *see also* First law efficiency; Second Law efficiency
Thirring, Hans, 78–9
time, one-way direction of, 8–10, 13, 16–18
transportation, 37, 61, 65, 164–183, 205–6, 208, 219; accident rates, 171; application of solar energy to, 128; capital productivity data, 168–9, 170–1, 172, 174, 175, 176–7; energy demands of, 61, 145, 164; energy productivity in, 145, 168, 169, 172–3, 174–6, 205–6; failure of U.S. system, 176–83; freight, 168, 169, 170–1, 172, 174, 175, 179–82, 205, 206; labor productivity in, 168, 170–1, 174, 175, 181–2; overall productivity, 167–8, 172–6; passenger, 168, 169, 170, 171, 172, 174–175, 176–9, 181–2, 205–6; petroleum fuel consumption, 30, 34, 61–2; pollution from, 171,

174, 175, 178–9; public funds in, 176, 180; *see also* air travel; automobile; buses; railroads; trucks
trolley, 174, 175, 177–8, 205, 219
trucking industry, 176
trucks, 175, 181, 205, 211, 212; air pollution, 175, 181; capital productivity, 170, 175; energy productivity, 169, 175; labor productivity, 170–1, 175

ultraviolet radiation, 117, 118
unemployment, 31, 142–3, 165, 213, 225, 230, 231; causes of, 3, 159, 212–13, 220, 221–2
Union Electric Company, 244–5
Union of Concerned Scientists, 87, 88
Union Pacific Railroad, 181
uranium, 77–80, 113, 203, 208; enrichment, 79, 81–2, 99, 110–111; mining, 81, 92, 111; ore, 79, 92, 99, 100; price, 92, 93, 99, 106, 107, 110; reprocessing, 81–2, 85, 99
Uranium-234, 79
Uranium-235, 77–80, 81, 93
Uranium-238, 79–80, 81, 93
U.S. Chamber of Commerce, 227, 235
U.S. Congress, 87, 136; and oil crisis, 31, 32, 108
U.S. Department of Agriculture, 157, 162
U.S. Department of Commerce, 194
U.S. Department of Interior, 32, 45, 49
U.S. Department of Transportation, 179, 181
"U.S. Energy Outlook" (NPC study), 120
U.S. Geological Survey (USGS), 45, 46, 49
U.S.S.R., 238, 246; breeder reactor explosion, 97, 109
utility industry, 72, 93, 105, 208, 244–5; capital needs, 200–1, 216

"value added" concept, 188–9
Vietnam War, cost of, 235
vinyl chloride, 68, 185, 186, 190

washing machine, 28, 64
Washington Monthly, The, 238

Washington Post, 247
waste heat, use of, 37, 63–5, 91, 122, 136, 173
water heating, 28, 34, 63, 64, 121, 136–7, 145; solar, 124, 125–6, 127, 128, 136–40, 142
water pollution, 67, 195; oil spills, 71
water power, 120, 123–4
water transport, 169, 170
wealth, distribution of, 219, 225
Weinberg, A. M., 84
Westinghouse Corporation, 110
Wiener, Norbert, 20–1
wind and windmill, 119, 130
Woodruff, D. M., 151, 153

wool, 161, 191, 194, 196, 208, 218
work: defined, 9–10; matching of energy source to, 28–9, 35–37, 63–5, 121–3, 145, 146–7, 202–3; rate of, 10; Second Law of Thermodynamics on, 4, 19, 20–2, 24–8, 35, 121–2

X-rays, 115, 117

"yellow cake," 92
Yudow, Bernard, 137, 139, 140

Zapp, A. D., 47–9
Zarb, Frank G., 83–4, 86
Zener, Clarence, 130

ABOUT THE AUTHOR

BARRY COMMONER was born in Brooklyn in 1917. He graduated from Columbia University and received his M.A. and Ph.D. degrees in biology from Harvard University. He is university professor of environmental science at Washington University in St. Louis and is director of its Center for the Biology of Natural Systems. He is chairman of the board of directors of the Scientist's Institute for Public Information, and a founder of the St. Louis Committee for Environmental Information. His two previous books are *The Closing Circle* and *Science and Survival*.